Differentiation and
co-operation

in an Israeli veteran moshav

Elaine Baldwin

Lecturer in Social Anthropology
in the University of Salford,
formerly Research Fellow in Social Anthropology
in the University of Manchester

Differentiation and co-operation

in an Israeli veteran moshav

With a Foreword by Max Gluckman

Manchester University Press

30.35
B181d

© 1972 Elaine Baldwin

All rights reserved

Published by pq
Manchester University Press
316–324 Oxford Road
Manchester M13 9NR

ISBN 0 7190 0438 1

Distributed in the U.S.A. by
Humanities Press, Inc.
303 Park Avenue South
New York, N.Y. 10010

Printed in Great Britain by
Butler & Tanner Ltd, Frome and London

Contents

Tables

Acknowledgements

I thank the Bernstein Research Trust for providing the means which enabled me to undertake research in Israel. I thank my colleagues on the Bernstein scheme for their comments on this work, especially Dr. Emanuel Marx of Tel Aviv University. I also benefited from the work of Dr. J. Abarbanel, who did similar research to my own. I am deeply grateful to Professor Max Gluckman of the Department of Social Anthropology in the University of Manchester, not only for his reading and criticism of this study but also for the teaching and training I received in the Department.

In Israel I was helped by many organisations and individuals. I thank Mrs. Lea Brakhin of the Moshav Movement who helped me to find Kfar Hefer. I am grateful to Dr. S. Tapuach of the Central Planning Department of the Ministry of Agriculture who gave me the benefit of his knowledge of Kfar Hefer. Mrs. Alisa Levenberg gave invaluable help in 'smoothing my path' in Israel, I thank her for this and for her generous and lively hospitality.

My biggest thanks are to Kfar Hefer. I shall not forget the warm-heartedness and willingness to help that I received from its members. Kfar Hefer is not the real name of the village and so I cannot make all my thanks personal but I do thank the village secretaries; members of the Executive committee and Council who patiently answered my questions and bore my presence at almost everyone of their meetings. It is impossible for me to adequately express my thanks to them, to all the members of Kfar Hefer, and to my friends in the communities which I call 'Gavish' and 'Dunia'. Rahel and Shmuel of Kfar Hefer deserve my special thanks. They gave me a home in the village and made me one of their family. It is a pleasure for me to record my gratitude and my affection for them.

Finally, I thank my parents who have always encouraged my anthropological interests and who have given tremendous help in the preparation of this manuscript.

Foreword

This is a study of one of the oldest co-operative villages (*moshavim*, sing. *moshav*) in Israel. Surprisingly, though there have been many sociological and anthropological studies of the co-operative villages formed to cope with the inrush of immigrants to Israel after 1948, this is the first detailed study of a long established moshav; and it is a very good first indeed.[1] The moshav itself, which Dr. Baldwin calls Kfar Hefer, was established, with great difficulty, in 1929: Dr. Baldwin's field research was carried out between 1966 and 1968. By that time the original pioneers were well into their sixties, if not their seventies, and some of their children were in their forties, with a third generation moving into maturity. Here one can speak in fact of layers of generations, since the ages of the pioneers at settlement covered a very narrow span, so that there are strata of sharply defined 'age-sets' with comparatively few people of intermediate ages. Hence many of the problems which now beset the village are seen by the villagers to result from what is more widely called a 'clash' of generations: in this moshav it is phrased by some of the elderly as a departure of the young from the ideals of the moshav, and by the young as the failure of the elderly to understand the problems of modern agriculture—even though, as one young man exclaimed to Dr. Baldwin after a heated debate, 'Oh, these old men; and (yet) they are not fools, you know.' For various reasons, this 'clash' began to become critical just at the period of Dr. Baldwin's research. In this book she analyses how far the villagers' view of the situation accurately assesses what had happened and what was happening, and where that view is not accurate she explains why they adopt it. This leads her to make her own analysis of the process of differentiation of interests within the moshav, under the pressure of factors internal to the moshav but greatly aggravated by changes in its external environment.

The idealism contained in moshav ideology was that individuals

[1] I stress that I speak of a full detailed study. In their *Moshava, Kibbutz, and Moshav: Patterns of Jewish Rural Settlement and Development in Palestine*, D. Weintraub, M. Lissak and Y. Azmon give an historical and sociological account of these various types of settlement, including a relatively brief account of Nahalal, the first moshav. This book, which was not available to Dr. Baldwin before her own study went to press, is an invaluable background to the present study, particularly the early phases (up to 1948) of the history of the moshav which is analysed here, mainly at a much later phase of its development and problems.

should have equal access to the means of production and equality of opportunity, while they should be free to develop farming on their own initiative within a co-operative framework for marketing and for purchase of supplies, for mutual aid, and for municipal services (such as schooling). This idealism characterised the pioneer settlers, most of whom originally were young Russian Jews inspired by revolutionary socialistic ideas in combination with a Zionist hope of rebuilding a Jewish homeland in which Jews worked on the soil. Dr. Baldwin in her introduction describes the pioneers: highly self-selected, devoted and determined, making a new life mainly as agricultural labourers while they waited for a grant of land, and thereafter struggling against all sorts of difficulties in establishing their own settlement. Eventually the settlement prospered because there was a demand for its products; and its members too mostly prospered. As one of the pioneer groups at a time when those who worked on the land were among the elites of Jewry, pioneer members of Kfar Hefer figured among Jewish leaders in Palestine. In the initial years after Israel was founded in 1948, they were even more important, for they were part of a tolerably well-educated, in Western terms, relatively small population in a new State which was almost overwhelmed by the immigration of large number of—again in Western terms—under-educated people. It is little wonder that the members of Kfar Hefer take great pride in their achievement as a moshav, and in their contribution to Israel.

The beginnings of considerable differentiation among the members of 'old' moshavim of this type, despite the stress on equality, co-operation and mutual aid, were subjected to a preliminary, but characteristically acute, sociological analysis by the late Professor Yonina Talmon-Garber in an incisive article on 'Social differentiation in co-operative communities' (1952).[1] The further development of the effects of this differentiation has also, of course, been discussed by those involved, not only orally but also in print; and the resulting technical agricultural problems have been analysed by specialist agronomists. But—again it is with astonishment that I record this— Dr. Baldwin has produced the first full study of developments in the social organization of a single moshav of this type. The result is a book penetrating in its technical analysis and compelling in the reading as it presents, in detail, this story of the seemingly inexorable development of conflicts of interests between categories of members, and the attempts of members and village officials to cope with the new situation, within the co-operative framework in which they work

[1] *British Journal of Sociology*, vol. 3 (cited by Baldwin).

and also within the sets of moshav laws and morals in terms of which they argue and to which they wish to subscribe.

Dr. Baldwin shows how their new dilemmas are rooted in the variable chances of life as these operate in the setting of demographic and economic constraints. Since even the relatively small area of one moshav is to some extent a patchwork of soils of varying fertility, and since crops on that patchwork are variably affected by climatic factors, environmental differences, however small, cause men to develop their farming with varying success. The luck or ill-luck of diseases of plants and stock takes varying toll. Farmers, not raised to the job, proved more and less skilful and/or more and less able to sustain the hard physical work. Above all, the chance by which farming couples have been affected in health, or have had or not had sons and daughters, enabled some to have more labour or less labour at hand to help in farming. While for many years the moshav as a whole prospered, some individual farms did not. As the pioneer generation aged, those farms which lacked members of the second generation (children and children-in-law) to undertake part of the hard labour, and ultimately to take over, fell increasingly on hard times. Eventually one-third of the 154 farms were thus imperilled through lack of family continuation: this was the crisis of the clash of generations, not a straightforward clash of age-grades, but one between families where there was such continuation against those left in the hands of the elderly without younger helpers. Where there has been continuation, relationships between the elderly and their children are mostly, but not of course always, amicable; and both old and young seem to side with the interests of successful farmers. Dr. Baldwin works out this thesis in detail, and shows that it is the farmers who fall into the categories of successful and unsuccessful, who are struggling to maintain their relationships within the co-operative despite the fact that they have both developed conflicting interests.

This conflict of interests arises largely from the fact that since 1958 'orthodox' agricultural production in Israel has exceeded the demands of the local market and of overseas markets, partly because of production by the many immigrants who were settled in co-operative villages— ironically, with the help of instructors produced by old moshavim like Kfar Hefer. The government's response has been to impose quotas on agricultural production; and, since a farmer can only make a living if he has a fair quota, in the new and more specialised agriculture, competition has developed between villagers for shares in the village's quotas for various types of farming. Hence some farmers can prosper more if other farmers do not use up their share of the village's quotas of production—and of the village's land and allocation of water. Though the village guarantees a minimum income to all its agricultural members, the prosperity of some seems to depend on the penury of others: and this appears to the latter to favour prosperity of the young and able-bodied at the expense of some of the elderly. These recall early periods of mutual helpfulness, so important a part of moshav ideology: they allege that in the past they gave such aid to one another, and that in some moshavim it is still given in the form of the village working the land of the old and weak. The younger generation sympathise with the lone elderly, but are struggling themselves with the problems caused by shrinking markets, vacillations in government policies, rising costs, and shortage of resources (including quotas of production) and of home labour and of time.

Dr. Baldwin shows how some of the elderly farmers, as well as a few unsuccessful or aspirant young farmers, tried to re-establish the base of their incomes through co-operative farming groups which aimed, or talked of aiming, to produce new types of products within the overall co-operative framework of the village. If successful, such efforts would claim back land 'temporarily' lent to successful farmers through the village, and would use anew their share of the village's allocation of water: this effort would thus threaten the output of successful farmers. She traces the consequences of this situation through a series of meetings of the General Assembly, the Executive, the Council, and the specialised Committees of the village; through articles and letters in the village bulletin; and through the gossip within the village. We are shown the dilemmas of these various committees, as they try to be fair to all as far as they can when clearly the economic viability of the village depends on the successful farmers. Some of the latter, though seriously disturbed, perforce are moved to admire the spirit of the elderly. But, as the external pressure from government's efforts to help all Israeli agriculture constrains village initiative—and these pressures change rapidly in response to local mishaps and outside markets—the Executive is compelled to try to narrow the range of its commitments to the very individuals who are trying to increase communal responsibility for their risks and losses while at the same time they are trying to restrict the Executive's powers. The villagers look to their officials for help within the co-operative: the officials who in other contexts represent the co-operative's values and powers, try to reduce its liability to individual villagers and to shift this to outside agencies.

The story of this clash of interests might of course be paralleled from many agricultural, and indeed industrial, regions. In Kfar

Hefer the clash has specific elements, and it is exacerbated by the fact that its members feel themselves to be a community, who are closely bound together by shared experiences in pioneering and/or growing up together. Naked 'self-interest' must at least be clothed; and the clothes it wears are tailored by the co-operative framework. Even the individuals who are aware of the conflict of interests within the co-operation, wish for the co-operation: like men elsewhere, they tend to see the conflict as resulting from the breakdown of the moshav spirit, and thereby (Dr. Baldwin argues) endeavour to reverse the process of what has actually occurred. Yet her conclusion is that she was observing the beginnings of a process whereby more and more 'pockets' of co-operation will develop among sub-groups of farmers in order to meet changing conditions by entering new forms of agriculture. These sub-groups may become innovators, and move Kfar Hefer out of the well-grooved rut dug by her very success as an early initiator. Here, too, the village models what has happened to pioneers in industrial, as well as agricultural, development elsewhere.

Given these seemingly irreconcilable conflicting interests, we need not be surprised that Dr. Baldwin's meticulous accounts of village meetings show sometimes heated reaffirmations of opinions and not reasoned debates, or that frequently a debate was ended by the appointment of a special ad hoc committee which was instructed to look at the problem concerned, while efforts were made to create a scrutinising committee to oversee the Executive. These events show in microcosm processes that occur also in governmental and parliamentary procedures of large states. The background to these processes in Kfar Hefer is delineated in a fascinating analysis which takes in the manner in which minutes of meetings were kept and interpreted, etc., and how the two secretaries, internal and external, of the village operated. The internal secretary, as a member and a son of Kfar Hefer, was subjected to a variety of pressures and inducements from the accumulated history of community living; little wonder that he told Dr. Baldwin: 'Specialists are all right for giving advice but they never solve anything.' They cannot, for they are not aware of, let alone a part of, the web of personal interrelationships which affect the working of village institutions. On the other hand, the external secretary, who handled the village's relationships with outsiders, had a chance to operate decisively precisely because he was outside that complex web, because he was not a member of the community. Dr. Baldwin's report and analysis thus bring out the difficulties of these, and other, village officials, and the apparent inability of village meetings, committees, and negotiations to reach compromise decisions by objective reasoning: we may therefore have to reconsider the balance of judgments on similar institutions in the new co-operative villages which were settled by *Reluctant Pioneers*[1] in thousands during the waves of immigration after the founding of Israel in 1948. Studies of these new villages have described how badly most of their political institutions worked, and how the settlers often undercut any attempt to exercise authority by their own officials. These studies referred these political conflicts to multiple factors present among new immigrants. I feel now that these studies assumed, perhaps unconsciously, that in these respects veteran moshavim worked well. If that was the assumption, this first full study of a veteran moshav must to some extent call that model into question.

This is but one of the many problems of general importance for social anthropologists, sociologists and political scientists, as well as for planners, which I can only indicate for those specialists, problems which Dr. Baldwin works out in intricate analyses that make this book a substantial contribution to general social theory as well as to our knowledge of Israeli society. Of great significance here are her discussions of contrasting theories of gossip, and of the problem of how a group which feels itself to be a community of equals becomes incapable of imposing effective sanctions on those who break many of the tenets of its moral code: how does a co-operative control a member who refuses to work within the constraints of the organisation? This theme too is illustrated with searching, and poignant, cases.

All human life is a scramble of self-interest and idealism: idealism if it is to be realized must absorb self-interest, and self-interest in a small group must be phrased in terms of its code—or at least parts of that code. Dr. Baldwin shows us some of the long-term and short-term oscillations of a community's members between these two poles. Where members of the moshav used to take pride in learned people becoming farmers, they have, from their present social perspective, begun to distrust higher education as a threat to the moshav way of life—an inaccurate perspective, says Baldwin. Where a general meeting was once the locus for solving common problems, it becomes the place where conflicting interests are cried. Where the village Execu-

---

[1] The graphic title for A. Weingrod's study of immigrants in some post-1948 villages (Ithaca: Cornell University Press, 1966). M. Shokeid's *The Dual Heritage: Political and Familial Interaction of Immigrants from the Atlas Mountains in an Israeli Village*, Manchester: Manchester University Press (1971) does not assume that the difficulties in the new pioneer villages sprang from problems of newness or of composition of their settlers. See D. Weintraub and others, *Social Change and Rural Development: Immigrant Villages in Israel*, Manchester: Manchester University Press; Jerusalem: Israel Universities Press (in press) for a general analysis.

tive was the aid to pioneering innovation, for a period at least it becomes the protector of consolidation; and so forth. Kfar Hefer is a microcosm for us all. The Barotse with whom I lived in Africa, told me of their problems: 'What God gives with the right hand, he takes away with the left.'

Dr. Baldwin was repeatedly told by villagers that it was important for her to understand the 'atmosphere' of Kfar Hefer and that she could not do so just by collecting information and asking questions: indeed, she was bound to fail. She goes on to say: 'Mostly people were kind enough to add that this was not a personal failing on my part and presumably to console me they said that "No outsider can understand Kfar Hefer. . . ." "It is our way of life in a moshav." ' And when they were referred to other moshavim, different in pattern, they retorted: ' "They are not really moshavim; Kfar Hefer is a real moshav".' Through her detailed analysis of social problems she does bring out this 'atmosphere': and it is an indication of her acceptance by the villagers that, as she tells us in one of her many humorous asides, she was counted as three-quarters of a person, rather than a half, when a general meeting jokingly brought her in to count towards a quorum. Those who know Israel better than I do, assure me that I am right in feeling that she became an insider in the moshav; but she remained enough outside to understand the views of both sides involved in the conflicts that beset the villagers' feeling that they were a 'community', where being a community and have 'harmonious relationships' was 'almost synonymous'. What perhaps may be a mythical view of the foundation years provides a charter for the synonymity. Her moving description of its revival in the crisis of the War of June 1967 relates how the myth, if myth it was, temporarily became reality and was thereby strengthened. It also made the continued bearing of the results of the inevitable internal conflict less tolerable.

I write this foreword in Israel, where I moved mainly among urban dwellers. They speak often of the high price of food: I must note that the accounts of typical incomes cited by Dr. Baldwin bring out that even the successful farmers in Kfar Hefer do not prosper unduly.

Dr. Baldwin's work was financed by the Bernstein Israeli Research Trust of the University of Manchester. I have, in the first book to emerge from our researches,[1] thanked at length the donors (Lord Bernstein, Mr. Alex Bernstein, and Mr. Cecil Bernstein) for their generous gift. I can also say again that, when they read this book, I

---

[1] 'Foreword' to S. A. Deshen's *Immigrant Voters in Israel*, Manchester: Manchester University Press (1970).

am sure they will feel that their gift has brought forth rich fruit.
I also thanked there the many scholars, in Israel and Britain, who
have assisted in our whole programme or research.

Max Gluckman

Department of Social Anthropology
Victoria University of Manchester
December 1970

Introduction

In the early part of this century 'pioneers' from Eastern Europe came
to Palestine with the aim of establishing Jewish agricultural settlements based on the ideals of socialism and co-operation. This is a
study of one of the settlements founded by these 'pioneers'. Kfar
Hefer, as I call the village, was settled forty years ago by immigrants
from Russia and Poland. The village is a co-operative, farming
village (a *moshav*) and is built on the principles of moshav organisation formulated by the 'pioneers'. Each member of the moshav
receives a plot of land equal to that of all other members and similarly
an equal quota of water and an equal quota for production. The care
of the individual farm is the responsibility of the farmer and his
family but the total produce of all moshav members is marketed by
the village administration. The 'pioneers' advocated 'mixed' farming
in moshavim for 'ideological' reasons of self-sufficiency; but this
ideology was supported by practical fears of crop failure, the uncertain security situation and a shortage of money to buy on the open
market. Kfar Hefer still maintains a pattern of mixed farming and
the village economy is based on dairy, citrus and poultry.

This study of Kfar Hefer covers the years 1966–68, the time when
I was in the village. During this time there occurred a series of events
which led to a process described by one of the village's members as a
'revolution' in the family farm. In part this 'revolution' was the
result of developments which had been taking place for several
years in Kfar Hefer, but which were precipitated by government
action, and in part the result of [this government action itself.
However, although government policy was directed solely to agricultural production the repercussions in the village affected both social
and economic relationships.

In the years immediately preceding Statehood Kfar Hefer gained
considerable economic and political power, a position which was
reinforced on the creation of the State. The village economy prospered
from the increased demands for production to provide for the large
numbers of immigrants. And the village members played an active
part in the settlement of these immigrants in new moshavim. Yet,
twenty years of Statehood have affected the role and the standing of
collective settlements in the country and Kfar Hefer like other
settlements has been influenced by these developments. One of the
most significant changes for agricultural settlements has been the rise

B

of centralised government direction of agriculture, through various government agencies and departments. The power residing in government, especially in a small state like Israel, has greatly diminished the independence of individual settlements to plan their own economy. This restriction has been intensified by the concomitant growth of administrative power in government which has lessened the effectiveness of purely political power of the type previously exercised by Kfar Hefer.

In the years 1966–68 the effect of government power was felt by the agricultural settlements—the 'revolution' in farming mentioned above. In these years there was considerable over-production of dairy and poultry in Israel. The government introduced measures to cut back production and to encourage farmers to switch to other branches of agriculture, especially to production of sub-tropical fruits and vegetables for the export market. The measures introduced by the government to restrict production included the imposition of strict quotas of production for each settlement with the imposition of financial penalties for exceeding this quota and also an increase in the price of feeding-stuffs for poultry and dairy. These actions affected all Kfar Hefer's farmers but not only in the economic sphere, there were also social repercussions in the village. Through a series of specific incidents, related to the existing social and economic relationships in Kfar Hefer, I examine how these measures operated in the co-operative framework of the moshav. The pressures of economic affairs coincided with the results of certain demographic processes in Kfar Hefer. During 1966–68 some thirty farmers in Kfar Hefer ceased production in dairying; this number combined with those who had already ceased production resulted in a state where almost a third of the village's farms were no longer involved in dairying. The overwhelming majority of those giving up dairy production were elderly farmers whose son(s) or daughter(s) had left or were expected to leave the farm. Despite mechanisation the up-keep of a dairy farm demands considerable physical labour beyond the capabilities of an elderly farmer alone. Moreover, the modern techniques of farming demand increasingly large-scale production if the farmer is to benefit from economies of scale. These two factors taken together resulted in many elderly farmers giving up dairying. The system of village allocation of quotas of production resulted in the dairy quotas of these non-dairying farmers being transferred to the remaining dairy farmers, who thus benefited from other farmers ceasing production. The farmers giving up dairying suffered a fall in income; an income which they were not able to supplement through compensating increases in poultry production. The village policy of equal allocations to all members prevented one section of the community receiving more than others, and furthermore the national situation of excess production prevented the village as a whole increasing their output. Thus, although the restrictions affected all farmers in Kfar Hefer, for some members the pressures were alleviated by increased quotas received from other farmers who did not fulfil their quotas; while these others with already reduced farming suffered from an inability to recompense their loss from another farming branch.

Within the village this led to a struggle for the limited resources of the moshav; farmers who farmed all three branches of agriculture and benefited from additional quotas argued that the economics of modern farming demanded even larger-scale farming; others argued that they should be compensated for transferring their rights in dairying to members who prospered from this gain. Much of this struggle focused around differing interpretations of moshav law and principles, and the village administration came under fire from both groupings for failing to understand their arguments and for failing to take the necessary action. Because of the age difference between the two groupings the dilemma was often stated as a difference between the generations, with the 'two-branch' farmers who were on the whole elderly accusing the second generation in the village of failing to live up to moshav ideals. In return the young farmers retorted that these farmers who were now retiring from farming did not understand the problems of modern agriculture. I argue that the dispute was in fact between two different socio-economic groupings who had different interests in the moshav. None of the participants in this dispute questioned the viability of the moshav as a way of life, at least not publicly, and so this struggle went on within a system of economic and social relationships in which members are committed to co-operation.

I examine this struggle from several different standpoints: (i) the operation of village administration; (ii) the national and local situation; (iii) the principles of moshav organisation; (iv) the village's relationships with outside bodies. Through the analysis of these various and differing relationships I show a clustering of factors, some chance, some inherent in the natural process of the moshav, which created the necessary conditions for the emergence of this paradox in moshav life—the paradox of competition and struggle between members bound together by an ideal and an organisation of co-operation.

Transliteration

Except for words with accepted transliterations into English—for example, Zion, Israel—I have used the following method of transliteration:

א not noted
ב and ו = v
ה not noted when muted
ז = z
ח = h
ת and ט = t
י = y or i
כ = k or kh
ע not noted
צ = ts
ק = q

List of persons mentioned in text

Almagor. A first generation farmer of Kfar Hefer, he farms his land with his only son. A member of the village Council 1966–68, and a former village secretary. First mentioned page 90.

Amiram. A second generation farmer in Kfar Hefer, who farms his own farm in the village. His elder brother works the family farm. Amiram has only a small dairy herd and has not achieved much financial success in his farming. Initially he was associated with the 'new farmers' in their scheme to grow alfalfa, later he transferred to the group of farmers growing avocado. First mentioned page 113.

Arad. A first generation member of Kfar Hefer, no longer dairy farming. A member of the village citrus committee 1966–68, and a member of the social committee in the early years of settlement. First mentioned page 15.

Ben. The village's External Secretary, a 'professional' (non-agricultural) member of the village. Formerly a member of a kibbuts he came to Kfar Hefer in 1961 to take up the position of external secretary. First mentioned page 98.

Ben-David. A first generation member of Kfar Hefer without continuation of the second generation in the farm. He was not actively involved in farming and was one of the outspoken critics of the village Executive, which he criticised for failing to make adequate provision for members who were no longer able to work their lands. First mentioned page 90.

Ben-Natan. The leader of the 'new farmers', a group of members reclaiming their land from the village in order to cultivate the land themselves. Ben-Natan is a first generation farmer, the continuation of his children on the farm is doubtful and in 1966 he gave up dairy farming. First mentioned page 103.

Cohen. A first generation farmer who farms his land with the occasional help of his son who is resident near Kfar Hefer. Cohen has given up dairy farming and joined the 'new farmers' (a group no longer dairy farming) in their venture to grow alfalfa. First mentioned page 99.

Dani. A 'son-in-law' of Kfar Hefer, who farms his father-in-law's farm. In 1967/68 he was elected to the village Executive, after an earlier term of office in 1964–66. First mentioned page 136.

Dora. A second generation member of Kfar Hefer married to a Kfar Hefer farmer who farms her family farm which she inherited on the death of her parents. Dora is the only woman member of the village Council. First mentioned page 135.

Doron. Secretary of the joint 'third and Valley' settlement groups, and in the early years of settlement a member of the village Executive Committee. In the years 1967–68 he served as Chairman of the village's scrutinising committee (*'va'adat ha'bikoret'*); is in full time employment outside the village and the family farm is managed by his only son. First mentioned page 9.

Dov. Internal Secretary in Kfar Hefer. Previously he had served on the village Council and Executive and he followed his father in the position of village Internal Secretary. He and his wife and children lived with his parents on the family farm which he and his father farmed. First mentioned page 76.

Eden. Kfar Hefer's permanent representative to the Moshav Movement. He is no longer actively involved in farming and has transferred his farm to his only son Moshe Eden. First mentioned page 58.

Eden, Moshe. A second generation farmer in Kfar Hefer, now in charge of the family farm. First mentioned page 71.

Emanuel. A second generation member of Kfar Hefer. He and his father farm the family farm which has a large dairy herd. He opposed the village policy of membership in *Marbek* (a cattle marketing agency) and he was elected to the committee which was set up to examine this policy. First mentioned page 170.

Guy. A member of the scrutinising committee (*'va'adat ha'bikoret'*) he came to Kfar Hefer on his marriage to a Kfar Hefer girl and now farms the farm of his parents-in-law. First mentioned page 150.

Hadar. A young farmer married to a girl from Kfar Hefer. He farms the farm of his parents-in-law. In 1967 he was elected to the scrutinising committee (*'va'adat ha'bikoret'*) when the size of the committee was increased to five members. He was involved with Jonathan in the dispute which led to the resignation of the committee's chairman. First mentioned page 152.

Haim. A second generation member of Kfar Hefer but despite the purchase of a farm his main income has not come from farming. He is employed by the village as a service worker and in 1967 he was appointed manager of the agricultural supplies store. Haim joined the 'new farmers' in their alfalfa growing scheme. First mentioned page 113.

Ilan. The professional (non-agricultural) member of Kfar Hefer responsible for the village's citrus groves and the marketing of fruit. First mentioned page 98.

Isaacs family. The circumstances of this family are unique in Kfar

Hefer, both father and son have their own farm in the village, but the father's dairy herd is managed by the son. The accounts of the two farms, although separately compiled, are the joint responsibility of father and son. First mentioned page 69.

Ish-Shalom. A member of the alfalfa growing scheme of the 'new farmers'. Ish-Shalom is a first generation farmer no longer in dairying and it is doubtful if his son will stay in the family farm. First mentioned page 113.

Jacobs. A first generation farmer in Kfar Hefer. A member of the social committee in the early years of settlement in Kfar Hefer. First mentioned page 15.

Jonathan. A second generation member of Kfar Hefer. In 1967 he was elected to the scrutinising committee (*'va'adat ha'bikoret'*) when the size of the committee was increased to five members. Later he was involved in a dispute with the committee's chairman after which the chairman tendered his resignation from the committee. First mentioned page 150.

Josef. A second generation member of Kfar Hefer who farms his parent's farm with the help of a younger unmarried brother. Josef claimed compensation from the village Executive for citrus trees of allegedly poor quality. First mentioned page 143.

Levi. A first generation member of Kfar Hefer, formerly a farmer and now a full-time employee of the Ministry of Agriculture. The family farm is managed by his son and daughter-in-law. First mentioned page 77.

Levine. The secretary of the 'new farmers' and with Ben-Natan the initiator of the scheme. Levine and his wife live alone on the family farm, none of their children have continued in farming. First mentioned page 103.

Marks. A first generation member of Kfar Hefer he is still actively engaged in farming with his son-in-law who lives on the family farm. Throughout the years of settlement in Kfar Hefer, Marks has participated in village administration and in the years 1966–68 served as a member of the village Executive. First mentioned page 136.

Marks, Sonia. The wife of Marks who serves on the village Executive. A member of the newly formed scrutinising committee (*'va'hadat ha'bikoret'*). First mentioned page 150.

Meiri. A member of the alfalfa growing scheme. Meiri and his wife live alone on the farm, both their children have left the village. Meiri no longer has a dairy herd and supported the view that members without dairy herds should receive additional quotas of poultry to compensate for the loss of earnings from the dairy. First mentioned page 120.

Michaeli. A first generation member no longer keeping dairy cattle. He advocated a new system of distribution of agricultural quotas by which members who were not involved in one agricultural branch would be compensated by increased allocations in others. First mentioned page 113.

Oren. A first generation member of Kfar Hefer, he and his wife live alone in the farm and now are not active in farming. Oren is the village's tax expert and deals with the accounts of individual members and of village enterprises. Oren has been active in village affairs from the early years of settlement and he has many times served on the village Executive Committee. In the years 1966–68 he served on this Committee. First mentioned page 97.

Ori. A second generation member of Kfar Hefer, he is married to a Kfar Hefer girl and farms her family farm. A member of the village Executive Committee. First mentioned page 136.

Pinhas. A second generation member of Kfar Hefer. He is married to a girl from Kfar Hefer and they live in his family farm. For several years Pinhas and his wife have been in dispute with the village about their incubator for turkeys which they operate independently of the village co-operative. First mentioned page 195.

Ra'anan. A second generation farmer in Kfar Hefer who farms with his father. The farm has a large dairy herd and is one of the biggest milk producers in Kfar Hefer. First mentioned page 77.

Reuven. A second generation member of Kfar Hefer who inherited the family farm on the death of his father. Reuven does not play a big part in the development, and he supplements his income by acting as a carrier for the village. He joined both the alfalfa and avocado growing schemes. First mentioned page 117.

Ron. The head of the land committee (*'va'adat hamesheq'*) in Kfar Hefer. Ron is a second generation farmer and for many years has been in charge of the family farm. In the year 1967–68 Ron was involved in negotiating with the 'new farmers' in their claims for the return of their land. First mentioned page 103.

Schulman. A first generation farmer, he and his wife live alone on the farm. A member of the village Council. First mentioned page 146.

Sharon. Secretary of the original Kfar Hefer settlement group after the union of all settlement groups he served as a member of the village Executive Committee. First mentioned page 10.

Shauli David. A second generation member of Kfar Hefer, married to a Kfar Hefer girl and resident on her family farm, Shauli is a member of the *Knesset* (Israel's legislative assembly). Formerly he was a member of *Mapai* (leading socialist party) but he joined *Rafi*, the party formed by Ben Gurion after his break with *Mapai*. Several of the Israeli socialist parties (including *Mapai* and *Rafi*) have now united to form a new labour party and this is the party Shauli now represents in the *Knesset*. First mentioned page 135.

Shimoni. A first generation farmer who farms with his daughter and son-in-law. The farm has a large turkey holding which provides a good income for the farm. Shimoni is a member of the village committee reviewing Kfar Hefer's constitution. First mentioned page 92.

Shlomo. A second generation member of Kfar Hefer. He farms his own farm which he bought from a member who left Kfar Hefer. A member of the village Council. First mentioned page 196.

Shwartz. A member of both the alfalfa and avocado growing schemes—Schwartz is a first generation farmer working alone in the farm. First mentioned page 118.

Tagar. One of the 'first Twenty' on the land in Kfar Hefer and head of the village poultry committee. First mentioned page 91.

Videtsky. First generation farmer in Kfar Hefer, he lives on the farm with his wife and his youngest daughter. The continuation of one of his children on the farm was considered doubtful, and Videtsky was gradually decreasing the size of his dairy. He became the chairman of a group of farmers who began to grow avocadoes in 1968. First mentioned page 71.

Waxman, Ruth. A first generation member of Kfar Hefer. The first woman to be elected to the village Council. First mentioned page 15.

Yael. A 'daughter of Kfar Hefer' who is married to a 'son-of-Kfar Hefer'. She lives on his family farm. Together with her husband she is involved in the dispute with the village concerning their private incubator. First mentioned page 195.

Yoel. A man in his middle 40's, Yoel is married to a girl from Kfar Hefer and farms his father-in-law's farm. He serves on the village cattle committee and represents the village to the Cattle Breeders Association. He served on the village Executive Committee in the years 1965–67. First mentioned page 99.

Yuval. An unmarried young man who lives with his parents in the family farm. Yuval is in charge of the farm's poultry holding and was involved in two disputes with the village Executive and Council concerning the marketing of the farm's poultry. First mentioned page 189.

Zioni. Representative of the 'third and joint' settlement groups on the social committee of the Executive 1936–37. Chairman of the Regional Committee in 1934 and in 1936. 'Head of the Regional Council' when the regional committee received official recognition from the British Mandatory Government. First mentioned page 15.

I
Historical background

Kfar Hefer is one of the oldest co-operative farming villages (*moshav*
—plural *moshavim*) in Israel. The first settlers came to work the
land in 1929, but it was not until 1932 that the village was registered
as a moshav. The village is situated in the coastal plain of Israel, in
what is today the most densely populated part of the country. Two
main highways border the village and link it with the cities of Tel
Aviv and Haifa: the main railway line between these cities cuts the
village fields. Thus the village is well served by a network of communi-
cations giving its members easy access to the main centres of Israel.

The situation was very different when the first settlers came to
Kfar Hefer. In a special publication by the Moshav Movement to
mark the twenty-fifth anniversary of Kfar Hefer one settler describes
his first visit to the area, in the winter of 1928, when the land had
just been transferred to the Jewish National Fund (J.N.F.), and even
before the question of settling there had been discussed. Five men set
out on horseback from the private farm where they were working
and rode for several hours before they came to the site. The journey
was difficult and arduous, over sand dunes and through swampy
ground. The writer describes how the group came to the river border-
ing Kfar Hefer. It was swollen with heavy rains and when they tried
to ride across one horse slipped and the rider fell in the water. Today
this journey along either of the main roads takes about fifteen
minutes by bus or car.

The people who founded Kfar Hefer were part of the wave of
pioneering movements for settlement in Palestine which started in
Eastern Europe in the latter part of the nineteenth and the early part
of this century.[1] Almost all the settlers in Kfar Hefer are from Russia
and Poland, and they and their children born in Palestine form the
majority of the village's population. Most of the original settlers
came with the 'third aliya' to Palestine in the early 1920's, and they
were greatly influenced by the ideal of working the land and setting
up Jewish agricultural settlements based on socialism and co-
operation.

In the early 1920's several agricultural settlements had been
founded according to these principles. Most were of the 'kibbuts'
type, although under the influence of the thinking of Eliezer Jaffe[2]

---

[1] In Hebrew the waves are called '*aliyot*' (singular '*aliya*') 3rd *aliya* (1919–23)
[2] See Labes (1962)

there were also settlements of the 'moshav' type. There are many descriptions of these varying types of settlement in Israel,[1] but briefly the difference between the 'kibbuts' and the 'moshav' can be described as the difference between 'communal' and 'co-operative'. In the kibbuts all aspects of social, domestic and economic life both for production and consumption were organised communally: no member worked individually for his own benefit, and the attempt was to abolish the holding of private property and work for individual gain. In the moshav more latitude was allowed to the individual: each member was allotted a parcel of land which he worked individually, for the benefit of himself and his family; but all marketing and buying were performed jointly through the village. The village was administered as a whole by a village council elected from its members. Both types of settlement adhered to the three main 'principles' which were set down as characteristics of these types of settlement: that there should be no private ownership of land (all the land is owned by the Jewish National Fund and leased either to the kibbuts as a unit or to the individual member of the moshav); that there should be self-work without hired labour; and that there should be mutual aid between members of the settlement.

Several organisations existed both inside and outside Palestine to further Jewish settlement in Palestine. In the diaspora there were groups recruiting young people for settlement and also organisations raising funds to buy land in Palestine for Jewish settlement. Within Palestine there were several organisations, notably the J.N.F., which both recruited membership for settlement on the land and helped groups of prospective settlers to find areas for settlement and to finance their ventures.

One of the groups which was to form a core of Kfar Hefer came together from a town in the Ukraine with the purpose of settling on the land. As was typical at this time, these young people looked for work to support themselves until they could settle on the land. Initially they worked as agricultural labourers on privately owned Jewish farms; they then moved to road building; and finally they worked as labourers in the drying out of swamps on the land of Nahalal (the first moshav in Palestine). Throughout their time in Palestine they had been in contact with the agencies for settlement and it was from Nahalal that they organised their own settlement movement. Members were recruited from other places in Palestine and were informed about progress: all met from time to time to discuss their settlement plans. At this time they had no fixed idea which form of settlement, kibbuts or moshav, they should adopt. It

[1] Orni (1963)

is reported that the debate between the members of this group on the merits of these different types of community was heated and fierce. After much discussion it was decided to choose the 'moshav' type of settlement; and two or three people who opposed this left the group. At the same time it was also decided that the group should affiliate itself to a political party, *Hapoel Hatsair* (the Young Worker), where previously the group had been non-political. Aid for settlement, for which there were many claimants, was directed through the political movements and so party affiliation was essential for an aspiring settlement group.

After the decision to set up a 'moshav' and the affiliation to *Hapoel Hatsair* the group's plans for settlement became more definitely determined. Members were carefully screened to assess their political suitability and their aptitude for moshav life. Reminiscing about this early period, one member recalled how he was approached by a young man who asked to join the group. This young man said that he had applied to another settlement group but they had turned him down because he was too young, since he was 22 years old while they were all 24 to 25 years old. Also he was a member of *Ahdut Avoda* (a political movement also promoting settlement on the land) and they were all members of *Hapoel Hatsair*. The member of the Kfar Hefer group said he would investigate and let the applicant know, and asked for the names of people who knew him and who could testify about his suitability for moshav life. Presumably, despite some reservations about the applicant's political attachment, the investigations were successful and he was acceptable. The applicant became a member of the group and was one of the first to settle on the land of Kfar Hefer.

As the membership of the group increased a secretarial board was elected from the members present in Nahalal. Their duties were to recruit members for the group, and to find a suitable place for settlement. They also organised discussion among all the members of the group to agree upon the details of their life in a moshav. It was agreed that agriculture would be the main basis of their work, and that the village land would first of all be worked co-operatively as a single unit. But it was recognised that initially the village economy would not be able to support all its members and so some would work outside the moshav: therefore the secretariat of the village would help them in finding jobs. During their stay in Nahalal the members of the Kfar Hefer settlement group learnt at first hand some of the problems involved in establishing a moshav, and so they were anxious from the beginning to lay down rules of conduct for their own settlement.

Three years after the settlement of Nahalal a meeting was held in Nahalal of all the Heferites. Altogether there were now sixty members, many of them working in Upper Galilee. This meeting was important for the group because they chose a site of settlement and also decided upon their way of farming. They chose a mixed pattern of farming along the lines of that pursued in Nahalal. At this meeting it was further decided that the nucleus of group members in Nahalal should leave to find work elsewhere. They had come to Nahalal by chance because it was short of labour. While they had been there they had gained practical insight into the problems of moshav management, but now they should take steps towards forming their own settlement. The meeting decided to form a moshav near Nahalal and to ask the J.N.F. for all help in achieving this. It was also decided that the group's members in Nahalal should seek work in private farms in the area as a first move towards achieving settlement in the Jezreel Valley.

This decision to settle in the Jezreel Valley close to Nahalal brought the Kfar Hefer group into a political dispute which had far-reaching consequences both in Palestine and in the party organisations in the diaspora. At this time, in the late 1920's, the two main political parties, *Hapoel Hatsair* and *Ahdut Avoda* were engaged in a bitter 'war' about the development of the country and their respective rights in this development. Inevitably this struggle affected the settlement movement within Palestine. The Heferites were affiliated with the minority party (*Hapoel Hatsair*) that was trying to increase their power at the expense of the majority party (*Ahdut Avoda*).

When Kfar Hefer applied to the Agricultural Settlement Department of the J.N.F. to settle in the Jezreel Valley they were told that another group had priority for settlement. This group, which was associated with *Ahdut Avoda*, had earlier been allocated another area for settlement which had proved unacceptable. Kfar Hefer claimed that they had seniority as a group for settlement and so they had a prior right to the land. This dispute spread to the party organisations: the final decision was in favour of the *Ahdut Avoda* group.

It was also decided that Kfar Heferites should be settled at some later date. This was a setback to the Heferites who were anxious to settle, especially as now some of the members had married and had young families to support. They applied again to settle in the Jezreel Valley, and were again refused, this time because the land was earmarked for a group affiliated to a third political party (*Hapoel Hamizrahi*—religious). So the Heferites gave up hope of settling in the Jezreel Valley and decided to look for another area. But though some members were disheartened and left the group, the great majority remained as members to await a further opportunity for settlement on the land.

Until this time the main area for settlement of co-operative settlements had been in the Jezreel Valley, because of its apparent natural advantages for farming. Yet the desire for further settlement compelled the J.N.F. to look elsewhere for other suitable areas for settlement. At the time when the Heferites were planning to settle close to Nahalal the settlement authority was extending its lands into the Yehuda and Shomrom areas. In this venture the J.N.F. hoped to enlist the aid of private agencies who would be interested in development. One of the chief agencies involved was Yachin, a company which marketed citrus and therefore planted citrus groves for new settlements.

The land on which present-day Kfar Hefer is built was one of the areas in which early Zionists dreamed of settling Jewish settlers. In his memoirs Ussishkin tells of his visit to the area and remarks upon it as one of the places important for the future of the Jewish people. The area was owned by an Arab family. According to tradition the Arab settlers said that they had originally come from the west of Trans-Jordan with their leader who had killed or driven out the original settlers. In the time of the Ottoman Empire the local Turkish official was Mustafa el-Kubani who gave his name to part of the land. But later the land was sold to a Christian Arab who built the first stone house in the area, the house which the first settlers of Kfar Hefer occupied during their first years on the land.

The J.N.F. had a perennial problem of finding money to buy land for settlement; and when a price was agreed for the area of Kfar Hefer and its surroundings, the J.N.F. did not have enough money to complete the contract. The money was raised on a fund-raising tour in Canada, and it is reported that in July, 1927, in Winnipeg at the 21st conference of the *Histadrut Zionit* (Zionist Organisation) Ussishkin spoke about this area and appealed for donations. The fund raised the money and the land was bought from its Arab owners by the J.N.F. Notwithstanding the sale there still remained some Arab squatters in the area and Bedouin who periodically came up from the area around Be'ersheva. Settlement was delayed for a time because of riots and disturbances in 1929 between Arabs and Jews.

The Kfar Hefer group heard of the purchase of this area and also heard favourable reports on its suitability for intensive farming. Water was available, there were both light sandy soils and heavier darker ones, and the land was said to be excellent for citrus. Urged on by the members of Nahalal and by their own failure to find a settlement in the Jezreel Valley, they decided to apply for settlement in this area. Their application was successful and it was decided that Kfar Hefer should develop the land in the area for settlement and also receive a parcel of land for the settlement of their own village.

It was recommended by the settlement agency that Kfar Hefer should be helped by another group. This group, 'the third group', had applied to join the Kfar Heferites whose quota of places (80) was already filled; and the settlement agency advised that this group should form a settlement in the area near to that of Kfar Hefer and that they should form a joint association with Kfar Hefer for studying the problems of a moshav. This second group was joined by a further group, 'The Valley', who were all members who had left kibbutsim and now were anxious to settle in a moshav. By themselves this last group did not have enough members to form a settlement and as they did not want to recruit a large number of members in a short time the settlement agency suggested that they join together with another group. The union with the 'third group' was organised with the help of the settlement agency, and it was planned that this united group should settle close by Kfar Hefer. The members of 'The Valley' greatly outnumbered those of the 'third group' and also differed from them in that they were married and had young children. These members had left the kibbutsim because of their dissatisfaction with the kibbuts way of life and their desire for the greater individual freedom of life in the moshav. In all some fifty members left the kibbutsim. Initially they had petitioned the settlement agency to allow them to take some land from the kibbuts to form their own settlement but this was refused. The *Histadrut Zionit* decided that it was impossible to alienate the land of a kibbuts to form a moshav and, so one member involved in the affair told me, 'In those days the *Histadrut Zionit* [or the *Mosadot* (Jewish Agency in pre-state days)] was more powerful than the Government today, so we left.' But they left reluctantly despite 'eight years in which we had only disputes' and their consequent loss of faith in the kibbuts. The decision to take their families away from the relative security of a permanent settlement into the uncertainties of unemployment and waiting for a new settlement was not easily taken. The first lot left the kibbuts in the winter of 1928 and others followed in the spring of 1929. Immediately they formed themselves into a settlement group and requested that they should be allowed to form their own moshav. The *Histadrut Zionit* recommended that they should be given priority in settlement: one member of the group said to me, 'They were interested that we should leave the kibbuts: we were a nuisance and were causing a disturbance.' The union with the third group enabled them to form a big enough unit for settlement but in the meantime until they were settled they were given work as labourers by the Palestine Electric Corporation on the construction of the Jordan Valley Power Station. Despite the agreement of the Agricultural Settlement Agency to the settlement in this area of the joint group, the J.N.F. recognised only the right of the Kfar Hefer group to settle and refused financial aid to this other group. They overcame this difficulty by receiving loans from other sources and at the end of 1929 the two prospective settlements decided to send representatives to begin working the land.

Twelve members of Kfar Hefer and eight from the joint group were sent to the area to lay the foundations of the settlements and to prepare the way for others to follow. Meanwhile the other members of the groups continued working in their jobs in other parts of the country. The 'First Twenty' on the land, as these original settlers came to be called, were all bachelors and lived in the 'big house', the stone house built by an earlier Arab owner of the land. Even today there is a 'mystique' attached to the 'First Twenty' and although no formal recognition is accorded to them, it is still undoubtedly regarded as an honour to have been one of the first twenty on the land. Part of this feeling has to be seen against the background of the settlers with their upbringing in the Zionism and revolutionary socialism of early twentieth-century Eastern Europe. The settlement of a Jewish agricultural population in the land of Palestine signalled the rebirth of the Jewish people and a way through socialism and co-operation to a new and better form of society. This can be seen to this day in the way in which members continue to speak of the 'conquest' and the 'liberation' of the land. There was also a sense of adventure in being the first settlers building this society on land where they were the first Jewish settlers.

But for these first twenty the work was difficult; and even though it may have been exciting, this excitement was lost in the tasks of preparing the land and in skirmishes with the local Arab population. In a diary[1] kept by one of the first twenty there is recorded some of the frustrations of these early settlers. The writer describes the feelings of boredom and impatience at the apparent lack of progress, and also his despair at the enormity of the task. Writing on 20 November 1930 almost a year after their settlement, he notes that another group of settlers were due to come in March. The J.N.F. were urging that the settlement be founded quickly because of their

[1] *Tlamim* (1955)

c

lack of funds, but he wrote that it was clear that if more members did not join they alone could not manage the work.

Other members did join the original nucleus in the 'big house' and together they planted a vegetable plot and grew wheat. A little later they began to plant citrus trees. Conditions were difficult. They often had disputes and problems with the Arab squatters who tried to damage and hinder the development of their work. They also had to work in drying out the swamps; and on 1 March 1931 the diarist wrote that for the third time he was suffering from malaria. On 9 March 1931 the settlers suffered their first casualty when a member was killed when the tractor he was driving fell into the river.

Gradually other members joined them and they set up temporary houses around the 'big house'. Not all the settlers worked in the preparation of the land: funds were short and many members went outside the area to find paid work in order to supplement the settlers' resources. At this time work was difficult to find and there are reports[1] telling of members walking for two or three hours to reach their place of work. Others were more fortunate and found work nearer at hand as employees of Yachin, the company planting citrus groves on land that had been bought by American Jewry as a settlement for American Jewish immigrants to Palestine. Several of the members had young children and a school was formed for them near the 'big house'. Later, the children had to attend school in the nearest town which was more than an hour's journey away, by donkey. Relationships between the two settlements were often strained: it was said by the others that the members of Kfar Hefer resented their presence and feared the loss of claims by Kfar Hefer to some of the land. In a publication of the village bulletin, a farmer in Kfar Hefer who was a child at this time, reports the squabbling between the children of the two groups and the exchange of names which reflected their identification as groups following the lines of division between their parents. The children of Kfar Hefer called the children of the joint group 'bananas' while they retorted by calling the Kfar Hefer children 'camels'.

Agricultural development was slow. Because the J.N.F. was not able to provide adequate capital for development and because of the members working outside, it was not possible to have an adequate labour force to push ahead with the settlement. Many members could only work at night after they had returned from work or could only work full-time when they were unemployed outside. Financially the members had to be self-supporting and had to rely on loans from private financial organisations. Citrus trees were

[1] *Tlamim* (1955)

planted for all the potential members of the two settlements, including those who had not yet joined the settlement. Many meetings
were held to discuss the development of agriculture and a record[1]
of one of the meetings conveys the settlers' doubts whether they
would ever reach a stage where it would be possible to earn a living
from agriculture and when outside work would not be necessary. The
settlers had begun a dairy but many cows imported from Switzerland
died; a specialist called in to give advice said that because of the
conditions in the area he doubted if the families would ever be able
to have more than one cow and one heifer per farm.

By 1932 there were about fifty families living in and around the
'big house'. At this time the idea was put forward, primarily by the
J.N.F., that the two settlements should unite to form one big village.
Already a tentative division of the land into two villages had been
agreed but nothing had been finally settled. Some members approved
the idea of one village and like the J.N.F. stressed the advantages of
a single strong moshav against two weaker ones with the wasteful
duplication of services and administration. Those opposed to the
idea said that the village formed by the combination of the two
groups would be 191 family farms and it would be too big to be
controlled as a unit. In addition the fields would be far from the
houses and organisation would be difficult. Doron, who was secretary
of the joint 'third and Valley' group, told me that the main opponents of the union were Kfar Hefer and that the basis of their
opposition was 'egoistical'. They claimed that they had the rights of
settlement on the land and they were opposed to sharing their budget
with the others. The joint group on the whole supported the union:
the ex-members of the kibbuts were anxious to be settled and were
agreeable to anything which would hasten this; the 'third group'
knew that alone they could not form a settlement so they too were
willing to form a bigger unit of settlement. The arguments were
long and bitter but at a general meeting of all the members
of the two groups it was decided to unite. The voting was most
probably seriously affected by a statement issued by the Agricultural
Settlement Agency that if the two groups did not unite then they
would have to put off settlement because of shortage of money for
two villages in the one area. Some members left Kfar Hefer after
this decision. And others who had not yet joined the settlement
informed the secretariat of their withdrawal. It was suggested to me
by Doron that some members left Kfar Hefer because of genuine
opposition to the union but that for others this was only the osten-
sible reason. As I have described, the early years of settlement were

[1] *Tlamim* (1955)

physically exacting and this proved too much for some. Others who had not yet settled the land were employed in jobs outside and as they often had young children to consider they were unwilling to give up permanent work for the risky alternative offered by Kfar Hefer. The union of the two groups was yet another turning-point in the history of the village settlement and offered them an opportunity to leave the settlement group on a question of principle without acknowledging their weakened attachment to agricultural settlement. Sharon, the secretary of the Kfar Hefer group, continued to oppose the union even after the formal vote for union, but he remained in the village as one of the controlling figures of the village secretariat, with responsibility for social matters in the village.

The size of settlement after the union of the groups was unprecedented, and to this day Kfar Hefer is one of the biggest moshavim in Israel. In addition to the arguments of members for union (cited above) the settlement also benefited from economies of scale and presented a powerful organisation in negotiations with the bureaucratic agencies of the time.

The united group still had to wait until the land in the area was divided for settlement. Many political parties and Zionist organisations were involved in this division, each wanting an area for its own settlers. Today this region has settlements representing a range of political interests: *Hashomer Hatsair, Ahdut Avoda,* and *Hapoel Hatsair*, religious settlements, and even ethnic interests with the settlement of a 'Russian Zionist' group. The land now allocated to the Kfar Hefer group was basically that given to the original group with the addition of part of the land planned for the others. Yet after the division of the land settlers still remained for a time around the 'big house' which was in fact now outside the boundaries of their land. Outside work still remained the main support of the community but agriculture had developed and the settlers worked communally a vegetable plot and grew alfalfa and fodder for the embryo dairy of the village. Late in 1932 the settlers began moving their houses to permanent sites on the land which was to be their home. All the houses were moved by putting them on wheels and towing them into position by tractor. A Heferite who was a child at this time described how her family was the first to move to the new site; they remained alone all night in their new position, surrounded by sand dunes and guarded by one young settler who had been appointed to watch over them and ensure their safety. Within a short time all the members moved to the new site of Kfar Hefer. Not all the members of the various groups took the opportunity to settle: some chose to move to other agricultural settlements while others remained outside agriculture and took jobs with organisations directing Jewish settlement in Palestine. In all it was expected that 191 families would settle in Kfar Hefer but in actual fact only 154 families came to the village.

This move to permanent settlement also brought changes in the economic situation of the village. Many members still continued to work outside while others were engaged in village administration and upkeep of the village lands. But in addition, each family received an allocation of poultry and a cow to form the basis of their individual farm economy. Until 1940 all the village land was farmed communally and fodder was also grown jointly to provide for each family's cow. As in the kibbuts the emphasis was placed on equality, and work was divided by the village secretariat according to family conditions: those families with several children were given the first opportunity of jobs. In some cases only the wife and children of a family were actually settled in Kfar Hefer while the husband worked outside and returned to the village only occasionally. In this event it was the wife's responsibility to run the farm and to work in the village fields. At this time the women, like the men, took outside jobs and worked on the land with the men. Where there were children in the family these were looked after during working hours by a woman member appointed by the village.

Communal buildings for the benefit of all the members were put up in the village. The village school was a prefabricated hut brought by the members of the 'third' group from their previous place of work prior to settlement in Kfar Hefer. A village store was installed in a hut. After considerable argument a synagogue was also established in a hut, for there was much opposition in the village to the setting up of a synagogue: many members objected that they were 'free-thinkers' and did not need a synagogue. But the view of those who said that they were establishing a Jewish, as well as a socialist, way of life prevailed, helped (I was somewhat cynically told by an opponent of the scheme) by a grant from the settlement agency towards the cost of the building. Until this day Kfar Hefer has no full-time rabbi or other religious official. The first larger permanent building to be erected was a supply store for agricultural equipment, though it was rudimentary, a few tractors and pipes for irrigation; but like the land it was communally owned and used. At first camels were used for transporting fodder, but with the growth of individual family farms these were replaced by a horse or donkey and cart owned by the individual family.

Agricultural progress was slow now that members, in addition to working communally the main lands, were trying to build up their own individual farm economies. In the late 1930's work outside the village was difficult to find and families with several children suffered hardship because of insufficient agricultural support. Social relationships in the village also became strained because of this situation. There were complaints about those who had jobs outside earning well, while others, through no fault of their own, were having a difficult time. At a village meeting it was decided that all those who had permanent jobs should be left in them but that they should contribute an amount equal to two days work to those who were unemployed. The secretary responsible for economic affairs of the village was Doron and he told me of his difficulties in arranging adequate financial support for each family. There were accusations of favouritism in the division of money and those who worked outside the village were suspected of holding back money for their own private use. I was told by one woman settler whose husband worked in full-time employment outside the village that for over a year she did not dare bring to the village a radio that she and her husband were given as a present because of the gossip and accusations that would follow. Similarly, another woman whose husband also worked outside the village told me of the gossip and unkind remarks that were made when they built their house with a lavatory inside instead of outside the house as was customary in the village. She said that she dreaded going to work with other members of the village because of their gossip and their insinuations that her husband and she were keeping money back from the husband's salary to spend on luxuries in their own home while other members did not have enough to support themselves.

In 1934 there was a population of 534 in Kfar Hefer (see also below Table 1 showing population growth). Of this number, 510 were agricultural members and their children; 8 professional residents (employed as teachers in the school or as agricultural advisers); and 16 temporary residents. In the village school there were 7 classes and 70 children were receiving education (see also Table 2).

In addition to the formal administrative and other bonds created by common membership in the village, the settlers were also linked by numerous sentimental ties. There was the tie of group affiliation before the union to form Kfar Hefer; associations had also been formed through work prior to coming to Kfar Hefer; many members were also acquainted through ties formed in the diaspora before coming to Palestine, either by membership in Zionist youth groups or through residence in the same town. In addition some members were related to one another by kinship ties. Amongst the 154 families who came to Kfar Hefer there were 11 pairs of brothers, 4 pairs of sisters and 4 pairs of brothers and sisters (19 pairs of siblings). Through their marriages, a larger number of Kfar Hefer's members were linked by affinal or consanguinal ties. Moreover there were also more distant kinship relationships, so that many told me that they knew they were related to other members of the village but they did not know the exact relationship.

The influence of these various ties can still be seen today in Kfar Hefer. In the laying out of the plan for permanent housing, members chose their neighbours, and these choices ran broadly along the lines of former group affiliations. Within the limits of the settlement choices were made according to kinship ties (brothers settling next to each other) or along the lines of friendship formed in association at work outside Kfar Hefer. Perhaps more significantly, these ties acted in a very effective manner (as described above) as a force for social control in the village. The members were all intimately known to one another and all shared the common difficulty of building the settlement. It would have been difficult to use any formal sanctions against families who were felt to be breaking the rules of social conduct, partly because such formal sanctions were hard to establish, short of actually expelling the family, but also because of their precarious situation in a settlement and their emphasis on the village as a 'community' in the social as well as economic sense. To use formal sanctions would only emphasise differences in the village and make continued co-operation difficult in other aspects of life at a time when the village was most concerned with fostering the ideals of co-operation and mutual help. The Hebrew word *haver* (plural *haverim*) which I usually translate simply as 'member' does in fact imply these desirable characteristics of social life and carries with it the idea of 'comradeship'. Thus the only sanction that could be applied was criticism through informal channels, mainly by gossip, and village members were quick to comment unfavourably on behaviour or actions which seemed 'out of place' or made members noticeably different from others. By implication at least criticism was so voiced at general meetings; and I was often told, usually nostalgically, by older members of the village, of the tremendous interest which in the past all members took in such meetings, and of their hundred per cent participation in village affairs. Further efforts were made to ensure equality by deciding at such a general meeting of all village members that all income from both agricultural work and outside work should go into a common fund which would then be distributed according to family need by the village secretariat. It was further decided that in times of unemployment a certain minimum income would be guaranteed to each family. Each family had an account held in the village co-operative where it was debited loans received from the various organisations while income from outside work or from agriculture was credited. But this minimum sum would be paid regardless of the state of the family's account.

In 1936 the village received a grant from the Jewish Agency to build a home of two rooms for each family in the village, plus a foundation of a terrace. Originally this money was to have come from a private financial corporation, *Paza* (Palestine Zionist Association), but Kfar Hefer quarrelled with *Paza* over its refusal to give equal loans to each family. *Paza* refused to give money to all the settlers because of differences in their economic situations, for some members had brought money to the village and others were earning outside the village. The villagers stood firm on one of their basic principles, 'equality in the means of production', and insisted that the corporation should give equal sums to all the members. When *Paza* was adamant the village turned to the J.N.F. and received a loan from it.

Doron, who was for all this time involved in village administration, told me that he was often uncertain how much the village members agreed with the principles of moshav life as laid down in the constitution of the moshav. Nevertheless he believed that the conditions of the time, and the difficulties they experienced, compelled the members to live according to these principles. I discuss this proposition later and examine the consequences of the lack of formal change in moshav principles in spite of the changed conditions in which these principles now have to operate. I argue that the lack of congruence between these principles and the prevailing conditions has led, over the years, to a growing institutionalisation of these principles; services which were originally conceived in direct personal terms have now been taken over by village, municipal and national agencies. In the early days of Kfar Hefer, in the absence of these agencies, villagers had to rely upon informal mutual aid organised amongst members themselves. One of the first problems they had to face was the widowing of a member whose husband was killed by Arabs while working the land. This woman had two young children to support and would have found it difficult to do this and develop her farm. Several suggestions were made concerning her future: some suggested that she be given work in the village and the farm be transferred to a new agricultural member. But the final decision was that members of a moshav helped one another in all difficulties. It was the dead man's intention that his family should be brought up in farming, and therefore the family must remain in the village, on its farm, and the farm should be developed with the aid of the other members. For the future it was decided that in any future event of this kind the village would allow the farm to be developed with the help of hired labour and the farm would be freed from taxes until the children grew up and were able to work on the farm.

Responsibility for village administration was vested in six members elected from a general meeting of the village members. Until the middle 1940's these six holders of office were divided into two committees, one responsible for economic affairs and the second dealing with the social life of the village. In the year 1936–37 (the village year runs according to the Jewish calendar, usually from September to September), two members of the original Kfar Hefer group and one from the joint group held office in each committee. In the committee dealing with economic affairs a member of the Kfar Hefer group was responsible for directing work in the village fields which were still worked communally. The second Kfar Hefer member in this committee dealt with the problems of finding employment for members and the division of work. The member of the joint group (Doron) represented the village in negotiating with outside institutions, particularly in raising money for development. The social committee dealt with the settlers' problems, the care of children, and the provision of educational facilities. On this committee the joint group was represented by Zioni, who later became head of the Regional Council on its inception, a position he has since held without interruption. The Kfar Hefer group had two representatives, Arad and Jacobs. These officials had authority to run the village, but ultimate power in making decisions remained with the general meeting of all village members. In the following year (1937–38) an intermediary body between the village administration and the general meeting was elected from the general meeting. This body, called the Council (*moetsa*) had nine members, five of whom were originally from the joint group and four from the original Kfar Hefer group. There were several women candidates for the first election to the Council, one of whom, Ruth Waxman (the wife of a member of the economic committee), was elected to office. Six members (three from each group) were elected from the Council to serve on the economic and social committees. Working relationships between these two committees were seldom smooth especially in matters requiring the spending of money, which in fact was involved in nearly all their activities. The social committee was required by the general meeting to provide a certain minimum standard of living for each family, but the economic committee tried to keep spending to a minimum in order to invest in the farm economy of the village. The member responsible for allocation of money to individual families told me [and this was a recurring complaint that I heard from all those involved in village administration]

'Everyone had a good case why they should be given extra money, but there was not enough for everyone so howsoever one distributed it there were always those who were disappointed and disgruntled.'[1]

Members continued to join the settlement (see Table 1 below). I discuss these and other population figures further in a later chapter: here I present them only to show the increasing size of the settlement. Several of those joining the village had not previously belonged to any of the groups which united to form Kfar Hefer. As I described earlier not all the members of these groups took up their option to settle in Kfar Hefer. Furthermore some of those already settled in Kfar Hefer left the village. In some cases they disliked farming: others had jobs outside which fully occupied them, and rather than

Table 1 Population growth in Kfar Hefer in the first 25 years

	1934	1939	1944	1949	1954
Agricultural members and their children	510	641	695	692	800
Professional members	8	21	24	54	105
Temporary residents and others*	16	110	156	234	129
Total	**534**	**772**	**875**	**980**	**1034**

* These numbers were inflated in the years of World War II and in the immediate years after Statehood (1948) by groups of young people who were brought to Palestine (or Israel) without their parents and temporarily housed in Kfar Hefer until they could find permanent homes.

devote more time to building up their own farms they preferred to leave the village. There were not many of these, but their departure did allow new members from outside to buy farms in the village. New members continued to join the settlement until 1939 when the maximum number of farming units, 154, was reached.

Table 1 shows the growth in the numbers of 'professional' members in the village. Almost from the very beginning the village had enjoyed the advice of professionals who were resident in the village. As agriculture developed, albeit slowly, the need for technical advice and for skilled work increased. Actually the term 'professional' is somewhat misleading, since very few of these members had any formal qualifications. They were 'professionals' in the sense that they were paid by the village for their work, but probably the term

[1] For a discussion of this point see Gluckman (1955)

'skilled workers' gives a more accurate description of the functions they fulfilled in the village life. It became clear that these professionals were an integral part of the village even though they were not farmers and so the village decided to give them formal recognition. A category of 'professional' members (as compared with the farmers who were 'agricultural' members) was created, and the professionals were awarded certain rights and duties in the village. They were given the right to vote in village meetings (except on matters concerning agriculture); and they enjoyed full use of all the village services, including education for their children. They were not allowed to own fixed property in the village but were given a house, for which they had to pay a nominal rent to the village Council, in the village for the duration of their work there.

In the meantime settlement in the area around Kfar Hefer had got under way and as early as 1934 a joint meeting of representatives of all the settlers in the area was called in Kfar Hefer. The settlers agreed to form a union to press for representation in the *Knesset* (at that time the unofficial legislative body for the Jewish population in Palestine) and to this end they chose a committee which met in Kfar Hefer. This was the beginning of the Regional Council as it was later called, and Kfar Hefer as the economically strongest settlement in the region played the major part in its foundation. Twelve settlements were represented at the first meeting and they agreed to work together to help in drying out the swamps of the area and to exploit the water of the region's river for irrigation purposes. The headquarters of this association were established in Kfar Hefer, and Zioni (mentioned previously) from the beginning acted as chairman of the group, a position which was later changed to 'Head of the Regional Council' when the association received official recognition from the British Mandatory government. The settlements co-operated in the defence of the area which still suffered from intermittent Arab raiding and also in the provision of services such as drainage and sewerage. Later more formal rules were drawn up setting out the relationships between the settlements in the area and also between them and governmental institutions. The original committee acted as the representatives of the area to the British Mandatory government and also acted, *de facto* if not *de jure*, as the municipal authority of the area.

The outbreak of World War II brought changes to the area and to the village in particular. Apart from individual volunteers to serve in the Jewish Brigade and British Army, the village as a whole decided to send members to serve in the army. A general meeting decided the numbers and also the individuals who were to go. Those chosen were bachelors or, wherever possible, those without family responsibilities.

By 1940 the individual farms had begun to progress and even to make money. Now many of the 'second generation' in the village, the sons and daughters of the settlers, were old enough to give real help on the farm. Table 2 shows the school population and gives an indication of the numbers and age of the young people.

The establishment of a British and Allied army camp near the village had a considerable effect upon village life and its economy. The presence of the British Army gave opportunities for employment to the village members. But increasingly members were devoting more and more time to their farms at the expense of outside work. The blockade on the country during the war resulted in orders for foodstuffs and supplies for the army being given to Jewish settlements. Kfar Hefer, because of her proximity to the camp, benefited and villagers began to experience prosperity. Ties of friendship developed between the villagers and the soldiers for whom the

Table 2   School population in Kfar Hefer, 1934–54

	1934	1939	1944	1949	1954
No. of grades	7	8	10	11	12
No. of pupils	70	151	242	245	334

members of Kfar Hefer began to perform small services. This was welcomed and approved by the village Council and committees but in some cases the transactions were on a financial basis, for example shoe repairing or the renting out of rooms. This income provided a standby against the vagaries and vicissitudes of farming but was contrary to the principles of co-operation and non-exploitation on which Kfar Hefer was founded. The secretary of the village at this time told me that they had to put a stop to these activities when people began to put signs outside their houses advertising their services. The village also thwarted attempts at private sales of produce which circumvented the village accounts. All sales were organised communally through the village co-operative and there was no selling privately, or on the black market, by Kfar Hefer members. Nevertheless the conditions prevailing at this time did give a boost to agriculture at a time when the members were able to exploit this opportunity.

The growth in agricultural production is shown in Tables 3 and 4. Table 4 shows the reliance of the members on mixed farming, a decision which had been taken many years earlier in Nahalal. There were practical and idealistic reasons for this choice: on the one hand there was the proclaimed ideal that members be self-sufficient and work to produce their own livelihood; while on the other hand mixed farming provided a basic subsistence for the village and saved the expense of buying food from outside. Similarly, mixed farming also lessened the village's dependence upon market fluctuations, and stood up better to the unpredictable security situation which hindered the establishment of reliable trading ties. The citrus groves were an obvious choice because of the natural advantage of the region for growing citrus fruit. The settlers were unfortunate that at the time the trees began giving fruit there was a blockade on the country and

Table 3 Head of cattle and milk production (in 000 litres) in Kfar Hefer, 1936–54

	1936	1939	1944	1949	1954
Total head of cattle	246	168	609	1375	1569
cows	159	124	303	605	584
milk production	494·4	386·4	1,035·8	2,086·6	2,175·5

Table 4 Gross income according to agricultural branches in Kfar Hefer, 1936–1954 (in Israeli pounds and as percentage of total production)*

	1936	%	1932	%	1944	%	1949	%	1954	%
Dairy produce	5,225	65·4	4,178	25	50,938	30·8	165,819	36·2	548,264	31·2
Poultry produce	2,650	33·2	11,667	70	83,830	50·7	184,243	40·2	806,010	46·0
Citrus			120	0·7	2,887	1·7	53,516	11·6	333,130	19·0
Vegetable	303	1·4	688	4·3	17,536	16·8	54,905	12·0	67,456	3·8
		100		100		100		100		100

* pre-state Israeli pound was equal to pound sterling of that time

no shipments for export could be made. All their production had to be for the home market and in actual fact most of the fruit was given to the animals as feed. Meanwhile production of vegetables and tomatoes developed rapidly in the war years. Although these crops demanded a lot of work there was a ready market and a good return for a relatively small input of financial capital and a short period between this investment and return. The sons and daughters of the farms were now sufficiently grown up to provide labour additional to that of the member and his wife. Poultry was introduced into the village for two reasons: firstly, to provide work and an income close to the family house for the women of the moshav, and secondly, to provide a basic staple food supply for the family. Initially, as I have related, the women of the settlement worked with the men in all sections of the village economy, in work outside the village and in the fields. But the birth and care of children resulted in women becoming more and more tied to the house. Yet their work was still needed to boost the farm economy and so efforts were made to find a form of employment which would enable women to care for their families at home while continuing to contribute to the farm income. Poultry was chosen as a suitable enterprise because it fulfilled these conditions and also because it added to the diet of the family, especially of the children. It was not difficult to get staple food for a family but the members did not have the ready money to buy food. I shall show in a later chapter that until recently in the village the upkeep of poultry had been regarded primarily as women's work. The dairy was also established to ensure internal self-sufficiency in milk products. Despite the early difficulties already recounted this branch did develop rapidly in the early 1940's. The main emphasis was on milk production and only in the last few years has rearing of cattle for meat become a major branch in the village.

The effect of increased agricultural production and the sale of the produce led to a demand by some settlers that the land should be divided between the members and that each family should work its own individual farm. The families now had the means to develop their farms in a young labour force provided by their children and they had ready markets for produce. Not all members were anxious for the land to be divided. Some were doubtful of their ability to run their own farm independently in such a way that they would be able to make a living. Others, for demographic reasons, such as small families or very young children or only girls in the family, knew that they would have a physically hard and difficult time in managing their own farms. Others opposed the idea because the men of the family were still engaged in outside work which they were reluctant to relinquish. These argued that when at long last things were beginning to go well they would be foolish to change the system. The counter argument of those in favour of land division said that they had come to Kfar Hefer to be independent yet co-operative farmers, and this was the distinguishing feature of moshav life. They argued that the division of the land was an inevitable and essential part of the settlement's development; and it was this argument that won the day.

Over a period of years the land was divided into the family farms. The citrus plantations were divided with each family being allocated three dunams (one dunam is approximately a quarter of an acre) of land planted with trees. There was also a 'reserve' of two and a half dunams for each member to be planted with citrus trees at a later date. Once the groves were divided it was the responsibility of each member to look after his own plot. The other village lands were divided in the same way and gradually each member began to assume responsibility for his 'own land'. The division did not pass without disputes. Despite the relatively small size of the village (at this time there were about 4,000 dunams cultivated) there are differences in soil type and in availability of water; some areas are sheltered while others are exposed; yet others are low-lying and susceptible to night frosts. The farming experience of the previous years had made members aware of the differences in yields between these various areas and each farmer was anxious that he should receive a good plot of land. The land division was carried out by a special

Table 5 Land use in Kfar Hefer, 1936–54 (in dunams)

	1936	1939	1944	1949	1954
Dry land field crops (winter)	800	1,005	565	2,250	3,214
Irrigated crops	150	559	1,937	1,950	2,962
Citrus groves	620	692	700	750	828
Total cultivation	**1,570**	**2,256**	**3,202**	**4,950**	**7,004**
Paths, roads and uncultivated	2,030	1,589	1,542	1,182	1,329
Total area	**3,600**	**3,845**	**4,744**	**6,132**	**8,333**

committee appointed for the purpose and it tried to ensure that every farm received both good and less good parcels of land. Nevertheless there were complaints about the division, not least of which was the objection that each farmer's fields were situated in different places over the cultivated land and this involved him in much wasted time simply in moving from one area to another. Subsequently, further divisions and re-organisations have taken place in an attempt to rationalise each member's holding. Table 5 gives a picture of the total use of village land.

The full exploitation of land resources was held back in the early years because of lack of water. The installation of an extra water-pipeline in late 1936 helped cultivation to expand, and in the middle and late 1940's additional land was added to the village giving a total cultivated area of a little over 6,000 dunams. Eventually each member received a total farming area of 28–30 dunams: this contrasted with the 100 dunams allocated to each settler in Nahalal but it was considered to be an adequate amount for the type of farming carried out in Kfar Hefer. It was fortunate for the village members that all the expected 191 families did not settle in the village because undoubtedly there would not have been sufficient land for them.

The division of land meant that the individual families, although supported by village institutions, were now on their own in their responsibility for their farm's development. The greater part of the members gave up outside work and concentrated on agriculture as their livelihood. Some members still continued to work outside and in a later chapter I shall discuss the effect of this on the individual farm concerned and on the village as a whole. Thus, by the middle 1940's the settlers of Kfar Hefer had achieved their aim of establishing their own moshav. Each family had its own house, its own allocation of land, and its own livestock.

Each farm unit received an equal allocation of the 'means of production', in keeping with the moshav principle to ensure equality amongst the members. Poultry, like land, was distributed equally between the members of the village. Initially the distribution of dairy cows was on an equal basis, but as farms began to develop each family increased its dairy herd according to its financial ability. Other measures were taken to ensure equality of members and to minimise economic differentiation in the village, notably in the system of taxation. All members of the village (both professional and agricultural) paid both municipal and co-operative taxes to the village co-operative. The money was used to maintain and improve village services, in particular for education and the upkeep of the school which was owned by the village. There was a progressive system of taxation for agricultural members who paid according to income. Professional members all paid an equal sum, usually less than the average tax of the agricultural members. By this system the village tried to provide another form of mutual aid and socialist co-operation between members, for the economically strong farms thus subsidised the weaker farms.

Village administrative activities grew concomitantly with the development of individual farms. From the time when Kfar Hefer had begun production all the produce had been marketed collectively through the village administration. This system was an essential part of moshav life as laid down by the moshav constitution. Collective marketing maintained the working of the village as an administrative unit and re-affirmed the co-operative aspect of moshav life. Also, this system enabled the village to run a system of loans to its members. Members were given advances against their production and when payment was received for the produce marketed, these advances were deducted, and the remainder was credited to the farmer. For the operation of this system it was essential that receipts from the sale of the produce be channelled through the village co-operative. It was also in the interests of the villagers as a whole that they should market in this way, for without credit they could not continue in farming. Within the framework of this scheme it would have been beneficial for the individual member to market his produce privately without repaying debts to the village, and also avoid payment to the middleman. But I have been told that at this time there was seldom private marketing: it was restrained both by the commitment to moshav principles and by the fear of sanctions. If a member was found to be marketing privately then either the estimated income was debited in his account or for a time he was refused quotas of produce or feeding stuff. In a later chapter I shall discuss more fully the operation of sanctions and social control in the village. In actual fact it was difficult to market milk privately and for practical reasons the farmers preferred to market through the village. Citrus was also difficult to market privately, which was not really worthwhile. Vegetables and eggs were the most easily marketed 'on the side' but the village co-operative through its control and distribution of financial credit held a powerful weapon against this practice.

The village general meeting continued to be the ultimate constitutional body to make decisions and, as previously, a Council, now of 15 members, was elected to serve as an intermediary between village members and the village Executive. Until 1945 this Executive was divided into social and economic committees: thereafter five members were elected to manage all these affairs jointly. The jobs of internal and external secretary (respectively the heads of the social and economic committees) were full-time paid positions, and the members concerned received a salary intended to be equal to that of the average income from agriculture. These positions were open for election and re-election every year, but in practice the members of the Council and of the Executive committee tended to be drawn from only a few of the village members. Once a member was elected to one of these bodies he tended to be re-elected at once or at least return after a short break. This incipient development of a village 'bureaucracy' was considered by the village to be against the spirit of moshav life which demanded equal participation by all members in the running of the village. Therefore, in 1943 the annual general meeting decided that the Council and executive should be elected from village members who had not previously served on these bodies. But another characteristic of moshav life is the encouragement of individual initiative and autonomy within the boundaries of the moshav. Not enough members agreed to be candidates for election

D

so the idea had to be abandoned, and Council and committee members continued to be drawn from the same few. Many members were reluctant to take on the duties of village administration because of their total involvement in their farms. Demographic patterns, age of children, ill health, and the crop patterns of farms, all made for differences in a farmer's ability to serve as a committee member. Candidates and members of councils and committees tended to be drawn from those villagers who had additional sources of labour for the family farm, but there was also a core of members who had always been active in various organisations even before the settlement in Kfar Hefer, and who continued to volunteer or to be pressed to serve. These latter members, because of past experience, specialist knowledge, and ideological commitment to the Labour Zionist movement, regularly stood as candidates for election. Several women were elected to the Council but none were ever members of the Executive committee.

Other committees were set up by the General Meeting to serve the interests of the village. Committees for education and culture were formed as well as those dealing with various agricultural branches (poultry, citrus and dairy). These economic committees demanded a lot of work for their successful functioning and the secretaries of these committees each received a small monthly salary to recompense them for time devoted to their tasks.

The village's ties with institutions and organisations on a country-wide basis became more diversified and more formal. Earlier in the chapter I referred to the Regional Council; as settlements developed so did the work of the Council. The siting of the Regional Council office in Kfar Hefer meant that the village was always in touch with Council affairs and played a part in directing them. Jewish immigration into Palestine, which was heavy in the late 1930's and early 1940's, necessitated the growth and strengthening of existing Jewish organisations to help them settle. Even though Jewish settlement took place in the framework of British Mandatory government the various Jewish organisations did in fact form an autonomous government within this state. There was an elected body (the *va'ad leumi* (National Council) to represen tthe interests of the Jewish population to the mandatory government. Agencies for the promotion of immigration and settlement, and financial corporations and banks, served the economic sector of Jewish life. The very important *Histadrut* (General Labour Federation) controlled all labour interests as well as being involved in policy making. Political parties were also active and contended with one another for power in these various institutions. All the parties agreed upon the necessity and desirability of increasing Jewish immigration into Palestine but they hotly disputed about the best ways to do this. To serve the interests of moshav members there were federations of moshavim, based on political affiliation. Kfar Hefer was affiliated to what was to become the largest federation, 'The Moshav Movement.' Marketing and buying organisations existed to buy from and supply the moshavim. *Tnuva*, the biggest agricultural distributor, took all Kfar Hefer's produce; and the village bought supplies from *Hamashbir Hamerkazi*, the wholesale organisation owned by the *Histadrut*. Thus the '*Yishuv*', as the pre-state Jewish population of Palestine was called, was amply supplied with agencies to provide for its needs. Kfar Hefer, both because of her members' 'ideological' commitment to Labour Zionism and because of her position as one of the oldest moshavim, took an active part in these organisations. In the Moshav Movement delegates from Kfar Hefer sat on the executive committee and helped to determine policy. The village was represented on the central socialist political movement. Similarly, delegates from the village sat on the board of *Tnuva*. Commenting on this period Eisenstadt wrote: 'The political elite can be identified with leaders and the main officials of the various national institutions. . .'[1] and, 'Leadership of the *Yishuv* and the strata with the highest prestige did not belong to the high income group and emphasised their simple way of life as part of their legitimation of power.' He goes on to comment that,

it was only gradually that a second fully fledged ideology developed according to which economic power, wealth, etc., were in themselves the main justification for political power. Until the end of the mandatory period this was only secondary in the *Yishuv* social structure. Thus it happened that a large part of the office holders and influential people in the *Yishuv's* political organisation consisted of members of collective settlements, former workers in agricultural colonies and intellectuals of the various leaders of youth movements. At the outset not many holders of private economic power or of purely political or Trade Union bosses were amongst the first rank of leadership.

The *Yishuv* was not in fact so monolithic as the above quotation may suggest. Not all Jewish immigrants to Palestine were members of collective or communal settlements; many settled in towns and engaged in the professions, in commerce and in trade; others were private farmers working their own land. All these sections of the population influenced the development of Palestine, a fact reflected in the variety of associations and organisations they set up to serve

[1] Eisenstadt (1960)

their interests. Yet, as Eisenstadt points out, the dominant political role was assumed by delegates of kibbutsim and moshavim.

The main leaders came from kibbutsim who, because of their communal economic organisation, were better able to support full-time delegates sent to serve in these organisations. But Kfar Hefer also provided some leaders, and the village became known as one of the main pillars of pre-State organisation at this time. Thus concomitant with the growth of the village's economic significance in Palestine, its political significance also grew culminating in the establishment of the State when the village gained a nation-wide reputation as one of Israel's foremost settlements. It was in the village's interest to be amongst the policy makers; and the absence of any single central authority, and the diversity of its resources, enabled the village to exercise influence and pressure in many spheres. Yet equally there was a genuine ideological commitment and concern which prompted the village to take a part in directing these affairs. Their attempts to achieve within their moshav a new society which was in some way a redemption from the attributes of diaspora Jewry spread over into the wider area of Jewish life in Palestine, for they were anxious that this too should be built on the principles of 'spiritual redemption through redemption of the land, manual labour and co-operative enterprise'.[1]

These several institutions had to cope with waves of immigrants who came into Palestine after the end of World War II and emergency measures had to be used to deal with the further numbers of immigrants after the creation of the State of Israel in 1948. The second generation of Kfar Hefer fought in the War of Liberation which followed hard on the declaration of independent Statehood. In these two wars the village lost seven of her sons.

The existing national organisations in Palestine took on governmental duties with the creation of the State of Israel, and new organisations were formed as the functions of the mandatory administration were taken over. The achievement of Statehood 'gave rise to a whole new gamut of new political power positions which had not existed before',[2] a national army was set up, and bureaucracies were formed to administer the state administration and deal with the waves of immigrants that flowed into the country. Kfar Hefer's representatives and delegates now became members of state and local governmental institutions. As early pioneers they had worked for this achievement but nevertheless it proved a turning-point in the structure of *Yishuv* as they had known it. The economic and administrative resources of the *Yishuv* (now State) organisations

[1] Willner (1960)   [2] Eistenstadt (1960)

were stretched to the limit in dealing with the sudden enormous rush of immigration. For the first years the administration was carried out by 'beleagured improvisation': and the 'respective jurisdiction of national institutions was worked out only piecemeal and gradually during the 1950's'.[1]

For many and complex reasons it was decided to settle these new immigrants into settlements based on the moshav pattern. The mobilisation of the immigrants for land settlement began within months of the creation of the State and the existing bureaucracies had no time to plan for the changed conditions. The moshav was chosen partly because its organisation based on families was seen to provide a framework into which all types of immigrants fitted. Further, the political parties in the country each had a stake in the existing form of settlement through the affiliation of each settlement to a particular party. The parties saw this new settlement as a way of maintaining or possibly improving their relative power positions in the country. There were also expressed 'sociological' reasons for choosing the moshav system in preference to that of the kibbuts. The belief was held that qualifications higher than those possessed by most of the new immigrants were necessary for the establishment of a kibbuts. There thus developed the pattern whereby kibbutsim were established on the exposed borders of the state and the mass of the immigrants were settled in moshavim built to consolidate the territory newly acquired in the interior of the country. In spite of attempts to build up their staffs to cope with their newly acquired tasks and powers the bureaucracies could not adequately cope with the task of settling all the immigrants, and so an appeal was made to established settlements for their help. The youth of Kfar Hefer was amongst the first to answer this appeal and it is from this time that the village reinforced its reputation as a leading moshav.

Doron from Kfar Hefer was appointed the chief instructor for the Moshav Movement Federation and he had the responsibility of organising instruction for all the settlements affiliated to this movement. At first the second generation of Kfar Hefer was sent out as social and economic instructors, mainly to new moshavim in the Negev. Altogether 27 of the sons and daughters of Kfar Hefer acted as instructors over a period of several years, and one of these, a girl instructor, was killed in a new moshav by a grenade thrown by Arab saboteurs. In some cases the recruitment of these young people caused difficulties on the family farm, since the oldest members of the village were now in their late fifties and it was difficult for them to manage a farm by themselves. All the instructors returned to the

[1] Willner (1960)

village at the end of their service and all but three remained in Kfar Hefer as farmers. When the young people returned, some members of the older generation also volunteered to serve as instructors. Amongst the 26 of the older generation who served were six women who acted as social instructors and taught Hebrew to the immigrants. Closer to home, Kfar Hefer through the offices of the Regional Council, helped in the establishment of seven new moshavim in the immediately surrounding area.

Along with the rise in political significance the village also boosted its economic output (see tables 3 and 4). There was a great demand for food to satisfy the needs of the new population and because of the shortages food prices were high. Kfar Hefer consolidated her position as a major producer, and yields and output grew rapidly while the village obtained a large share of the home market. The end of the war also meant the end of the blockade and citrus products could be exported to Europe. The trees gave a very good crop of 8–9 tons per dunam and even more while 4–5 tons is generally considered good. Some farms now had two families working on them, for the second generation, whether son or daughter, with spouse, joined the parents on the farm. With this extra labour, the farms prospered.

II
Economic and social relationships

Today (1968) Kfar Hefer has a prosperous appearance and is considered by other moshavim, and in Israel generally, to be a well-to-do village. All the original houses have been extended. Many of the population have private cars, and telephones installed in their houses. The village is well laid out, with surfaced roads and paved footpaths. An impressive number of public buildings serve the population. There are many visible signs that the village as a whole enjoys a high standard of living.

Economically Kfar Hefer is still based on mixed farming of three main branches: dairy, citrus and poultry. The production of vegetables has declined and today the few members who do grow vegetables do so mainly for their own use. There have been some changes in holding of land within the village. In the late 1940's two additions were made to the area, increasing the village's holding from 4,000 dunams to a little over 6,000 dunams. The greater part of the cultivated land is irrigated (see Table 6).

Water is obtained from two sources: the village's own wells supply two-thirds of water consumption; the remaining third comes from *Mekorot* (The National Water Company). Water for irrigation comes mainly from the village's own resources, and only in special cases is water from *Mekorot* used in the fields. The provision of sufficient water supplies has always been a problem in Palestine and in Israel, because of climatic conditions and lack of surface and underground water. To a large extent this difficulty has been overcome, partially by increased supplies, partially by efficient use of the available resources. Nevertheless the village is restricted in its use of water and receives an annual quota of water determined by government agencies. Internally, this quota is equally divided amongst the members.

Comparing Table 6 with Table 4, which gives land use in Kfar Hefer in the years 1936–54, one sees that the total area of cultivated land increased until 1954, but since then the area has declined slightly, notably in field crops. After the foundation of the State and the establishment of settlements in the area of Kfar Hefer, the village had some land taken from her for these new settlements. The original number of settlers expected to settle in Kfar Hefer was 191. There was never enough land to provide for the needs of this number, but the area was greater than that considered suitable at the time for the

Table 6 Land Use in Kfar Hefer, 1966–69 (in dunams)

	Farmhouse and plot	Total land cultivated	Total land cultivated with permanent right to land	Temporary cultivation	Non-irrigated land	Fallow	Wooded
1966/67							
Field		2,485	2,485	80	80	80	
Orchard		1,786	1,706			80	
Total	**1,839**	**4,271**	**4,191**	**80**	**80**	**80**	**195**
1967/68							
Field		2,485	2,405	80	80	80	
Orchard		1,786	1,786			80	
Total	**1,839**	**4,271**	**4,191**	**80**	**80**	**80**	**195**
1968/69							
Field		2,485	2,405	80	80	80	
Orchard		1,786	1,786			80	
Total	**1,839**	**4,271**	**4,191**	**80**	**80**	**80**	**195**

154 farming families of Kfar Hefer. Consequently the land area was adjusted so that each member could receive the 28–30 dunams of land which was the accepted size of a farm holding in a moshav. The great increase in irrigation is also apparent, and today only 80 dunams are not irrigated. This development has greatly helped the farmer to plan his crops to a steady flow of work and a constant income. The cultivation under the heading 'orchard' in Table 6 refers mainly to citrus groves: of the 1,706 dunams of orchards planted, 707 dunams are planted with trees bearing fruit, and the remaining 999 dunams are planted with young trees. As will be recalled the first citrus trees were planted nearly 40 years ago and because of declining yields many have now been replaced by young trees. The increase in orchards shown in 1967 is due to the introduction of avocado, a crop new to the village. The land for the crop was prepared in 1967/68 and planting was started in 1968. Thus the village economy has expanded through increased efficiency in farming methods and through the shifting of attention to more valuable crops.

Dairy farming has grown very rapidly in Kfar Hefer and the village is one of the biggest producers among moshavim. Table 7 shows an inventory of farm livestock in 1966/67.

Table 7 Farm livestock in Kfar Hefer, 1966/67

	Beginning of year	*End of year*
Horses		
(Working animals)	12	8
Dairy cattle		
Cows	956	963
Heifers (calves(f))	829	871
Total	**1,785**	**1,834**
Bull calves		
(meat)	737	675
Fowls		
layers	36,742	74,426
breeding	51,104	
chickens	28,558	16,377
fattening	2,720	3,653
chicks	11,875	18,370
turkeys	28,192	24,960
cockerels		4,046
Total	**159,191**	**141,832**

From the one cow and one heifer originally conceived as an adequate dairy for a moshav farm, many farms in Kfar Hefer have now over 30 head of cattle, and the median number of cattle per farm is 22. The emphasis is still on milk production but increasingly farms are raising bull calves for slaughter. The poultry branch has also extended: about 10 million table eggs are marketed by the village each year, and the rearing of turkeys is a new branch that is profitable.

Production in the village has increased tremendously in the last five years and the gross revenue from the sale of agricultural produce in the year 1966–67 was about 7½ million IL. (Israeli pounds IL.8·40 = £1). Table 8 shows the production, gross return and amounts paid to members from the marketing of their produce (1965–67).

Table 8 gives the figures for 1965/66 and 1966/67 in a slightly different way, showing the comparative contribution of the farm branches to the total village income from farming.

Comparison with Table 4 shows that keeping poultry has lost its first position as the main source of income for the village: dairying has now taken over this position, and contributes about 40 per cent of the village's gross income. Vegetables which in 1944 formed 16·8 per cent of the total gross income have now declined completely and do not even appear in the Table for 1965–66 and 1966–67. With the formation of new settlements after the establishment of the State, most of the vegetable production of the country was transferred to them, since it is well suited to new farmers because of the small investment needed and the quick return on investment. Because of the availability of more profitable branches the members of Kfar Hefer are no longer prepared to give the large number of working days and manual labour required to grow vegetables. Table 9 shows the new development in Kfar Hefer of rearing turkeys: this branch has proved very profitable over the last few years and now provides almost 18 per cent of gross income. Citrus has declined in value, both relatively, with the growth of other branches, and absolutely because of declining yields from old trees, while newly planted trees are only now beginning to bear fruit.

The village administration manages very large sums of money. The fixed and co-operative costs of the village have grown from IL.4,009,554 in 1962/63 to IL.5,897,857 in 1966/67. Village financing is to a large extent from the members themselves, and from the assets they hold in various organisations and institutions in Israel, primarily those concerned with agriculture and marketing. The village also receives loans from banks and national organisations. In

Table 8 Marketing of produce of Kfar Hefer's members in the years accounted, 1965–67

	Amount	Gross return IL	Paid to members IL
1965/66			
Milk (000 litres)	4,290·2	1,678,401	1,575,506
Bull calves	769	834,299	820,595
Table eggs (000)	10,742·8	1,022,201	985,420
Breeding eggs (hens 000)	3,523·9	906,944	864,235
Breeding eggs (turkeys 000)	188·6	152,445	152,445
Poultry (hens, cockerels) (live weight tons)	269	422,540	397,173
Turkeys (live weight tons)	422·5	1,218,430	1,202,135
Chickens	12,080	43,485	42,483
Breeding cockerels	118	1,163	1,160
Vegetables (tons)	36,659	3,868	3,300
Citrus { Export	1,454·7	322,123	} 349,381
Home	491·5	38,973	
Clementinas (tons)	1,093·3	442,564	400
Lemons (tons)	2·1	981	966
Total		**7,068,417***	**6,395,199**
1966/67			
Milk (000 litres)	42,382	1,642,754	1,536,673
Bull calves	633	908,616	888,646
Table eggs (000)	10,755	1,043,166	1,004,706
Breeding eggs (hens 000)	3,395	878,466	821,416
Breeding eggs (turkeys 000)	137·2	154,784	151,075
Poultry (hens, cockerels) (live weight, tons)	225	320,522	298,292
Turkeys (live weight, tons)	573·2	1,333,025	1,300,157
Chickens	16,610	104,780	103,194
Breeding cockerels			
Vegetables (tons)			
Citrus { Export	1,980·6	462,533	} 521,849
Home		69,828	
Clementinas (tons)	1,178·4	493,126	454,776
Lemons (tons)			
Total		**7,411,600**	**7,080,784**

* Plus additional credits from 1964/65: table eggs—IL.15,195, turkeys—IL.7,181.

1966/67 the credit of the members in their personal accounts in the village was IL.452,212 but the indebtedness of village members to the village co-operative totalled over IL.1,000,000.

A village member writing in a special publication of the Moshav

Movement journal[1] said that Kfar Hefer was one of the first settlements which through her own efforts and experiences found the solution to the problems of the moshav. He comments that the moshav is built 'both socially and economically'. And '. . . a sound basis of the village is built on finances from the members themselves'.

One of the main factors affecting Kfar Hefer's economic situation is that agricultural production now takes place within the framework of governmental and national economic planning. Up to the creation of the State, village production increased largely according to the members' own abilities, financial and physical, to expand their production. After 1948 this situation still continued for a number of years, and production was actively encouraged by government in order to provide for the large increase in the country's population. However, by 1955 the food scarcity had been overcome, since new settlements were producing and fewer immigrants were coming into

Table 9   Comparative gross income from agriculture in Kfar Hefer, 1965–67

Produce	IL.	1965/66 %	1966/67 %
Dairy	2,959,150	40·0	38·9
Poultry	1,848,417	32·2	31·5
Turkeys	1,634,750	17·8	17·6
Citrus	712,600	10·0	12·0
		100·0	**100·0**

the country. For a time the effect of this change was not felt because of an exceptionally large number of years of drought. And, 'in addition consumption changes brought a prosperity in the livestock branches from which the moshavim profited mostly. Only in 1958/59 did the crisis come, leading to considerable losses in most of Israeli agriculture. From that time on administrative limitations of production have been introduced by the government for one branch after another and subsidies to agriculture grow.'[2]

Several government ministries and departments are involved in agricultural planning. The Ministry of Agriculture and the Central Planning Department of the government fix production figures in consultation with producers' representatives. Apart from the moshav and kibbuts federations which act as spokesmen for their members' interests, representatives from private farming are also consulted. In addition there exist several marketing agencies and councils for particular farm branches, such as the Poultry Breeders' Union and the Cattle Marketing Board, which seek to promote the production

[1] *Tlamim* (1955)   [2] Shatil (1966)

of their respective branches. Production quotas for individual settlements are by and large based on production in previous years though overall these quotas are affected by changes in government policy: thus, for example, a 10 per cent decrease in poultry on a national level results in a 10 per cent reduction in each settlement's production quota. In actual fact the workings of production quotas are seldom as simple as this and I shall discuss in greater detail the effect of quotas on the village, the extent to which the village is able to withstand pressure on production, and also the effect within the village and on the individual farmer of changes in national economic policy.

Despite efforts at control the nation as a whole now faces serious over-production in all the areas traditionally regarded as the main agricultural branches. In an article in the *Jerusalem Post*, 26 January 1968, there is the report of a statement by the director of *Tnuva*: 'Israel is no longer a land flowing with milk and honey. It is a land overflowing with milk and honey and the main problem is how to deal with the surpluses.' In a report from a *Knesset* debate,[1] Haim Gvati, the Minister of Agriculture, cited the difficulties facing citrus production: rising costs at home (in picking and handling the crop and in transport charges); uncertain prices abroad; difficulties of tariffs imposed by the Common Market countries. Per head farm income has fallen in the past three years by one and a half to 2 per cent. A member of *Gahal* (conservative right-wing party) said that only a re-structuring of agriculture could cope with their problems: the country needed larger units of production and small moshav units should be liquidated; he urged that 'ideological and political motives' should not stand in the way of these changes. This then is the context within which Kfar Hefer's production takes place: home markets are saturated; overseas markets are uncertain; and a re-organisation of agriculture is demanded. The following chapters show the village's response to this state of affairs.

The first generation in Kfar Hefer, the original settlers, were concerned not only to establish a new way of life different from the life they had known in the diaspora, but also to pass this way of life on to their children. In keeping with their Labour-Zionist background they had undergone deprivations and difficult times in order to achieve this. In 1968 there were 230 families in farm units and farming the land (Table 10).

The total population of the village in 1966/67 was 704 persons (Table 11).

More than a third of the village's population residing at the time of the census is between the ages of 21–59 years, those aged 60 years

[1] *Jerusalem Post*, 1 January 1967

Table 10   Employed in Kfar Hefer, 1966/67

	Farming families	Professional members	Hired Workers	Others
Farming				
in village	230*	5		
outside				
Industry				
in village				
outside				
Farming services				
in village	15†		54	
outside				
Other services				
in village		5	6	
outside				
Agricultural Occupations				
in Kfar Hefer				10
Total	**230**	**5**	**60**	**10**

* As there are 151 farm units it will be seen that of these 230 farming families some 80 have a second generation farming with their parents.
† These 15 people occur twice in the table—they are also included in the 230 farming families.

Table 11   Population in Kfar Hefer, 1966/67

	Aged 0–5	Aged 6–14	Aged 15–18	Aged 19–20	Aged 21–59	Aged 60–65	Aged 66+
Male	38	38	20	10	138	62	38
Female	42	40	14	4	145	60	55

and above form almost another third of the population, and young people, aged up to 20 years, are also slightly less than a third. This last figure may in fact be somewhat higher than shown here because of the probable under-representation of the age group 19–20, since this is the age-span within which young people are serving in the Army and some of these may return to the village. Although those in the age groups 60 years and above are still engaged in some form of agriculture and are classed by the village as agricultural members, because of the physically exacting nature of farming the bulk of the village production is by the age group 21–59 years, i.e. by slightly more than a third of the village population. Most of the age group up to 19 years are the third generation of Kfar Hefer, the grand-children of the original settlers. Already for a number of years they have given occasional help in the farms but in the near future they are potential new farmers in the village.

Table 12 gives in a more detailed form an analysis of population changes in the village over the last five years. This table shows that there has been a drop in the population of the village since the end of 1965. Comparing this table with Table 1 the fall in population is even more apparent. Yet the number of second-generation families farming in their parents' farms has steadily increased during the five-year period 1962–67. This is not an overall decline in population, since it is expected that further children will be born to the second generation in the village. Moreover, as I show, it is difficult for members to give up houses in the village; most prefer simply to give up farming.

There are several reasons for Kfar Hefer's overall decline in population. (1) The number of residents has decreased. Residents are persons employed by the village, or in service in the village, but they do not have membership in the village. This category includes (i) employees of the postal service and some teachers in the school, all of whom are government employees, (ii) workers employed in the village both as agricultural labourers and as service workers and (iii) the sons and daughters of the village who do not live in their parents' houses and who have not built their own house on the land of the family farm. These are mostly young people, some of whom work as probationary professional workers in village service, while the remainder work on their parents' farm but for reasons of lack of accommodation or family difficulties do not live with their parents. The fall in numbers in the category of residents is mainly among this latter group. If the young people are accepted as professional members they move into the category of professional members ('public workers' in Table 12), but if they fail to be accepted as professionals they leave the village. Those helping on their parents' farm usually build their own house on the family land when the financial state of the farm permits this, and then they are incorporated in to the category of 'Families on their parents' farm'. (2) There had also been a decline in the number of professional members, as a result of a twofold process: a fall in numbers caused by the retirement and death of members; and the failure to replace these persons because of improved techniques of village administration, chiefly through mechanisation. But the biggest drop in population is (3) among the agricultural members and their families. Social processes inherent in the constitution of moshavim and the natural processes of aging

Table 12 Analysis of population of Kfar Hefer 1962–67 (compiled from Annual Statement of Kfar Hefer, prepared for Government inspection)

	1962–63		1963–64		1964–65		1965–66		1966–67	
	No. of persons	No. of family units	No. of persons	No. of family units	No. of persons	No. of family units	No. of persons	No. of family units	No. of persons	No. of family units
(a) Heads of agricultural families and their children on farm										
Members (m. and f.)	289	152	281	152	281	152	274	147	276	141
Sons and daughters above 18 years	78		86		88		83		72	
Sons and daughters less than 18 years	76		59		52		40		45	
(b) Public workers and sons in house										
Members (m. and f.)	68	35	67	35	69	31	62	26	51	24
Sons and daughters above 18 years	7		5		10		16		14	
Sons and daughters less than 18 years	42		44		36		27		25	

(c) Families of children of agricultural members on parent's farm										
Members (m. and f.)	103	62	124	62	121	65	130	68	135	72
Sons and daughters less than 18 years	88		106		109		116		124	
(d) Residents										
Workers (m. and f.)	34	14	29	17	33	14	28	14	27	16
Sons and daughters less than 18 years	22		21		24		23		19	
Total	**807**	**263**	**822**	**266**	**823**	**262**	**799**	**255**	**788**	**253**

and death are responsible for this. This trend is particularly marked in Kfar Hefer because of the narrow age-span covering the original settlers. Table 12 shows that the number of heads of farms has dropped in the period under review: while the number of farm units is 151 (see Table 10), the number of occupied farm units is only 147.

Four farms were unoccupied in the years 1964–68. The vacancies were caused either by the death of both partners in the farm or by the death of one and the absence of the other. In all four farms there was no continuation by the second generation of the family. The law relating to co-operative farming settlements (moshavim), and the contract that each member signs with the J.N.F. on becoming an agricultural member in a moshav, specify that only one of the farmer's children may inherit and work the family farm. Writing about the existing moshav constitution and the proposed 'moshav law' to be put before the *Knesset*, a member of the *Knesset*[1] commented '. . . we have the stipulation that inheritance may not overrule the moshav's basic principle of equality in holdings, i.e. no member may hold more than one holding nor may his wife own a separate one; the proposed legal condition is that a person inheriting a farm holding on a moshav must move there and work the farm, himself accepting the conditions of moshav membership.' This has been customarily insisted upon by moshavim but now the attempt was to give this the force of legal standing. Indeed it was at the Moshav Movement convention held in Kfar Hefer in 1951 that it was proposed that there should be a moshav law giving the moshav a special status in national law. Shoresh goes on to add: 'There is a defined order of priorities in inheritance and no will left by the deceased may overrule this order . . . in all cases the surviving spouse, husband or wife, is top of the list. Both have equal rights as members of the moshav co-operative society . . . Next in order of priority is a son who has worked with his parents on the farm also helping to create assets. This applies irrespective of whether he is the eldest or the youngest son.'

Children do not wait until the death of their parents before making decisions about their future. The effect of the moshav constitution, which prevents both the accumulation of land by a member and the fragmentation of land into smaller units, is to allow only one child of the family to inherit the family farm. This means that other children in the family must seek their livelihood outside the farm.[2] The continuation of the moshav as a moshav depends on the solving of the double-edged problem: of retaining one child on the farm and

---

[1] Shoresh (1965)
[2] For a discussion of a similar problem in Ireland see Arensberg 193–200

the sending out of its 'surplus' sons and daughters into other occupations—as in many other rural areas. Some of these may be incorporated into the moshav as professional members, but as shown above these opportunities are limited. The population of Kfar Hefer has therefore declined, at least temporarily, because most of its children have found their living outside the village, and a new generation of grandchildren has not yet been bred from settlers of a narrow age-cohort. As I stated earlier in this chapter the success of the village, as judged by the members themselves was, apart from economic considerations, also evaluated by their success in transmitting the moshav as a way of life to their children. In Kfar Hefer in 1966 there were 88 farms where continuation of the second generation was assured. In these 88 farms, 73 sons have, or are expected to join their parents on the farm, while in the remaining 15 farms married daughters and their husbands have settled in the farm. In 1966 there were already 66 farms occupied by the parent(s) and married children and grandchildren. In 38 farms it was known that there would be no continuation, and in these farms the first generation live alone. In a further 16 family farms it was uncertain if there would be a further continuation but the probability was that the children would not stay on the farm. Taking this figure with the previous one it is seen that a third of the village farms are single generation enterprises and will not be continued by their children. Nine farms which became vacant in the village have been bought by members of the second generation of other parents and they work as independent owners. The significance of these figures and the effect on individual holdings and on the village, in the light of the economic situation described above, are discussed in the following chapters.

III
Continuation in the family farm

The preceding chapters recounted the history and the conditions under which Kfar Hefer developed as a moshav. An outline of the economic and demographic picture in 1966–68 was also given. In this and following chapters I am concerned to analyse more fully the interplay and consequences of economic and social factors in the village. In this chapter account will be taken of demographic factors (number of children in a family, their age and sex, age of the village itself, and the age of the village population); the influence of moshav principles upon social and economic life; and the effect of government and local internal village policy.

One of the recurring topics of discussion during the time I was in Kfar Hefer was a concern about 'the way of life in the village'. Many different meanings and interpretations were encompassed in this all embracing phrase but fundamentally the members of the village were concerned about the effect of moshav laws and principles and their applicability in the village under its prevailing conditions.

It will be remembered that the moshav as a way of life is concerned with the promotion of individual effort within a co-operative framework. Emphasis is given to equality. But from the outset it should be stressed that the moshav was not like the kibbuts which tended to see equality in terms of communal ownership of all means of production, and sharing of consumption. On the other hand, in the moshav, emphasis was always on 'equality in the allocation of the means of production', and consumption was by individual family choice. Differences between members are recognised by the moshav, even though certain devices are used to minimise these. Differences existed between members of Kfar Hefer from the very beginning. Some members were already married when they came to the settlement and had families; others were bachelors. Some members had small amounts of capital when they settled, so they did not have to get into debt and pay interest on this debt while they developed their farms. Some members continued to work outside the village even after the division of the land and so their farms developed more slowly than those of members engaged in full-time farming. Reference has been made to difference in the quality of land holdings: some members, by chance, received better allocations of land than others. Skill and aptitude for farming and general ability to perform manual tasks also greatly influenced the rate of progress on the farm. One woman commented unfavourably on her own financial condition compared with that of a neighbour, and attributed the difference to the differences in skill between her own husband and the other farmer. Whenever her husband performed a repair job or attempted to build anything on the farm she had to 'follow him with bandages and plaster to tend his wounds, and then afterwards call in a skilled man to do the job. But Moshe [the other farmer] can turn his hand to anything.' On a minor scale this reflects the villagers' recognition of the effect of varying degrees of skill on the finances of a farm.

Whenever discussions came up about differences within the village the first one to be mentioned was always the difference between those farms which had a continuation of the second generation and those which had not. During the time I was in Kfar Hefer much attention and concern were paid to this topic, usually in regard to the effect this had on the village as a moshav. A lot of the discussion went on in the pages of the bi-monthly village bulletin and members wrote their opinions and explanations about this aspect of village life. I was told that of late the problems created by the absence of second generation families had come to the foreground and the subsequent discussion was indicative of the interest shown. This is probably explained very simply: in past years those members who had no continuation in the farm still continued to work their farms, but with increasing age they found this progressively more difficult until many of them had to give up some areas of their farming activity in order to suit their tasks to their physical capabilities. Because the older generation of Kfar Hefer is very much an 'even-age' population this happened very quickly—in fact in the years immediately preceding and during which I worked in the village. Thus, in a short space of time, the village saw the practical effects of a lack of continuation on a farm. Perhaps here it should be emphasised that this phenomenon of older generation families being left alone on the farm is part of a wider characteristic of moshav life, that of sons leaving the village. In an earlier chapter I showed that the effect of moshav law was to compel 'surplus sons and daughters' in a family farm to seek their living outside the farm and in practice this usually meant outside the village. Thus the process of sons and daughters leaving the family farm is an acknowledged and indeed integral part of moshav life. Kfar Hefer's concern was not with this general principle but rather with the particular problem caused by a complete lack of second generation members in a third of the village's farms, that is by the failure to retain one son on the farm.

Sociologically it is possible to isolate and to suggest a number of factors which might account for this process. Thus demographic reasons might offer an explanation: the size and composition and indeed age or death of families born to the first generation affect the possibility of a second generation continuity in farms. Then there are the 'push' and 'pull' factors of life in a moshav and the wider environment. The effect of the moshav law cited above is one of the 'push' factors which compels a son or daughter to leave the family farm. Another influencing factor may be the state and composition of the family farm. There also are the influences of choices other than farming which are open to a young person: here educational opportunities and qualifications may be important. The choice of marriage partners and marriage patterns within the moshav may play a part in deciding whether or not a young person stays in the village. Writing in a newspaper article entitled 'Moshav sons knocking on the door', in 1967, Emanual Labes asks, 'What happens to the sons and daughters of the moshav?' He asks the further questions, 'Do they stream to the city? Do they return from the army to the farm? Can the moshav support a second generation?'[1] The answer to this last question in Kfar Hefer would be 'Yes'; but writing specifically about Kfar Hefer, Labes says that the village, 'has come through the critical generation changeover period very well. There is a married son or daughter on almost every farm.' This would seem to be at odds with the actual picture in Kfar Hefer where a third of the family farms have no son or daughter on the farm. Labes continues to discuss the position of university graduates in relation to the moshav: 'So far except in the case of teachers no way has been found to foster ties between them and the village after graduation. In point of fact this relatively small drain of moshav youth need not be detrimental because generally there is room for only one married son or daughter on the farm.' Here again the people of Kfar Hefer, particularly those who are without even the one married son or daughter, would take issue with Labes. In a later chapter I discuss how far these apparently conflicting views can be reconciled.

In order to analyse the processes involved in sons or daughters remaining in or leaving the village it is necessary to look at both categories of farms (those with continuation, and those without) in Kfar Hefer. Examining the size of the families born to the first generation members now holding farms in Kfar Hefer (a total of 142 farming families) the results shown in Table 13 are obtained. Thus on simple demographic grounds, because of no children in the family only one of the 142 farms has no continuation. In 13 family

[1] Labes (1967)

farms there is no choice of continuity between children but in the remaining 128 family farms there was a choice of successor in the farm. Conversely, in 128 farms at least one, or more, children had to leave the family farm and seek work elsewhere.

Of the 88 families in Kfar Hefer where continuation of the second generation in the farm is assured (see also previous chapter) there are 15 families where a daughter of the family has settled on the farm with her husband. In only one of these families was there a possibility of a son inheriting the farm: in the remaining 14 cases there were only daughters in the family. In the exceptional case where there was one son, this boy is much younger than his sister and she on her marriage remained on the farm with her husband; the boy is still of school age and gives only occasional help on the farm; the parents are in their late 50's. In 5 of these 14 farms the daughter was an only child, while in the remaining farms 5 eldest daughters have settled in the farm, and the second (and youngest)

Table 13 Size of first generation families in Kfar Hefer (those holding farms in 1968)

	Child-less	One child	Two	Three	Four	Above four
No. of families	1	13	59	45	19	5

daughter has remained on 4 farms. In the 73 farms where a son of the family has remained on the farm, 24 only sons have settled on the family farm, 27 eldest sons, 4 second sons (where there are more than two sons in the family), and 11 youngest sons. Later in this chapter other social attributes of these families will be discussed.

The second category of farms in Kfar Hefer, is the 38 farms where it is known there will be no continuation of the second generation. In this category is the one case in the village of a farm having no children born to the family. In 15 cases the families concerned had only daughters in the family, and in all cases these daughters, whether married or unmarried, are living outside Kfar Hefer and are not considered likely to return to the village. The remaining 22 families all had either sons or daughters who could have continued in the farm. In 4 cases these families do have a child who has remained in Kfar Hefer—in a farm he or she has bought and which is farmed independently of the parents, or in a farm where through marriage he/she settled with a spouse who has a family farm—or he/she serves the village as a professional member. There are 4 families where sons who might have stayed on the farm have died and a further 4 families where a son has moved to another farming settlement outside Kfar Hefer. In the 16 farms where continuation is a possibility but not a probability there is within each farm a son or daughter who may take over the farm. However, because of the following reasons these children are not expected to remain in the village. In 6 of these farms the remaining child on the farm has received or is receiving further education: 3 of these have already finished their university courses but have returned to the village, 2 are living on the family farm, and the third lives in a rented house in Gavish (Kfar Hefer's neighbouring moshav). Whatever their eventual decision about their future, village opinion was that they would not remain in the village, and their presence was regarded at best as only temporary.

In two of these three cases this son was the only possibility that the farm would continue. In the third case there was also an unmarried daughter in the family but she lived and worked in Jerusalem so she was not regarded as a real alternative. In one family the son who was expected to remain on the farm was killed in the War of Liberation, while the second son although much younger had already made plans for his future when he left the village. In fact this boy went to university and studied economics, and for a time he taught at the university and had a successful career. When his parents suffered increasing difficulty in farming he returned with his wife to the farm and while doing part-time teaching he also helped on the farm. When this particular case was discussed by village members there was a unanimous view that the young man would not stay in the village: indeed great surprise was expressed that someone with a university degree should return to farming.

Similarly, the son who lives in a rented house outside the village had completed a course in the university in philosophy. He worked part-time as a teacher in a government-supported college in Tel Aviv, and the rest of his time he helped his father on the family farm. This young man's spatial distance from the family farm, and the fact that he lived in the neighbouring village were interpreted by villagers to mean that he had no intention of staying in Kfar Hefer. When in fact he did apply to the village Executive for a home in Kfar Hefer the general reaction was one of surprise: 'What? Does he intend to stay in the village?' Moreover, the Executive were unwilling to spend the necessary money on improving the house which had been vacant for several years until they received an assurance that he would stay. They were reluctant to broach with the young man what they felt to be a delicate subject, so decided that they must take the application at face value as a sign that the young man did intend to stay on the family farm. Nevertheless each of the five members in the Executive expressed their disbelief that this would happen.

The third case is a son who also has a professional qualification and works full time in a job outside the village but in his spare time helps on the farm.

Thus in all these three cases the help given by these sons on the farm is only part time.

Several of the farmers in this category had only daughters in the family: these were either at school or were living at home with their parents but held full-time jobs outside the village. Only in the event of marriage with someone who is able and willing to become a farmer is there a possibility of continuation on the farm. In the case of those daughters living on the farm and working outside this possibility was considered very remote because all the women concerned were in their middle thirties and in the event of their marriage it was considered unlikely that their spouses would be willing to take up farming at this age. In these 16 families 46 children have been born to the families and yet it appears that not one of them will remain in the family farm.

When I asked a young second-generation farmer in Kfar Hefer what he believed were the factors responsible for sons and daughters leaving the family farm he replied, by, jokingly, telling me a Yiddish story that explains the conditions needed for a family farm to prosper. Such a family should have three sons: one with a good head for commerce who can bring prosperity to the family through business; a second son who is learned and brings honour and status to the family; and a third son who is stupid and incapable of learning, and he can continue on the family farm.

Although this story was told to me as a joke it does contain something of a feeling that was often expressed in Kfar Hefer, namely that educational attainment in university or in other institutions of further education is incompatible with continuation in farming. This was a common belief instanced in the three cases described above, even though I hope to show that this is in fact an incomplete and misleading view of the problem of second-generation continuation in farming.

Here it is important to stress the dilemma faced by parents in the education of their children. The parents cannot decide in advance which of their children will remain on the farm, and there are no rules of succession to the family farm, except the proviso that the farm must be passed on as a whole. Therefore parents try to give their children an education which prepares them both for a life on the farm and for other careers. This is a task which is hard to put into practice, especially in a system of education based on achievement in which gifted children are often drawn on to further education even if they do not wish to continue.

In Israel there is compulsory education for children from the age of six years to fourteen years, and from the age of five to six there is compulsory attendance at a kindergarten. In Kfar Hefer there is a primary school which provides for the village children until the age of fourteen, and there are also two kindergartens, one accepting children from the age of five years, the other for children younger than this. Primary school education in Israel is provided by the government and teachers are employed by the Ministry of Education: thus the primary school and compulsory kindergarten are controlled by the Ministry. Only in the voluntary kindergarten (before the age of five) does the village direct the classes and employ the teacher. Originally the Kfar Hefer school served only children from the village, but today four settlements send their children to this school and in fact the Kfar Hefer children are in a minority in the school. Figures for the year 1966/67 giving children in the two classes in the last grade of the primary school show that in a class of 27 children only four were from Kfar Hefer and in the other class, of 30 children, again only four were Kfar Hefer children.

At the age of fourteen children take an examination to determine whether they continue their studies in a high school. There are several schools which the children of Kfar Hefer may attend; most go on to the Regional High School which is situated on one of the main highways, about 15 minutes drive from Kfar Hefer. As the name suggests this school serves all the settlements (except kibbutsim) of the area. It is a big school with over 800 pupils. The children attend for four years at the end of which they take '*bagrut*', a matriculation examination. This examination is a necessary qualification for university and other institutions of further education and is usually required for professional training. Alternative schools are a vocational training school in a nearby town, where there is also an alternative high school. Children are not compelled to finish the four-year course in a high school and some transfer to schools offering specific training for a certain occupation, for example kindergarten teaching. Some pupils who do not wish to follow either an academic training or vocational training course (which is usually linked to industrial occupations) elect to attend an agricultural high school where the emphasis is on farming. Higher education in Israel is not provided by the government: parents have to pay for their child's attendance in a high school. In the moshav the cost of this education is borne by the members as a whole and is not the responsibility of the individual parent.

The above situation has prevailed in Kfar Hefer since the early 1960's when the school in Kfar Hefer was owned and directed by the village. Children from the other settlements paid the village according to rates laid down by the Ministry of Education. The changeover came for two reasons. Firstly, the numbers of Kfar Hefer children in the school declined: children from other settlements were in the majority, the school was expensive to run, and the cost per child was greater than that paid by children from outside. The other settlements refused to pay more than the government rates and so Kfar Hefer felt it was subsidising the children of other settlements at a time when their own children were in a minority of the school. Secondly, there were disputes with the other settlements about the standard and type of education given by the school. Members of the nearby moshav Gavish complained that the tuition offered in the school was not sufficiently academic and too much directed towards an inculcation of moshav ideals. As a result of these disputes Kfar Hefer decided to relinquish responsibility for the school which was transferred to the Ministry of Education, and now a joint parents' group from the four settlements takes a part in running the school. Kfar Hefer also had her own secondary school in the village but there were not enough pupils per class to justify the heavy expenses and also it was difficult to recruit able teachers. Most of the educational sphere is controlled by the government and salaries are fixed by law and increase with grades of seniority. This applies only to teachers in government schools and seniority in other schools is not recognised by the Ministry of Education. Therefore an experienced teacher in the Kfar Hefer school would on transfer to a government school receive only the salary of newly qualified staff. For this reason many teachers left the school to teach in government schools where prospects of promotion are better. Therefore at the time the primary school was transferred to the Ministry of Education it was also decided to close down the village High school and that in future the children should attend the Regional High School.

This decision caused something of a furore in the village. Despite the evidence of the heavy financial burden imposed by the upkeep of the school many were opposed to sending their children to the Regional High School. It was felt that shifting education outside the moshav's ambit would weaken the attachment of youth to the moshav as a way of life. Also the sending of the children into a government school was associated in the minds of some members with the '*bagrut*' examination. Writing in *Tlamim*[1] a member of Kfar Hefer described their attitude, '. . . they felt that a matriculation certificate in the hands of the graduates would lead their thoughts away from the path of continuation on the farm'. But he goes on to add that the village's 'three years of experience does not bear this out, there's no difference in the pattern of continuation'. The writer was describing the situation before the children were sent to the Regional High School, but I suggest that the same holds true today. It is not the possession of matriculation certificates alone which explains the lack of continuation on farms but rather the whole context of the education of the second generation that has to be considered. In fact most of the village members did elect to send their children to the Regional High School, but some, on principle, sent their children to the alternative school in town. In many ways this was a curious attitude for the opponents of the move to adopt. As was pointed out to me by a second generation member who is now studying in Jerusalem, there is nothing in the moshav constitution which prevents or forbids the acquiring of knowledge and even certificates by moshav members. Indeed from the inception of the movement the opposite has been true. The original settlers took a pride in emphasising their learning and culture and were quick to point out that there was no discrepancy in learned people becoming farmers. Why then in the 1950's did the moshav members evince such doubts and even opposition to higher education for their children? I suggest an explanation may be offered by the changed circumstances surrounding education.

Table 2 shows that in 1954 the village had 12 grades of classes. In point of fact the twelfth grade was established in 1952, i.e. only in 1952 could the children of Kfar Hefer reach the age of matriculation within their own school. By 1952 the oldest children in the village were over twenty years old, but some of these were even approaching thirty. (Although the first generation of Kfar Hefer is an even-age population, difference in age of marriage and birth of children and size of family have resulted in a considerable age span covering the second generation.) Thus these members of the second generation had to go outside the village to another school if they wished to take the examination. Again in *Tlamim*[2] a member of Kfar Hefer describes the reaction to the establishment of a twelfth grade in the school: 'Some people suggested that we should withdraw these last two years of classes, i.e. have only 10 classes in the village. Some argued that this would release the sons to work on the farm, others saw the extra classes as an additional financial burden on the village.

[1] *Tlamim* (1955)   [2] *ibid.*

Moreover the education of the children must be suited to their future life.' [Presumably in the moshav.]

The second generation who grew up at this time had to show special determination to pursue academic learning: a conscious decision had to be made to go outside the village to continue study. This involved the family farm in financial expenditure because education outside the village was not covered by the village as a whole. Moreover the period immediately before and during the late 1940's and early 1950's was the time of the greatest increase in agricultural production. This was the time when the labour of the second generation was most needed in order to fulfil the country's demands for extra food production. Furthermore this part of the second generation reached maturity in the immediate pre-state period, when the *Yishuv* was organising the *Haganah* and the *Palmach*, the fighting forces of young people, for their defence. The War of Independence brought this situation to a climax: these young people were actively engaged in the defence of the new Israel and in the formation of the State. Some young people even failed to complete 11 years of schooling because they volunteered to join the fighting forces. After the end of the war they were reluctant to return to studying especially because of the work needed to be done in building the state. In the first chapter I have already described how some young people went to new settlements to act as instructors. In these tasks academic attainments were of little value and the emphasis was on practical abilities.

Early marriage was also a characteristic of the period so that those with wives and families were unlikely to continue their studies in the conditions of the time. On their return to the village, these members of the second generation found much work to be done particularly as many of their parents were now unable to cope single handed with the farm. Thus all the conditions of the time mitigated against the acquiring of educational certificates. In order to pursue an academic or professional career a son or daughter of this period needed strong attachment to the idea of study and also parental encouragement, which (as the above quotations show) was not on the whole forthcoming in the village.

The situation contrasts markedly with the conditions experienced by children who went to High School in the early and middle 1950's and with the situation today. The introduction of the programme of instruction established by the government meant that the curriculum was no longer controlled by the village: thus the emphasis on 'moshav' education was lost. Also the planning of education by certain phases—primary school, examination; high school, matriculation

—meant that for many children progress was automatic. They no longer had to make decisions about schooling, they learnt in the framework of a pattern set by the government. Within the country there was also a shift in attitudes to education. The achievement of Statehood emphasised the need for skilled and trained people particularly to cope with the country's economy and with the problems created by large-scale immigration. In the pre-State period these tasks had been carried out by leaders who had no formal qualifications for these tasks, but it was soon realised that technical proficiency was also needed (see quotation from Eisenstadt, page 25). The effect of this change in the standing of the farmer was graphically described to me by Doron: 'At one time every boy wanted to be a farmer, suddenly everyone wanted to be an economist or a pilot.' Not everyone could be an economist or a pilot but with the establishment of the State new jobs were created and new skills needed (again see quotation from Eisenstadt page 25). Even though Israel is a small state she still needs many of the senior and middle-rank administrative positions in specialised organisations required by a bigger state: thus many new jobs were opened. In some cases these were filled (especially in government) by *Yishuv* leaders but there were also new positions requiring skills which they were not able to provide and in this opportunities for young people were suddenly increased. The newness of these jobs meant that there was rapid advancement for young people and they often assumed positions of responsibility and power at a relatively youthful age. This effect of this proliferation of opportunities and rapid promotion was neatly expressed to me by a young Israeli who quizzically asked: 'Have you ever yet met an Israeli who was not the manager of something or other?' Today there is no longer such an open field for advancement, but the emphasis on educational attainment has grown and the matriculation examination is often demanded as a condition of employment for non-technical and non-academic jobs.

Bearing in mind the different conditions under which the oldest and the youngest of the second generation in Kfar Hefer grew up, I suggest that it is incorrect to ascribe lack of continuation in farming to higher education, and to express the difference between those who stay on in farming and those who do not in terms of matriculation certificates. I consider that my suggestion is supported by a re-examination of the situation of those of the second generation who leave the village, in terms both of the factors suggested above and of other factors which appear no less important.

In all, 89 children were born to the 38 families where there is no continuation. Seventeen of these families had only daughters in the family. Even though according to moshav law sons and daughters have equal rights to inherit the family farm, in actual practice, because of the priority given to the child who has worked on the farm and 'helped to create assets' (see above), this tends to favour the son of the family. As I have shown there is only one case in Kfar Hefer of a daughter remaining on the farm at the expense of her brother; and in this instance the son is much younger than the girl and because of this he has never contributed much to the work of the farm. Nineteen of the second generation in these farms had matriculated from high school, so the majority (70) of these second generation children left the family farm despite their lack of academic qualification. The figures for married daughters with their husbands show that of the farms in Kfar Hefer to which only daughters were born, 45 per cent of these girls have remained in the farms, three of whose husbands are sons of Kfar Hefer. In part this may be explained by the difference in age between the girls, those remaining in the farms tend to be older than those leaving. This may be related to differential marriage patterns. There are 17 marriages between pairs of children of Kfar Hefer, all between 'older' members of the second generation. In recent years there have been no marriages within the village. Moreover most marriages even in the earlier period tended to be with farming members of other agricultural settlements, so that there was the possibility that husbands of Kfar Hefer girls would be recruited to the family farm. Later marriages have been to men from outside Kfar Hefer who typically did not even come from other agricultural settlements: compulsory army service from the age of 18 to 20 has had a considerable influence on choice of spouse. Nevertheless, even the figures for all the farms, including the earlier period, show that the likelihood of daughters settling on the family farm was small compared with that of sons. In these discontinuous farms there were only seven sons in five families who have gone on to further education, and in the case of three of these seven sons they all had a period of farming with their parents on the farm. In one case the second son of the family went to settle in a new moshav (founded after the creation of the state). On the death of his brother he returned to the village to work with his father on the farm, but there were family difficulties and the son could not settle in the village so he left Kfar Hefer and went to study at the university. He now lives near the village and gives occasional help to his father but there is no question of his returning to the village. In a second case in a family of two sons and two daughters the eldest son planned to stay on the farm, and the second son had no aptitude for, or inclination to stay in, farming. However the eldest son suffered an accident which made it impossible for him to continue farming; the second son was already studying at university and had no wish to return to the farm, and in fact the eldest son joined him at university. The third case is slightly different from the above. The son returned to the farm after obtaining professional economic training, and he planned to work in the village as an adviser. He did so for only a short time. I was told that he left because it was impossible for him to work in the village, since the members would not accept his advice. In another case the eldest son bought his own farm in the village to allow the second son to remain on the family farm, but the second and younger son did not like farming and so he decided to leave the village despite his lack of other qualifications. The father is now left alone on the farm.

Amongst the 38 families with no continuation there were nine families where the first generation woman was living alone, either widowed or separated from her husband. In seven cases these women had been alone for many years, their farms had never been fully operative, and their children were not brought up with a particular interest in farming. In addition the financial state of these farms was usually weak and not an attractive prospect for the second generation.

A similar situation existed in three other farms of this category, where, despite the presence of both parents, the family farm was never really developed. In one case the father of the family remained working outside the village, until the late 1940's and on his return to Kfar Hefer he did not work in the family farm but in the village administration. Both the children (son and daughter) have left the village despite the fact that neither have matriculation certificates: one is married to a second generation member of Kfar Hefer. In a second case the parents actively encouraged their son to study and to leave the village. It was explained to me that the boy had been an outstanding pupil in the school and even though his parents were farmers they took only a minimal interest in their farm. The boy's mother was a teacher in the village school. Even so, after completing his studies the boy returned to the village, and worked full-time in the moshav federation and after work helped his father on the farm. He left the village because of social difficulties: I was told he said that there was no place in Kfar Hefer for sons who had completed further education, they would never be accepted by the village. I discuss the problem of retaining these educated sons in the village later in a chapter on social control and social sanctions. The third instance is of a family of three sons, two of whom have remained in Kfar Hefer but none of whom are in the family farm. One son has married into another farm in Kfar Hefer and on the death of his wife's parents he now runs the farm. The second son is a professional member of the village and does not help on his parents' farm. The youngest son has left the village and works in Tel Aviv. It was said that all these children had quarrelled with their father about running the farm: as children they had worked on the farm, but as they grew up they felt they were being worked too hard, especially as their father directed all operations without paying regard to their opinions. None of the sons has formal academic qualifications.

On examining the situation in the 73 farms where sons have remained, two facts are immediately apparent. First the majority of these sons are of the 'older' second generation and so grew up in a period when not only was less emphasis put on formal learning but also when opportunities for study were far fewer. The second fact is, that of the 'younger' second generation there are many who have remained in the village even though they have matriculated from the High School. The size of this category makes it difficult to establish any pattern in the inheritance of farms. Where more than one son wished to stay in farming, then efforts were made to find alternatives to the family farm for the 'surplus' sons. Amongst the 'older' second generation the pattern so far as I am able to determine it seemed to be that the eldest sons were found accommodation outside the family farm either by the purchase of farms vacant in Kfar Hefer or by their going to settle in new moshavim established in the early 1950's specifically for the sons of moshavim. Thus within these families it is the youngest son who stays on in the farm. In the past few years possibilities of settling in a new moshav have been limited, although this picture has changed slightly since the 'Six Day' war of June, 1967, as new settlements are now being established in former Arab territories. In recent times there seems to be a change in the pattern of staying on in the farm. Now the eldest son tends to remain on the farm and the younger sons have to find occupations outside the farm. I find it difficult fully to explain this change, but I suggest that it is connected, firstly with the age of the parents and with their family status (widowed or separated), and secondly with the diminishing attractiveness of farming as a career and its lowered prestige within Israel.

When an eldest son of the 'older' generation was able to take a full part in the running of the family farm, his parents, and especially his father, were still able physically to run their own farms. Thus in fact if these sons had remained in the family farm the son would have been a subsidiary farmer, second-in-command to his father. Also at this period there were younger children who helped on the farm:

F

thus in some cases there may have been excess labour, more hands than were needed for the farm's production. Indeed it is a stipulation of Kfar Hefer's own constitution (discussed later) that no more than two families should live on a farm because the economy is not big enough to support more. On the other hand when the 'younger' of the second generation were old enough to stay on in the farm, their parents were older and full-time management of the farm proved a difficult task. These parents needed immediate help on the farm if it was to continue. Thus, I suggest that in this situation the eldest sons tend to be recruited into the farm and the youngest sons are the ones who go outside. These young people typically do not find their living in agriculture. Opportunities for settlement have diminished while the extension of the school system enables young people to prepare for a greater variety of jobs.

There is an added facet to this pattern: that in the past farming in another moshav was considered the alternative to Kfar Hefer and so it was useful for the eldest son to gain some practical insight into farm management while he worked with his father. This no longer holds true and another moshav is no longer a practical alternative for Kfar Hefer's sons and daughters. They enter into careers for which their background in the village can give them no preparation: therefore they are in a hurry to leave to start their careers.

I suggest that the changed conditions surrounding the moshav contribute to the ambiguous attitude towards education that is held by many of Kfar Hefer's members. The standing of agricultural settlement has declined in Israel and so has income from farming. There now exist many alternatives to the way of life the older generation wished to perpetuate. I have shown that increased education has no more effect on second generation continuation than have demographic and economic factors. But what has changed is the way of life of sons who have left the village. Previously there was a continuity in the way of life even if it was not in Kfar Hefer. Now the choices of career which are made by young people represent a break with this pattern.

This suggestion may explain the remark made by one of Kfar Hefer's old-timers, who is a delegate to the Moshav Movement and a staunch upholder of moshav values. He said that those who continue in higher education, 'are not traitors to the moshav, but something approximating this'. The topic of further education is still discussed very heatedly in Kfar Hefer. Now there can be no question of preventing sons from studying, and the emphasis has shifted to attempts to recruit them back to the village. But it will be recalled that those sons who had completed further education were markedly unsuccessful in their efforts to remain in the village. Here education is still regarded as a threat to the moshav. A young member of Kfar Hefer wrote in the village bulletin that he was afraid that in the future, 'only those who can't learn will stay on the farm'. This expressed regret about the quality of people who will live in the moshav but usually the fear felt is even more basic. It is that the moshav will not continue as a moshav. Commenting on my presence and work in Kfar Hefer I was told very lugubriously by a first generation member: 'You'll fail. You are bound to fail. If you wanted to study a village you should have seen the Russian and German villages. There life went on for hundreds of years, while with us it will be all over in ten years.' If one forgives the exaggeration, this view was shared by many in Kfar Hefer. They recognised and admired the achievements of those who studied but they deplored what they believed to be the conse-quences. Despite the lack of evidence to support their contention— and indeed the positive evidence against it—they continued to equate matriculation with the first steps to leaving the village. The attitude of young second generation farmers who had not matriculated was different. There were several young men who had responsibility for family farms and who continued to study both for matriculation and afterwards at night school. These young men did not think of leaving the farm: in all cases they were the main support to the family of origin and their own families. One of these young men told me that he went on studying to prove to himself and to others that he was not in Kfar Hefer because he had no alternative—but I was often told that this particular man would leave the village. In such cases the blame for continued study was placed on the young men's wives, who (as pointed out in my earlier analysis of later marriages of the second generation) on the whole have come from outside the village and not from agricultural settlements.

Disparaging remarks have been made that 'outside' wives wanted to 'uproot' their husbands from the village. Putting the blame for undesirable happenings on 'outsiders' and so re-affirming the unity of a group is a common feature of community life.[1] And indeed it was a common idiom in the village to describe those who pursued further education as being led astray and beguiled by its attractions. They had given up the life of the moshav for an easier life outside: as one young farmer put it, 'Today the best branch in agriculture is to go to University.'

Table 14 shows the residence of the second generation of Kfar Hefer.

The Moshav Movement's policy is that educated sons should

[1] See Frankenberg (1957)

return to their settlements as professional workers or to work in the Moshav Movement. The kibbuts federations give grants to their members who study on condition that they give a certain number of years of service to the kibbuts after graduation. There is no such system in the Moshav Movement. They have tried to solve the problem in another way by building, with the Jewish Agency's help, additional houses in moshavim. The *Jerusalem Post* of 19 September 1966 reports that the Jewish Agency Settlement Department is engaged in a large-scale building programme in Galilee to absorb their younger generation. Twenty to thirty new dwelling-units are to

Table 14   Residence of children born to first generation of Kfar Hefer, 1968

Resident in the village	
Married, in the family farm	88
In the family farm, not married	70
Own farm in Kfar Hefer or resident in another	17
Professional members	2
Total	**177**
Resident outside	
In farming	26
New moshav	19
Urban area	111
Dunia*	14
Army	3
Total	**173**
Overall Total	**350**
(plus 17 children dead)	367

* Dunia: residential area built close to Kfar Hefer. See below.

be added to each moshav to absorb young members who pursue non-agricultural trades in the region and in the commercial centres. Discussing a similar suggestion for Kfar Hefer, Eden dismissed the idea out of hand. Eden, the village's permanent representative in the Moshav Movement, is now a fairly old man and no longer actively engaged in farming because his only son had taken over the family farm. In village meetings he could be counted upon to express views strictly adhering to moshav principles and was regarded by village members as one of the proponents of traditional moshav ideas, as well as being totally uninformed about what went on in the village. He said[1] that some sons who did not intend to follow in the family farm might find a place as public workers in the village; such sons might find a place to live in the village or they might also be per-

[1] Reported in the village bulletin, 17 February 1967

mitted to live outside the village, but in no case should such a son be given a plot of land for a house on the family lands. Eden expressed his sorrow over sons whose main income comes from outside of the village since this development in the village entailed that some farmers were left without continuation on their farm. Eden said that the sons of settlers whose main income was from outside are no different from 'strangers' in Kfar Hefer and they should not be given special treatment. He added that non-farming personnel always by their presence caused difficulties in the village and these difficulties would only be exacerbated if non-farming sons of the village were involved.

One attempt to help sons who left the village was the acquiring of land from the J.N.F. in the residential area established on the Nor-Nor-Western side of the village. This settlement, Dunia, was intended to be reserved for professional members attached to all moshavim in the region, and for Kfar Hefer children who had left farming but who wished to live close by their parents. The settlement has by and large followed this intention although there have been houses built by owners who do not fit into either of the above categories. Yet in Kfar Hefer's case the experiment has not been a great success: many plots intended for Kfar Hefer's children have remained vacant and some have been sold. In 1966 only 14 of the second generation of Kfar Hefer lived in Dunia. This, I suggest, happened because of a mistaken view about the type of people who were leaving the village. Several times it has been stressed that few were professionally qualified and the great majority of those leaving were girls who, on marriage, took up residence with their husbands. Of the remainder who left the village many went into farming and so were not interested in houses in the residential area.

The fact that more than a third of the village's farms are without continuation is very unpleasant for the parent generation in these farms. It has been my concern in this chapter to suggest and to analyse the causes of this discontinuity. I argued that one cannot give priority to any one factor alone. I have also been concerned to show that, contrary to the general belief in Kfar Hefer, education has played no bigger part in this process than the other factors men‧ tioned. Indeed, recent developments show that for this younger generation matriculation and settlement in a farm are not mutually exclusive. Within Kfar Hefer there are young farmers who have matriculated and now (1968) several young people from Kfar Hefer who have matriculation certificates have gone to settle in new settlements established after the Arab–Israeli war of June, 1967. For these young people matriculation is part of a process and an accepted part of schooling in Israel, and does not imply any decision about their future in settlement. For these young people in the village who have not taken matriculation, matriculation reflects new status values in Israel and so is desirable. But I suggest that for the older generation their expressed fears about education are only the idiom in which general mistrust is expressed concerning the alternative highly regarded systems of living which have now superseded the moshav's pioneering in Israel.

IV
Dilemmas of specialised farming

In his report to the Annual General Meeting of Kfar Hefer (October 1967) the head of the committee responsible for land in the village (*va'adat ha'mesheq*) told members that they were in the process of a revolution. Just as there was an industrial revolution in Europe, so Israel today was undergoing agricultural revolution and nowhere was this felt more than in the family farm. He added that it would not be an exaggeration to say that in all the 30 years and more of the village's history they had never experienced such changes as those they had experienced in the last year.

This chapter examines the farm economy in Kfar Hefer in the years 1966–68 and illustrates the effects of the 'revolution' in farming. All members of Kfar Hefer were affected by these changes in farm policy, but not all in the same way. The response to the changed situation differed from family to family, according to their interests and needs. In this chapter I point out the broad division between dairy and non-dairy farmers, but also illustrate the competition between members falling into these broad categories. As a result of these divisions and this competition the village Executive was charged with achieving a balance between the interests of conflicting groupings within the moshav and with the general problem of reconciling private interest with public good.

Climatically the area in which Kfar Hefer is situated is well suited to farming. Table 15 gives the average temperature and rainfall for a ten-year period. (The source of the climatic figures is the Meteorological Service, Bet Dagon.)

These figures are average figures and do not accurately reflect the exceptional years which can have a great effect on agricultural production. The average number of nights during which the temperature falls below 41 degrees F. (5 degrees C.) in this area is given as 10 to 15 per year, but in 1963 there was a prolonged series of frosts and one very severe attack killed many young citrus trees. Also, from time to time there are heavy winter storms which can seriously damage fruit-bearing trees. Despite these occurrences, the area is generally considered to be very favourable for agriculture, traditionally for citrus growing and now for the new development of growing vegetables under plastic cover.

There are three major soil types in Kfar Hefer: a loamy sand and sand stone; sand dunes; and a small area of alluvial soils. In the

Table 15 Average climatic data for the region of Kfar Hefer, 1955–65

	Jan.	Feb.	Mar.	Apr.	May	June	July	Aug.	Sept.	Oct.	Nov.	Dec.
Mean max. temp. °C	18	18·5	21	24	27	30	31	31	30	28	25	20
Mean max. temp. °F	65	66	70	75	81	86	88	88	86	87	77	68
Mean min. temp. °C	7·3	7·5	9·0	10·5	13·5	17·0	19·0	20·0	18·4	14·5	11·5	8·5
Mean min. temp. °F	45·1	45·5	46·5	51·0	56·3	62·5	66·5	68·0	65·0	58·0	53·0	47·3
Rain m.m.	160	83	33	8							75	105

early days of the settlement the sandy soils were difficult to farm, but now, with increased supplies of water and more efficient means of irrigation, they have proved to be very amenable to agriculture.

It has been said that agriculture in Israel has passed through several stages. Initially there was the problem of finding land, and I have recounted the efforts of agencies in pre-state Palestine to acquire land for Jewish settlers. The next stage was marked by the problems of water shortage, and again I have shown that although this remains a difficulty it is no longer a pressing problem for the country. The third stage began in the mid-1950's, and is marked by the shortage of markets for Israeli produce. The small home market cannot absorb any more agricultural produce. Moreover political hostility denied her the markets of neighbouring Arab States, though of course she was protected from the competition of their cheap produce by the closed borders. Therefore markets must be found further afield; but here too there are difficulties. The markets of Europe are more than self-sufficient in dairy and poultry products from their own suppliers, and Israel faces strong competition from other countries, notably in citrus and sub-tropical crops. In this Israel is handicapped, the preference given by Common Market countries to territories (like North Africa) which have a special relationship with the Market, while British Commonwealth preference hinders Israeli marketing. And not least important is the cost of transportation. Israel is a long way from her main markets in Europe and this adds to the cost of her products. Kfar Hefer like all other agricultural producers suffers from this state of affairs, but I suggest that her position is exacerbated because unlike the country as a whole, which has largely overcome the problems of land and water, the farmers of Kfar Hefer continue to labour under these difficulties. The resources allocated to Kfar Hefer are being fully utilised and under the existing forms of agriculture in the village no further expansion is possible. I will show that these have been alleviated only by the growth of different forms of production among village members.

Under the system of government planning of agricultural production, a series of five-year plans for agriculture have been introduced, the last of these for the years 1965/66 to 1970/71 (the government year runs from April–April). The aims of these plans is to set a certain total production for the various branches of agriculture. Each settlement is allocated by the Ministry of Agriculture, through the agencies of production boards, a certain quota for its own produce. In the past these quotas allowed for a certain growth; but under the conditions of glut prevailing in recent years these have tended to be restrictive quotas, either maintaining present production or even cutting down on production in some branches. The policy in Kfar Hefer is to allocate these village quotas equally amongst the members engaged in production. No account is taken of family circumstances or of production in the agricultural branches: each member receives an equal quota. This has always been the practice in Kfar Hefer and is in keeping with the moshav principle of 'equality in the means of production'. The responsibility for division lies with the secretary of the village in consultation with the heads of committees responsible for the agricultural branches in the village, and the decisions must be ratified by the village Executive and the village Council. In practice a small amount of the village quota is 'held back' by the secretary for distribution, on application, to those who are felt to deserve additional opportunities for production. Where a member does not

Table 16   Account of milk marketing in Kfar Hefer, 1966/67

	Income	I̲L̲.
from *Tnuva*		1,671,462
addition for quality of milk		3,670
		1,675,132
less because of low fat content		46,004
		1,629,128
less Tnuva expenses		2,307
		1,626,821
add from local sale		15,923
Total		**1,642,744**

fulfil a particular quota, then the remaining quota reverts to the village to be distributed between other members who farm that product. If in a year there are additional producers in a certain branch, then the quota of all the other producers is adjusted accordingly to ensure these new producers an equal share of production possibilities. The aim of this system is an attempt to minimise differences in production and to give an equal chance to each producer. However, in practice there are considerable differences of production by members in the same branch, chiefly because not all members fill their quotas and this enables others to exceed their personal quota. Increasingly because of government restrictions the emphasis has been on maintaining and not exceeding the overall village quota, but within this quota considerable differences of production do exist.

Dairy production and the rearing of cattle contributed approximately 40 per cent of Kfar Hefer's gross income in the years 1965–67. The emphasis is still on milk production but beef cattle are increasing in value. Table 16 gives the village's account for milk marketing and shows that of the IL.2,959,150 (gross income) which the dairy branch contributed to the village economy, IL.1,642,745 came from the sale of milk.

Kfar Hefer receives a quota of 4,300,000 litres of milk per year from the Ministry of Agriculture. This is intended to be the maximum quota for the year 1970/71 when the five-year plan ends. This is the largest quota for any moshav or kibbuts in the region and even the biggest producers in the settlements around Kfar Hefer receive less than half this total. I have already described the allocation of quotas and this large amount reflects Kfar Hefer's reputation as a big producer over a number of years and the village's political influence

Table 17 Report prepared for the Ministry of Agriculture showing dairy and cattle holdings in Kfar Hefer, 1966–69

			Composition of branch					
	cows	Heifers	Young calves	Bull calves	Total	Milk quota	Marketed (000 litres)	incl. local
1966/67	963	70	801	675	**2,509**	4,300	4,196	80
1967/68	970	70	800	660	**2,500**	4,300	4,300	80
1968/69*	970	70	800	660	**2,500**	4,300	4,300	80

* Proposed.

in the policy making bodies responsible for the drawing up of the system of quotas.

Table 17 shows the composition of Kfar Hefer's dairy and cattle branch in 1966/67 and 1967/68 with the proposed figures for 1968/69.

Kfar Hefer remains within her quota of milk production and in 1966/67 did not reach the total permitted. Below I discuss how milk production in the village is kept at a steady level despite the growth of dairy farms. The village is already producing at a rate intended to be reached only in 1970/71, and so further growth is impossible. If Kfar Hefer's quota was equally divided, according to village principles, between all the farming units, this would give an individual quota of a little under 29,000 litres/farm/year. An average milk yield for milkers is 4,000–4,500 litres/milk/cow/year, which means that an average dairy farm in Kfar Hefer would have 6–7 milking cows. In the case of high yielding cows (6,000–7,000 litres) this number would be even smaller. However, most of the farms in Kfar Hefer have 12–14 cows per farm and there are some with 16–19 cows. This is possible because not all farms in Kfar Hefer have a dairy branch. During the year 1965/66 there were 113 farms engaged in milk production, but by the end of the year this number had dropped to 107. Table 19 below shows the composition of the dairy herds held by those farmers at the end of the year 1965/66. Not all those engaged in milk production rear cattle for slaughter, so this figure is slightly smaller (104) and there is one farm which rears only for meat. Table 18 shows that milk production was still the main activity of Kfar Hefer's cattle farmers. The one farmer who raised cattle only for slaughter is a young farmer who was building up his farm and was interested at that time in a quick return on his invested capital.

At one time in Kfar Hefer everyone had a dairy but at the end of 1956/66, there are 40 farms without cattle, yet this reduction does not have the effect of cutting down village production as a

Table 18   Analysis of dairy holdings in Kfar Hefer, 1965/66

Head of cattle	No. of farms	Head of milk cows	No. of farms	Head of bull calves	No. of farms
up to 4	1	up to 4	8	up to 4	18
5–9	7	5–9	42	5–9	60
10–14	11	10–14	53	10–14	25
15–19	11	15–19	1	15–20	1
20–24	22				
25–29	33				
30+	22*				

* Of this number 3 farms now (1968) have over 40 head of cattle.

whole. Quotas are allocated in the village as a unit and not according to the number of producers, so the consequence of a fall in the number of farmers engaged in dairying has been to increase the possibilities for production by those remaining. Today the internal quota for milk production per dairy farmer is 46,000 litres. But the above table shows, apart from the major differentiation in the village between dairy farmers and non-dairy farmers, there also existed differences in production between the dairy farmers themselves.

The farms without dairies in Kfar Hefer were those where there was no second generation continuation (see previous chapter), with the addition of four other farms. One of these farms was in the category of 'continuation doubtful' (see also previous chapter). In this case the parents married late in life and the husband is now 65 years old; they have two teenage daughters, one still at school and one in the army. The second case is unique in Kfar Hefer and has also been referred to in the previous chapter. Here the eldest son bought his own farm in preparation for the second son to continue in the family farm but this boy left the village and the father is alone on the farm. The eldest son now in fact runs both farms, although accounts and quotas of production are allocated separately. He had a small dairy on his own farm but found it too much work to run both dairies and so sold his own. The young man is engaged in dairying but not on his own farm. The other two cases are those of a *Knesset* member who lives in Kfar Hefer, and a farmer who now works full-time in village services.

It is not chance that the two categories of non-dairying and non-continuation coincided so much: there is a direct causal link between them. Despite the introduction of mechanisation, the maintenance of cattle demands hard physical work which is beyond the capabilities of an aging couple left alone on the farm. Although the introduction of feed concentrates and the mixing of feed in the newly improved village silo saved both time and effort for the individual farmer, the growing of fodder is arduous work. Moreover, considerable financial investment is required if dairying is to be profitable, and the farmer has to wait for several years before a return on his investment is achieved. Aging families who have no child to carry on the farm are not willing to involve themselves in this considerable expense.

As a result of these processes 36 families in the village have chosen to leave dairying and the number increased in the year 1966/67 when a further 14 farms gave up dairying, all of them from the farms where continuation by the second generation was not likely ('continuation doubtful' category in previous chapter). In all, in 1968, 54 farms of Kfar Hefer have no dairying. The result is that the biggest contribution to village gross income is from 93 farms, a little less than two-thirds of the village's farm units.

The position today in dairy farming in Israel is expressed in the following quotation:

A continuous cycle of change is constantly in progress: changes in equipment; feeding systems, breeding plans and goals, artificial insemination, management methods, new construction, all dictated by the demands of economics and consumer's preferences and the creation of new and better products by the milk industry. These and other factors dictate increasing herd size; additional investments. If and when the weaker farmer fails to compete the more skilful farmer continues. It is hoped that this procedure will lead to economically sound, efficient and producing farms. [Further, a] typical well-to-do moshav herd develops on much the same lines as that of the kibbuts herd. The number of cows per individual is being increased from 5–6 to 12–15. Closed barns are rapidly being replaced with sheds with slatted floors and portable milking machines and milking parlours are more numerous.[1]

---

[1] Israel National Committee of the International Dairy Farmers (1967

This situation holds true in Kfar Hefer: now all the farms have milking machines and several now milk into a central wheeled container instead of into individual cans. There are big differences in the standard of the dairy buildings, but all the big producers have conditions approximating to those described above. In the 14 farms which left dairying while I was in the village (1966–68), the conditions in their dairies were noticeably less good. Many did not have their own individual tractor but hired a tractor from the village which added to their costs, and four of these members still used the traditional horse and cart for work about the farm. Conditions in the dairy branch are such today that mechanisation is essential for profitable farming, and even though these 14 farmers may have made the best of the available resources, they were not efficient in the profit-making sense.

In addition to the effect of mechanisation, national policies regarding dairy production had a considerable influence on the profitability of dairy farming. There is over-production in Israel's dairy branch and the Ministry of Agriculture is making determined efforts to reduce production nationally. In a direct attempt, quotas are maintained with no provision for growth and in the event of production above the quota the extra litres of milk receive only 14 agorot[1] per litre, an amount which does not cover costs. In 1965/66 the price paid for a litre of milk was 39 agorot but this was reduced to 36·3 agorot/litre in 1967/68. Indirectly the Ministry tries to reduce production through price control of feed and in the latter part of 1967/68 prices were increased by 10 per cent. Prices of fertilisers for land and of agricultural equipment have also risen. The effect of these measures on the dairy branch in Kfar Hefer has been far-reaching. Until recently government policy was to encourage production and in response to this many members invested heavily in their dairies. The later change of policy, and the fact that the village has now almost reached the limits of expansion, have led to a fall in profits and the expected return on investment has been turned into a loss. Changes in government policy mitigate against the development of specialised farming; while farmers can insure against natural disaster they are almost powerless against government changes. The margin between profit and loss is now very small, and any drop in production can cause heavy losses. In fact the reason why in 1966/67 Kfar Hefer did not reach her quota was because of a sudden drop in production caused mainly by the effects of the June war when care and feeding of the dairy passed from the young farmers to the old and to women and children. Similarly in the early

[1] 100 agorot = IL.1; IL.8.40 = £1.

part of 1968 the Kfar Hefer dairy suffered from a fall in milk yield caused by a change in the feed provided from the village silo. One farmer who had a dairy of 12 milking cows complained to me that he was losing 20 litres a day and this was all his profit gone. In fact for the year accounted 1966/67, of the 107 farmers still remaining in dairying 64 suffered a loss on their milk account, although none suffered an overall loss on their cattle branch. These losses affected big and small producers alike, and were a result of a combination of factors, including falling production and inefficient feeding methods, which were largely a result of the June war, and also from the reduced price paid per litre of milk.

The following examples illustrate dairies showing profit and loss in milk production in the year 1966/67.

Account 1
This is the account of a family referred to earlier in the text, the Isaacs family. The farm is occupied by the husband (66 years old) and wife (64 years) but the running of the dairy is by the son (aged 38 years) who also has a farm but no dairy. This farm showed a small loss on milk production. The table below shows the composition of the dairy at the beginning and the end of 1966/67.

	1966	*1967*
cows	10	10
calves (f)	6	5
bull calves	12	14
Total	**28**	**29**

In this year the farm produced 47,520 litres of milk, a little above the average quota of village members. The labour force in the farm was provided by the father, the son, and his son, a boy of 12 years. It should be stated here that in this and all other following accounts no reduction or allowance is made for labour costs, except where hired work from outside the farm is used. The profit/loss account is obtained simply by deducting costs of animals and of foodstuffs, insurance, inoculations, interest (if any) paid on debt and the buying of cattle. In this farm the simple credit/debit balance shows an income of IL.17,500 from the sale of milk, while debited is IL.17,796. From the sale of the cattle there is an income of IL.10,243 and from this is debited IL.938 for the buying of cattle (two bull calves). Overall from these transactions the farm had remaining IL.9,009 plus an added investment of IL.800 in the value of its cattle. By far the biggest outlay on the farm was on feed for the cattle amounting to a total of IL.12,457. The milk yield of the cows was slightly above average (4,752 litres) and the amount spent on feeding stuffs was not excessive. Nevertheless there was a slight loss on the dairy branch though overall from the sale of cattle the branch gave a good return. As cattle-farming in Kfar Hefer has increased in number of stock and in value to the village the costs of care have increased and so the cost per cow (calf) is much greater than in past years. For example this farm paid insurance of IL.1,701 during this year, and all these costs have to be covered by the return on sale of produce.

Account 2
This is the account of a two-generation family in Kfar Hefer. The parents aged 69 years and 74 years live in the farm with their married daughter and her husband and the couple's children. During the year accounted this was the state of their dairy.

	1966	1967
cows	11	12
calves (f)	6	10
Bull calves	8	8
Total	**25**	**30**

The milk production for this year stood considerably above the Kfar Hefer quota at 53,132 litres, with a production of about 4,500 litres/cow/year. The gross revenue from milk production was IL.19,805 but expenditure was IL.22,783, giving a loss on milk of IL.2,978. As in the last case the biggest expenditure was on feed (IL.13,337) and insurance cost IL.1,617. A noticeable difference from the last account is in the large amount of hay and straw bought for the dairy at a cost of IL.3,134. (In Account 1 most of this was provided by the farm itself and so it was not involved in this expense.) Buying of cattle also cost this farm IL.1,800. The losses on milk were compensated for by a net income of IL.7,350 from the sale of cattle. Comparing this farm with the last in which there is a similar labour force it is seen that despite larger milk production the loss on milk was ten times greater in the second farm. If, as on the previous farm, hay and straw had been provided by the farm's own lands then the farm may just have broken even on the milk account. In the sale of cattle the receipts were very similar but the greater investment of the second farm in the buying of cattle reduced the immediate return.

Account 3
This account shows a farm with a very similar balance to that of
Account 2.

	1966	*1967*
cows	10	11
calves (f)	8	10
Bull calves	7	8
Total	**25**	**29**

This is the farm of Eden's son (see previous chapter) and he and his
wife run the farm together. Eden has transferred the farm to his son
and takes no part in running it, in fact he is out of the village for the
greater part of each week working in the moshav federation. Even
though the structure of the dairy in this farm is very similar to that
of Account 2, there is one big difference. In 1966/67 this farm had
a credit of IL.1,039 on the sale of its milk. The total milk production
of the farm was 53,227 litres, very similar to that above, and the
gross return of IL.19,824 is almost identical with that given above.
But production costs and expenditure are much lower on this farm,
only IL.18,785 as compared with IL.22,738 above. The major
difference is in the cost of feeding supplies: the amount spent on this
farm was IL.11,772, a difference of IL.1,600. Another difference was
in the provision of hay and straw, this farm spending only IL.132
on buying and producing its needs, approximately IL.3,000 less than
farm 2. Sale of cattle was greater in this farm giving a net income of
IL.13,421 (cf. IL.7,350) but investment in the branch was almost
the same, IL.3,350. This young man is known in Kfar Hefer as a
very industrious and hardworking farmer and he is helped considerably by his wife who works in all the branches of the farm. The
account for milk production alone shows that this farmer had a
bigger yield/cow (about 5,000 litres/year) from less feed than the
above farmer. His greater efficiency and his own provision for the
needs of his dairy reflect the slight margin between making a loss
and making a profit on milk production. But despite his efficiency
this farmer had a profit of only just over IL.1,000 and again this
reflects the difficulty, in the prevailing conditions, of making a large
profit on milk production.

Account 4
This is the account of Videtsky, one of the farmers in the 'continuation doubtful' category of the last chapter. He and his wife, aged
60 years and 52 years respectively, live on the farm with their

G

youngest daughter, a teenager. Both the elder daughters are now married and live outside the village. Videtsky farms alone and the size of his dairy farm is about the average for Kfar Hefer, although in number of milking cows it is below average (see above).

	1966	1967
Cows	7	6
Calves (f)	9	5
Bull calves	10	12
Total	**26**	**23**

In this year Videtsky produced 34,666 litres of milk, and had a good yield/cow: yet he ended the year with a deficit of IL.4,763 on milk production. The gross revenue of IL.12,599 was exceeded by expenditure of IL.17,589. His use of feed was slightly above average at a cost of IL.10,771 and certainly not as efficient as that of Moshe Eden (Account 3 above). He was also involved in an expenditure of IL.1,648 for hay and straw, while insurance cost IL.1,654. His main income came from the sale of cattle which totalled IL.21,382 gross. Not all of this was simply from sale of cattle for slaughter, because as the above table shows Videtsky was decreasing his dairy. His annual milk production was much smaller than the quota of 46,000 litres allotted by the village and these figures suggest that, because of the high fixed costs and also running costs of a dairy, milk production below a certain minimum level is not profitable. This limit is being steadily pushed upwards and in the conditions prevailing today in Kfar Hefer it seems that this limit is about 52–53,000 litres/year. This view seems to be shared by Videtsky for he is gradually running down his dairy and since I left Kfar Hefer I have heard that he intends to give up milk production.

The following accounts are of big producers of milk in Kfar Hefer, that is over 60,000 litres/year.

Account 5
This account is of Kfar Hefer's biggest producer, whose milk production in the year 1966/67 totalled 75,060 litres from an average of 13 cows.

	1966	1967
Cows	12	14
Calves (f)	7	7
Bull calves	9	8
Total	**28**	**29**

The yield from the cows was very good, over 5,000 litres per cow, and the farm ended the year with a profit of IL.5,284 on milk production alone. This was the biggest profit on milk in the village. The farm has a big labour force: the parents who are aged 64 and 60 years both continue to work on the farm and there is also a married son, aged 40 years and his wife, and a second son, unmarried and in his late 30's. This unmarried son has a full-time job working in the Ministry of Agriculture, but helps in the farm after work and at holidays. Thus the farm has both financial and physical resources to increase and improve their dairy herd, and the standard of buildings and equipment is high. In fact the number of milk cows was only slightly above average and the high yield per cow was the result of intensive care (afforded by the labour force in the family) and also of the high standard of equipment. The farm was in a position, because of these two factors, to increase the size of its herd and in the following year it grew to above 30 head of cattle.

Account 6
This last account is of another two-generation farm: the parents aged 67 years and 66 years, a married son in his early 40's, and his wife and their teenage children. The parents now play little part in running the farm; most of this is done by the son, with the help of his sons after school. In 1966/67 the structure of the cattle herd was as follows:

	1966	*1967*
Cows	14	16
Calves (f)	14	12
Bull calves	5	9
Total	**33**	**37**

This is one of the biggest herds in Kfar Hefer, and in the following year the number grew to above 40 cattle, chiefly through the addition of milking cows. In 1966/67 the farm produced 63,609 litres of milk, so the yield per cow was much lower than that of the farm cited above. There was a slight profit of IL.753 on milk. The use of feed was very economical, perhaps too much so, because the yield of about 4,000 litres per cow is smaller than those in the other accounts given above. Insurance was a heavy cost at IL.2,188, but most of the hay and straw were provided by the farm itself.

The above accounts show that the production of milk in Kfar Hefer was an uncertain proposition; and in all the farms the main income came from the sale of cattle—bull calves and fully grown cows. This also has its difficulties: in the last five years in Israel there has been a decrease in the sale of fresh meat and an increase of frozen meat, chiefly because of the high cost of fresh meat on the consumer. With the change in public demand towards frozen meat there was an excess of fresh meat in the market and in farms, and consequently there was a heavy fall in price to the producer. The sale of cattle for meat is now heavily subsidised by the government. Farmers in Kfar Hefer increased their holdings of calves for slaughter in response to the high price obtained but this has fallen and the farmers' expected gains have not materialised. At the beginning of 1969 the cattle committee of Kfar Hefer worked out an estimate for the general rearing of cattle because of complaints from farmers that this branch was not sufficiently profitable. This estimate of the cost of rearing bull calves is given below (in Israeli pounds).

Fixed Costs	IL.	*Rearing costs*	Kg.	IL.
Price of bull calf	420	Up to 40 days feed	38	67
Insurance—14 months	40	Feed up to 120 days	266	84
Cost of selling	30	Feed up to 225 days	455	127
Interest	100	Feed up to 420 days	975	273
Buildings (over 10 yrs)	30	Straw	1,560	234
Total	**620**	**Total**		**775**

These are average costs and as shown in the above accounts for milk production the amount can vary owing to the farms' self-sufficiency in feed, but on these figures the return for 14 months of rearing is less than IL.300.

In actual fact few farms ever make such detailed accounts, and the profitability of branches is judged roughly from a previous knowledge and experience of yields and use of feeding stuffs. Thus an increase in the costs of feeding supplies is added to the costs, and profit declines. In an effort to combat this the village is experimenting with new methods of feeding which will give a good yield for a more efficient method of feed utilisation. Commenting on this situation a research association said

... the account [of dairy and cattle] closed with a loss, but the desira-bility of the branch cannot be judged from this aspect alone. In effect it is necessary to distinguish between the computation of the cost of production which is expressed in a profit or loss and the contribution of the branch towards covering the fixed costs ... so long as the farmer has no alter-native employment which brings in more than IL.20/day there is no advantage in another occupation.[1]

---

[1] Institute of Farm Income Research (1967)

In fact, because of profits from the sale of cattle, all the farmers in the village do make this amount, but in Kfar Hefer only one farm (Account 5) reached this amount in milk production.

From the accounts above it is seen that in the middle-range of producers, 45,000–54,000 litres of milk per year, profitability is marginal and whether a farm makes a profit or loss depends mainly on the efficiency in using feed. The farms below this level of production have a very difficult task in achieving a profit: their scale of farming is too small and costs/unit are too great for their production ever to be financially rewarding. At the other end of the scale the big producers shown in Accounts 5 and 6, did make a profit. In Account 5 this was because of very high yields owing to investment in the farm and good care of the cows. Account 6 shows that despite a low yield per cow the size of the dairy alone can bring a profit. And indeed other farms in the village reflect this trend that large producers, even with only average yields, have a better return than those with smaller herds.

Table 19, compiled by the Institute of Farm Income Research and

Table 19 Factors influencing the profitability of family farms in the various side groups (Institute of Farm Income Research (1967))

Size of groups (cattle units)	up to 5	5–10	10–20	over 20
Produce composition: milk in total output %	59	63	58	54
Food composition farm grown fodder %	51	43	33	33
Food utilisation: standard milk/ farm unit (100 litres)	988	1,142	1,212	1,361
Milk yield/cow (litres)	3,425	4,490	4,649	4,804
Meat output/cow (kilos)	73	156	156	219
Meat output/bull calf (kilos)	378	307	371	314
Output value/IL. spent on feed (IL.)	1·61	1·79	1·73	1·89
Irrigated fodder crop area/cattle unit (dunams)	3·4	3·1	2·2	1·8
Work productivity in dairy farming— standard milk/day (litres)	193	203	305	442

the Central Bureau of Statistics, shows the economies of scale achieved by large producers. In the table 'cattle unit' is compiled as follows:

(i)   Cow with milk yield up to 4,500 litres/year = 0·9 cattle unit;
(ii) Cow with milk yield up to 4,500–5,500 litres/year = 1·0 cattle unit;
(iii) Cow with milk yield over 5,500 litres/year = 1·1 cattle unit;
(iv) Female calf or heifer of average age = 0·45 cattle unit;
(v)   Bull calf of average age = 0·5 cattle unit.

At a special General Meeting held in the village in January 1967 (agricultural year is 1966/67), the village secretary, Dov, reported that production of milk was running 10 per cent higher than anticipated; the villagers were 40,000 litres above their quota for the period. Eighty members of the village were present at the meeting, a number above the average attendance for village meetings, and the vast majority of those present were milk producers. The village secretary reported that in view of this situation in milk production the village Executive in conjunction with the cattle committee recommended that a differential scale of prices be paid within the village. These prices would be paid when the village exceeded its permitted quota, and in the event that at the end of the year the village as a whole had stayed within the quota then adjustments would be made accordingly to the accounts of the members affected. The proposal was, that the full price (39 agorot) should be paid to producers of amounts up to 46,000 litres/year; to producers of 46,000–60,000 litres/year, a price of 35 agorot per litre would be paid; producers above 60,000 would receive 12 agorot/litre. The intention of these measures was to ensure that production of the bigger producers would be penalised and not those who kept within their quotas. However, the effect of the measure was to freeze the pattern of dairying in the village and to maintain the production of farmers who produced within the quota and not encourage them to develop their farms, while those above this amount were urged to cut back on production despite their heavy investment. This is in keeping with moshav principles — that the stronger members should not produce at the expense of the smaller ones, and that efforts should be made to minimise differences within the village. Under this proposal payment would remain unchanged for 50 members engaged in dairying because their production was below 46,000 litres, but for the remaining 49 farmers there would be a substantial drop in income.

The announcement of the decision caused great controversy

although in fact most members had some knowledge that the announcement would be made. The composition of the meeting reflected this. When the proposal was thrown open for discussion all the members who spoke opposed the resolution. One member said that this was the picture at the moment but this could change; they all knew that Ministry plans changed from moment to moment and they would be foolish to take action which they would afterwards regret. The second speaker was Levi, a full-time official of the Ministry of Agriculture who represented the moshavim to the Ministry. He told the meeting that far from getting better the situation would be worse in the future. He went on to say that in that year there would be an excess of 1,200 tons of butter produced that could not be sold and he believed that the price paid per litre of milk would fall below that paid then. [Subsequent events proved that this assessment was correct.] And he added that in his opinion it was not worthwhile for a farmer to produce more than 60,000 litres per year. The next two speakers, one a woman, both declared their interests as big producers of milk and opposed the scheme. One proposed that ½ agorah should be deducted from all production above 25,000 litres and this should be added to producers of amounts above 60,000 litres. The woman's husband then added that this was a general problem for the village and not an individual one; the village had encouraged production and now could not avoid the results of its actions. This speech was supported by a third speaker who urged that compensation should be paid to those who exceeded the quota. They were not guilty: in the past they had been encouraged to increase their production. A counter proposal was put by Ra'anan, a previous speaker and a large milk producer; he suggested that two, not three, prices be paid—milk up to 46,000 litres the full price and production above that level to receive an 'average' price. On a vote, the proposal of the village Executive was defeated and the counter proposal accepted by 33 votes for and 2 against, the remainder abstaining. The 2 votes against the proposal were those of the village secretary and another member of the village Executive who had recently given up dairy farming.

In the event, these measures were not needed because village production fell owing to difficulties in getting foodstuffs, but the pattern of the discussion above shows several interesting features. All the speakers from the floor declared their interest, which was, in any case well known to the members present. All the arguments, including that of the village secretary, were couched in the terms of moshav ideology. The secretary appealed to the principles of mutual aid, with the stronger helping the weaker, and also to the moshav ideal of minimising differences between members. The speaker from the floor also used the argument of mutual aid but interpreted it in a different fashion. He emphasised the responsibilities of the village Executive, as the representative of all the village, to ensure the well-being of all members. He reiterated a demand for the village Executive and its committee to accept responsibility for their actions: they had encouraged an increase in production, now they should stand by the decision and not let members themselves suffer. They argued that without this guarantee there would be no moshav life and that the village as a co-operative would be meaningless. If individuals had to bear the responsibility then they must have the freedom to make their own decisions in their own interests and not be bound by the village co-operative. With the full backing of the village they had invested in the dairy production and they felt it was only justice that they should be allowed to have the benefits of this investment.

The position of the village Executive and the village secretary is discussed more fully in a later chapter. But this incident shows one of the difficulties inherent in their roles, namely the reconciling of the economic and social welfare of the village as a whole with that of the individual members. In the early days of the settlement it was easier to ensure that these ran concurrently; but differentiation in types and quantities of production has led to members having different interests which do not necessarily coincide with the interests of the whole population. The effects of these different interests existing in a co-operative settlement have in recent years been emphasised and re-inforced by national planning policies in terms of allocating quotas for glutted markets.

The situation in the dairy and cattle branches of Kfar Hefer under the fixed village quotas is that producers can only increase their production if other members either cut their production or give up branches. The incidents described above show that not only is there a major difference between the interest of dairy farmers and non-dairy farmers in Kfar Hefer but that also within the dairy branch the members are in competition. Kfar Hefer, as I have shown, was built for practical and ideological reasons on mixed farming and the ideal was that all 154 farm units should be involved in all three major branches. For various reasons this has not happened and now the increasing trend to mechanisation and economies of scale call for bigger units of production. The 'mini-farm' as it was affectionately or ironically called in Kfar Hefer is against all these trends.

The desire of dairy farmers to produce more has brought them into conflict with other members of the village. It will be remembered that until now the farmers who have left dairying, with three exceptions, were elderly farmers of the first generation. In many cases it was felt by these members that the dairy farmers were anxious to 'push them out' of dairying in order to receive an additional quota of production. This antagonism was popularly expressed in the village as a dispute between young and old, although in fact most of the dairy farmers did share a farm with their elderly parents. An editorial in the village bulletin, 1967, expressed the current position in Kfar Hefer:

... a member who invests a lot of money in his dairy wants to increase his dairy but is prevented from doing so by his quota, for him it is better for dairies to be given up and not taken up. Today with the present means of production in our hands we could have 20 milkers per farm but we are limited by a quota which says, 'up to here and no more.' Why is this so? The answer is that there are 'too many farmers in our state, in a modern state fewer and fewer farmers are able and required to produce the country's needs'. There is a difference between a basic branch and a profitable branch, and this results in a situation where ambition and inclination want fewer and fewer to be involved in production. In Kfar Hefer today this situation is not recognised simply because we do not speak, at least not openly, what we think and feel inwardly. Here the things are written and spoken openly . . . in order to develop dairy as a profitable branch we have to increase its size . . . Kfar Hefer is not yet based on dairies of 16–20 milkers and so it is necessary to run down the number of dairies and in this way increase the quota of others . . .

Certainly the above described situation was well known in Kfar Hefer and people, especially the 'old', talked about it. But no public announcement was made nor until this time was anything written about it. The editor at this time was a young man described in the previous chapter. He lived outside the village but helped his father on the farm. His position in Kfar Hefer as I have indicated was a marginal one: although he was 'of' the village he was not 'in' the village. Analysis of the role of 'the stranger' in communities has been discussed elsewhere.[1] And here I suggest this young man served on this role to bring to public debate an issue which everyone knew about but which they were reluctant to recognise and whose implications they were reluctant to discuss. In fact after this article there was a spate of letters in the bulletin, many criticising the editor for writing anti-moshav ideas and denying the report. But from the 'old' there were letters agreeing with him and expressing the feeling that the old were being discriminated against and the young no longer wanted to see them in farming.

This feeling of the old was reinforced because it was not simply the question of dairy farms that was at issue, but also the holdings of

[1] Frankenberg (1957)

village lands and the use of water. In addition to land for citrus and the family plot surrounding the house, each family has about 15 dunams of land for growing field crops, and each family receives an annual water allocation of 17,000 m³ water. This land is used for growing fodder crops and occasionally for vegetables. When a member gives up dairy production he customarily also relinquishes his holding of land. This is not a necessary consequence but in practice the reasons which compel a member to give up his dairy have in the past also precluded him from working his fields. The land is leased to the farmer on a 49-year lease from the J.N.F.: this lease is normally automatically renewable but there is a clause in the lease which says that lands must be worked. Therefore, within Kfar Hefer, the custom in the past has been for the land to revert back to the village to be redistributed among village members. There are no 'private financial arrangements' between members of Kfar Hefer; all the land is taken over by the village Executive. Two main justifications are given for this practice. First, the lease stipulates that land must be worked, and second, the moshav laws stress co-operation and mutual aid. It is considered wrong of a member to hold on to land which he does not farm. However, when a farmer transfers his land to the village he still retains his rights to the land, and on reasonable notice can claim it back at any time. This custom is reinforced by the use of financial measures. If a member does not transfer the use of his land to the village after he has finished using it then he is charged by the village at the rate of IL.15/dunam. These charges are said to be the cost of depreciation of pipes and installations in the land and also the member's share in the first costs of water, in spite of the fact that he does not use water in his fields. In 1966/67, in all there were some 580 dunams of land given back to the village for use by other members. A member who transfers his land to the village receives after it is allocated a sum of IL.5/dunam from the person who receives the land. This is a nominal payment and is in no way related to the value of the land to the receiver nor does it adequately compensate the giver for his years of work on the land and the installations he has made. But this level of payment was set because it was said that Kfar Hefer did not want a class of entrepreneurs or rentiers who made money from the loan of lands. Further, it was pointed out that the donor did not own the land but merely leased it and the village as an agent of the J.N.F. had a claim upon it. The village Executive, especially the internal secretary of the village, has the job of dividing the land between applicants. Dairy farmers are anxious to have more land for fodder growing for their cattle, and so they are the main applicants. The land is not divided amongst applicants equally, but according to 'need', as determined by the village Executive. During the years I was in the village, 'need' seemed to be defined in two ways: preference was given both to those members with large dairies and to the new farmers, usually young men who had bought a farm and were trying to build it up. The land given to the rest of the applicants tended to be roughly equal. Thus, in 1966/67 78 members received extra allocations of land, the big dairy farmers and young farmers as much as eight dunams of land and the others from three to five dunams. As a result of this process dairy farmers not only benefited by receiving extra quotas of dairy production when members left dairy farming but also received supplements of land, in some cases as much as 50 per cent of their own holding. This allocation reflected the village Executive's recognition of the advantage to the village of large dairies.

Similarly, the water of those not using their quota reverted to the village Executive, though the member did not relinquish his rights to it. In 1966/67 there was a considerable difference in water use, ranging from 7,105 m^3 in the case of a widow who did not farm her fields and who had no poultry, and who therefore used water only in the citrus groves, to, at the highest point of the scale, a water consumption of 36,849 m^3 on the farm of a young farmer who had a large dairy, a large poultry holding and citrus groves on sandy soils. The remaining farms fell between these two extremes, but big dairy farmers all clustered together around 26,500–27,000 m^3/year, an amount 10,000 m^3 bigger than their individual quota.

A case study at the beginning of the next chapter shows in detail how one typical non-dairying farmer reacted to the above situation. Here it is sufficient to say that these farmers were disgruntled and complained that far from their exploiting others they themselves were being exploited. The above cited complaints about the ingratitude of the young and their wish to push them out of production were all reiterated.

The second major branch in terms of gross income is poultry, again a part of Kfar Hefer's mixed farming. Within this one branch several types of rearing and breeding are pursued. These types of poultry farming are usually combined in a farm to give a spread of earnings and to guard against losses in one branch. The combinations are as follows: layers, turkeys (for meat) and 'anak' (a heavy bird developed in Israel as an egg producer and broiler fowl); layers and turkeys (meat); layers and anak; turkeys (meat) and anak; turkeys (meat and hatching eggs); anak. Most farmers in the village have some poultry. In 1966/67 there were 135 farms engaged in poultry farming, distributed as shown in Table 20.

Table 20   Distribution of poultry among Kfar Hefer's poultry farms, 1966/67

Number of farms	Turkeys	Quotas (chicks) Anaks	Layers
24	350	425	450
42	650		550
23		900	450
22	450	500	
10	740		
4		1,300	
5			1,400
5*			

* Turkeys for breeding—special situation discussed below.

Members choose which types they will rear and some alterations are possible from year to year but generally not during the year. The village policy is that each farm should have only two types of poultry, but the granting of supplements during the year and the market conditions often result in the establishing of three branches in particular farms even though this is frowned upon by the village Executive and the village poultry committee. They oppose it because each type needs its own special care and feed, and they consider that a farmer cannot give adequate attention to three different types. In the allocation of quotas between these different types they plan to achieve an equal income for each farmer irrespective of his choice of poultry. However, writing in the village bulletin in 1967 the secretary of the poultry committee commented upon the above distribution: 'It is known that there is not enough income here for members but we have tried to make the various combinations equal.'

Until two or three years ago production of poultry, and especially of table and hatching eggs, was encouraged in Israel. Exports were large especially in the European market of Italy and Germany and they seemed likely to continue. Even at the end of 1965 the Ministry of Agriculture feared there would not be enough eggs for the markets and they encouraged production. But the situation in Europe changed and those countries which had previously imported eggs now began to export and in March/April 1966 there was an excess of eggs in Israel, both in production and in stored eggs. At this time a plan was put forward that all fresh eggs should be exported to Europe and stored eggs should be used at home. This plan suffered because on 1 July 1967 the tariff barriers on agriculture were removed in the Common Market countries and in addition a tax barrier against outsiders was erected. Efforts were made to find other markets and agreements were reached with Yugoslavia, England

and Austria. Here again difficulties arose. After the 'Six Day' war of June 1967, the Yugoslavs refused to pay the price agreed and also cut down the amount previously agreed upon. The English market was still open but at a very low price. In November 1967 the state of the egg market was 70 million frozen eggs in store and every week there was a surplus of 5 million eggs (i.e. in excess of home demand). The country did not know what to do with all the eggs and these were now fed back to the chickens by mixing them in with chicken feed. The only answer was to cut down on production and also to re-allocate production between settlements. In the Jerusalem area there are settlements which have no agricultural income other than that from poultry, and attempts were made to soften the blow by re-allocating extra production to them.

This last factor is very important for Kfar Hefer, because in addition to being dependent upon national planning, a process which they can and do attempt to influence and direct through their affiliated agencies, they are also dependent upon other settlements. If other settlements decided not to keep within their allocated quotas, or to market on the black market, then the ordinary controls of the Ministry are no longer effective and the price of produce falls in the market. The usual penalties imposed by the Central Poultry Council are fines upon the settlement concerned; but as these are only in the range of IL.200–250 they are totally ineffective.

The Ministry of Agriculture and the relevant agencies used the same tools to deal with over production of poultry as they used for dairy surpluses. They increased the price of supplies by 10 per cent; they cut back quotas by 10 per cent; and they penalised production in excess of quota by reducing the price paid. The restrictions applied to the production of table and hatching eggs; turkeys which suffered less from over-production, were affected only by the increase in the cost of supplies. Table 22 below shows the effects of these measures on Kfar Hefer's production in amount produced and in revenue.

An analysis of this table shows that comparative income has dropped in table eggs and hatching eggs, the two types of poultry most affected by government action. On the other hand turkey production, both for meat and for breeding, has increased and the revenue from these has resulted in an overall gain for the branch in the years compared. Marketing of turkeys in the village is handled differently from marketing of other poultry branches. Kfar Hefer has relatively only a few turkey producers and as a village they were late in taking this up. Therefore they feel it is not to their advantage to handle their produce through the Poultry Council and the marketing is arranged by the village Executive (not the village poultry committee) with non-government agencies. Over the past few years Kfar Hefer has systematically over-produced the quotas she is allocated, and in the last year or so this has been by as much as 90 per cent. As a result of this turkey producing has been a profitable enterprise for individual farmers in the village.

Twelve families in Kfar Hefer were not involved in farming of poultry, or turkeys. With one exception they were all single generation farms, whose children were outside the farm. The one exception was a two generation farm, which was involved in poultry breeding but not under the auspices of the village. The circumstances of this case are discussed in detail later in another chapter. Of the remaining farms eight were occupied by a first-generation member living alone, while in two other cases both first generation members were present but one of the partners suffered ill health. The care and upkeep of poultry was thought of as the domain of the women of the family and in these two cases the woman, because of chronic ill health, had been unable to work on the farm. In the remaining case the wife of the farmer had a full-time paid job in Tel Aviv and so was not able to devote time to the farm. In ten of the cases the farms had also given up dairying and so their only agricultural income came from citrus. The 'special' case mentioned above and the farm with a working wife both had small dairy farms.

The effect of government policies did not fall as expected on the village, nor were all those interested in poultry equally affected, nor did all of them feel equally the significance of these measures.

Forty farms engaged in poultry and turkey raising in 1966/67 had only two branches of agricultural production, citrus and poultry, and in 1967/68 a further seven farms gave up the dairy branch and entered this category. The discussion of citrus growing (below) shows that most of these farms did not take an active part in citrus cultivation: hence for almost a third of the village's farms, poultry was the branch in which they were most actively engaged.

The village was faced with a double problem: to ensure an adequate income for its members and not to produce more than its quota. Even though village distribution is carefully allocated to avoid excessive production, in actual fact a number of factors make it impossible to control the situation completely. There are differences in laying standards and the usual calculations are not always accurate: sometimes members, not always intentionally, fail to market birds after 14 months, and the added period of laying increases village production. Moreover in the past, members have from time to time been allowed to buy chicks from outside the village for extra production. This practice has depended upon the state of the

Table 21 Production of poultry in Kfar Hefer, 1966–68

	Production 1966/67		1967/68		Comparison 1967/68 with 1966/67			
	Amount	Revenue (IL)	Amount	Revenue (IL)	±Amount	%	±Revenue (IL)	%
Table eggs	9,124,804	846,469	8,056,095	775,797	−1,068,709	−11·7	−70,672	−8·34
Hatching eggs	2,947,553	639,509	2,430,381	619,534	−517,172	−17·5	−19,975	−3·1
Broilers (tons)	283	263,104	177	308,272	−26	−12·8	+45,168	+17·6
Chickens	14,270	98,479	10,031	42,353	−4,239	−29·7	−52,179	−52·9
Cockerels		856	1,095				+239	
Total (1)		1,848,417		1,747,031			−101,386	−5·5
Turkey meat (tons)	441	94,723	523	1,350,054	+82	+18·6	+438,311	+38·0
Turkey hatching eggs	159,628	123,067	153,487	134,284	−6,141	−3·8	+11,217	+9·1
Total (2)		1,034,790		1,484,318			+449,528	+43·1
Total 1 & 2		2,883,207		3,231,349			+348,142	

market and in view of the situation it was decided that this should not be allowed in the future. In an attempt to mitigate the effect of government action upon income in the village, the poultry committee tried to shift the balance of marketing into the summer season when a slightly bigger price is paid for poultry products. In addition the village Executive reached agreements with two other moshavim, in one case to exchange a part of their quota of table eggs for a quota of hatching eggs. The second case involved Gavish, Kfar Hefer's neighbour who had a large order for turkey chicks for export to France; owing to other commitments, Gavish could not meet their order so Kfar Hefer took over a part of the consignment. Both these arrangements were to the village's benefit, the one with Gavish enabling some members to devote all their poultry branch to turkeys, while the exchange gave the village an increased supply of the profitable 'anak' birds.

The accounts given below show poultry production in several of Kfar Hefer's farms.

Case 1

This farm concentrates on the rearing of turkeys only, both in the production of meat and on hatching eggs. This was the first farm in Kfar Hefer to start, by chance, the breeding of turkeys. During the years accounted the farm had 1,600 turkeys at the beginning of the year and had a gross income of IL.76,563 from all turkey products. This amount was split almost equally between the income from turkey meat and the income from hatching eggs. The farm is a two generation farm: the father has a full-time job outside the village but both parents help their married son on the farm. On the account of the turkeys the farmer had a net remainder of IL.30,898 and an added investment in the branch of IL.3,139. These are very big sums, in excess of the total income from all branches of farming on some farms of Kfar Hefer. The family benefited from their early start and the good state of the market which in the early years enabled them to increase their production to the utmost of their capacity. Unlike dairying which needs heavy investment the poultry branch can be expanded quickly and not at great cost, so the family was easily able to increase growth.

Case 2

This is the account of a single older generation farm, where their agricultural income comes from poultry, turkeys and citrus. In fact this family do not take all their quota of poultry because this is almost the sole responsibility of the wife, a woman in her sixties and she finds it too much work to take all the quota. Her husband works in the village administration. The main emphasis on the farm was on the production of table eggs and hatching eggs, with over 83,000 table eggs and 20,121 hatching eggs which together brought in a net income of IL.5,367. Turkeys were reared for meat and this branch brought in a net income of IL.3,538. But this couple were decreasing their holdings of poultry because of increasing difficulty in coping with production and the value of stocks held fell by IL.1,595 which means that the following year's production will be smaller. This farm had no dairy and the only other agricultural income is from citrus.

Case 3
The next account is of a second generation farmer who now manages the farm alone, on the death of his parents. He is helped on the farm by his wife who runs the poultry section. This farm has all three main branches of agriculture. Like the one above this farm concentrates on table eggs, hatching eggs and turkeys. However in this farm the emphasis is on hatching eggs which brought in a gross income of IL.16,000, with table eggs bringing in a little over IL.4,000. Turkeys for meat, were of equal value with table eggs. From this produce the farm had a net remainder of IL.8,765. This is slightly more than the account above, chiefly because of the better prices obtained for hatching eggs as compared with the prices obtained for table eggs.

Case 4
This is the account of a farmer who is without second-generation continuation and who has recently given up dairy farming and is now concentrating on poultry. Towards the end of the year he applied to the village Executive for a supplementary quota and received a quota of turkeys, but his main income comes from table eggs and hatching eggs. In the year accounted he produced 187,003 table eggs, a figure which is three times as great as some farms in Kfar Hefer. The gross income from poultry totalled IL.46,342 and from turkeys IL.6,978. Overall on the combined branches he had a net income of IL.18,646. This is a very respectable sum, and reflects the emphasis he is putting on this branch as his main source of income.

Case 5
This is another account which shows a two-generation family whose main income in the poultry branch is from turkeys. In this family both parents and their married daughter and her husband work on

H

the farm. At the beginning of the year they held 950 turkeys, a number which increased to nearly 1,300 by the end of the year. From this branch they had a gross income of IL.68,792 of which the majority (IL.43,735) came from hatching eggs.

It is not chance that the farms involved solely in turkey raising are two generation farms. The care of turkeys demands a lot of specialised attention, since they are very susceptible to infection and must be carefully tended. Most poultry farms in Kfar Hefer have some turkeys, but most raise only for meat production. Breeding needs a heavier investment in equipment and in labour and even most two generation farms are not able to give this. In addition, especially amongst the older generation, there is still hesitation about total investment in one type of poultry; they wish to cover themselves against possible damage to one type by having at least one other branch to rely upon. This is despite the recent introduction of a village insurance scheme for poultry.

All the above accounts are for the year 1966/67, the year before government restrictions became fully effective in the village. I was unable to obtain complete figures for individual farms for the year 1967/68, because I left the village before the end of the agricultural year. However, village quotas, as Table 22 shows, were cut back considerably, and the villagers queried whether it was worthwhile, even in turkey rearing, to exceed their quota in meat production because of increased prices of supplies. Yet the table also shows that overall income from the poultry and turkey branches yielded an increase on the year 1966/67. This was due to a nation-wide attack of Newcastle disease (a respiratory infection) which caused considerable losses throughout Israel. Kfar Hefer's members also suffered though not as badly as some areas, and the members were also covered by insurance, so their losses were not total. The effect of this almost complete standstill in poultry production was to reverse the position from that existing in the early part of the year. From a situation of excesses in all branches, the pendulum swung to shortage in all branches, to the extent that eggs were imported from abroad and high prices were paid for chickens and turkeys.

Kfar Hefer expected the government measures to cost the village IL.100,000. This would have resulted in considerable cuts in income for all poultry raisers. In the eventual outcome this did not happen but within the village there are still members who complain that they cannot make an adequate living from poultry.

The cases given above show that recently turkeys have been consistently the best branch in poultry. Therefore farmers in Kfar Hefer all try to have an allocation of turkeys, but not everyone is allowed to do this, because if the production was equally divided then the numbers per farm of turkey would be too small to justify expenses. Inevitably this leads to accusations of favouritism directed mainly against the village secretary who is responsible for telling a member whether or not his application has been successful. Turkey breeders have not been affected very much by this trend, although at the beginning of 1967/68 three additional farms applied to raise only turkeys. This raised the number of such farms to eight and according to village policy the quotas of other farms were adjusted to accommodate the newcomers. The quota decided upon was 30,000 hatching eggs plus ten tons of meat, or 40,000 eggs alone. Complaints were voiced from the original raisers who said that anything less than 40,000 eggs plus meat was unthinkable (case 5 produced 43,500 eggs in 1966/67). On this scale of production revenue is very big and so there existed within the village a small group of farmers, all with two generation farms, who made a considerable income from turkeys. An amount of 8 per cent per quota is withheld by the village Executive for re-distribution as a supplement to members in 'need'. As in the case of supplements of milk, 'need' is broadly interpreted as help to farmers who cannot make a living from their current quota, and also given to members who are building up a branch. In the year 1966/67 sixty members applied for an addition to their poultry quota. These supplements have to be fairly substantial if they are to have any meaningful effect on the economic position of the receiver and an amount of less than 200 birds is generally not considered worthwhile. Thus one elderly member appeared before the village Executive to ask for another supplement to his poultry. He had already been given an addition of 250 birds of which 100 were turkeys, but he complained that 100 turkeys were not worth bothering with and he asked for another addition of 150 turkeys. When this request was turned down he appealed to the full Village Council, and said that his only source of income was from poultry because he had given up dairy farming and his citrus grove had been hit by frost and was not producing fruit. In fact in 1966/67 this man had an income of IL.10,000 from poultry, and the Village Council turned down the request because they said there were cases of greater 'need' in the village, as many members had a far smaller income.

It is recognised within the village, at least by the village Executive and the poultry committee, that some farms, notably those without dairy and where the first generation live alone, do not make a living from poultry. Writing in the village bulletin the editor said: 'A farm which lives on the production of table eggs and turkeys for meat on a yearly basis can for a day's work produce 250 eggs and 15 kilos of meat, and no one is rich from that.' At a very stormy and noisy village General Meeting held in November, 1967 (the start of the agricultural year 1967/68) to debate the poultry branch, this question of insufficient income was discussed. The issue was raised by Ben-David, a widower and a first generation settler who has no continuation on his farm and so has given up dairy farming. Ben-David is an experienced campaigner against village committees and in particular against the village Executive. Several years ago when he was able to work in the fields he started to grow green peppers as an addition to his income. These peppers he marketed himself and so revenue did not go to the village co-operative; the village Executive complained and said that he must stop these activities. He refused to do so and the village Executive ruled that he must not be given supplies from the village. They also threatened to cut off his water supply. Ben-David appealed to the Ministry of Agriculture who informed the village that the cutting off of water is forbidden and they also informed Ben-David that he could get supplies through their offices. For a time he did this but without the credit extended by the village this was a difficult task and in the end he gave up production. This incident is well remembered in the village and seems to have been a 'test-case' both for the individual and for the village's Council and committees. Ben-David's action was seen as a defiance of moshav principles and a direct challenge to the village Executive, and their eventual victory is interpreted as a triumph for the collective principle. Yet there is another side to this case: the action of the Ministry and of *Tnuat Ha'moshavim* (the Moshav Movement) who both refused to condone the type of sanction, showed the village Executive how limited are their sanctions against recalcitrant and refractory members. In this case they re-asserted co-operative principles because Ben-David was unable financially to stand against them. In a later chapter this issue of village sanctions is discussed in detail and a case-study will show the village's problems in dealing with a financially secure member.

At this meeting Ben-David spoke about the plight of members who had given up their dairy farming and were 'expected' to give up their land and to live on an income from poultry and citrus. He said that it was a crime that those whose lands are used by other members of the village to their benefit, should still continue to receive only an equal quota of poultry. At this point there was a lot of shouting from the members present, and above it all Almagor, a village Council member, was heard to say that there were provisions for extra quotas—Dov had 8 per cent of the total quotas to divide between such members. Ben-David retorted that he knew there were members who were willing and able to accept more, and further he criticised the division of supplements saying it was not always those in greatest need who received them. This view was supported by Michaeli, another farmer who had given up his dairy. He suggested that in this year there should be an examination of the distribution, then the village would see that it was unjust. Support for the village quota to be distributed according to the state of the farm came from Tagar, the head of the village poultry committee; he explained that the division of citrus groves gave a precedent for this. Over the years these groves had been adjusted to give approximately equal yields, and some members had given up rights in land for field crops in exchange for a larger holding of citrus groves. He thought that a committee should be elected to investigate similar possibilities in the case of poultry. All this time the meeting had taken place in the continuous sound of voices, sometimes reaching a point where it was impossible to hear the speaker. Members did not try to catch the secretary's eye to address the meeting but simply shouted their comments to those around them. Amid this uproar a young farmer stood up to speak formally to those present. He said that if 'need' was to be the deciding factor in allocations then one must look at the other side of 'need'. All those who had given up dairy farming had special family and demographic reasons (a statement which was not strictly true, see above discussions of dairy) and even though they may have had less income than other farmers, they also had fewer expenses because they had only two people on the farm to support. This young man was married with three young children and also his aged parents were on the farm, in all a livelihood for seven people had to be provided. He added that in many cases it is a mistake to think that the income from agriculture is the total income for these families; most have other work and this income does not go through the village co-operative. Again this was an exaggeration for while it was true that a number of farmers did have non-agricultural work, in only one case was this outside the village, and even in this particular case the income did go through the co-operative because the work was associated with the Moshav Movement. In an effort to calm the meeting Dov said that he was prepared to admit that in the past they may have been mistaken in their insistence on equal quotas, and he welcomed the idea of a committee to allocate the quotas. He was very willing to transfer all question of supplements to this committee; as far as he was concerned it was the worst job he had had to do and he was only too willing to give it away. A note of reason was introduced by Doron, who now has no connection with farming and worked outside the village. Doron pointed out that there was nothing definite about the figure of 8 per cent withheld for re-distribution; this could always be changed and he suggested that any committee elected to deal with the problem should consider this fact. The next speaker was Shimoni (see Case 5 above): he declared that there was no connection between dairy farming and poultry, and it was a mistake to think that deficiencies in one should be compensated for by increases in the other and he opposed the election of any committee. On a vote about the setting up of a committee the proposition was heavily defeated, only Dov and Ben-David voted for the motion. After this vote other members attempted to speak. Michaeli urged Dov to look again at the 8 per cent to which Dov said that all members may apply for a supplement but he agreed that perhaps 8 per cent was not a good figure and he suggested that they give it up. On this remark uproar again broke out in the meeting and everyone talked together. The meeting was called to order by the chairman who said that all discussion had finished with the vote and the whole question would be debated again, if desired, at a further meeting.

The meeting described above was the first public discussion of major differences and interests in the village. The meeting was called to discuss the state of the poultry market in view of the new government proposals but in fact not a word was said about them. The noisiness of the meeting was an indication of the interest involved in poultry distribution, and the description of the meeting shows the opposing views held by village members. The two extremes of production in the village are usually referred to in any discussion of farming. There are in Kfar Hefer a few farmers who because of luck, skill, labour force, financial resources and diligent application, have made and continue to make a lot of money from farming. In contrast to this, at the opposite end of the scale, are farms which for many reasons have not developed in this way and which have gradually run down production to such a level that the income is insufficient for a livelihood. Even though proportionately their numbers are small, their influence is considerable on village life. The big producers represent an example for young farmers, whose only hope of achieving a comparable situation is by increasing production. The elderly refer to both these extremes: they contrast profitable production with their own small income, and they see those with even less income as a warning about their own possible future. In order for them to increase their income they too have to increase their production, and their best chance of doing this lies in poultry production. For the most part they are no longer dairy farmers and an increase in citrus holdings involves a long period of waiting for return on the investment, but poultry holdings can be increased quickly for a small outlay and the return is relatively quick. The system of equal quotas with supplements cannot change their position, and they plead for a new means of distribution in the village. Those at the upper reaches of production are satisfied with the equal distribution which rein-forces and reaffirms their position at the top. Any system which was based on the provision of overall equal income would be detrimental to their interests. They, like the middle group, look to other members giving up production as their main source of increase. But poultry farming, unlike dairy farming, is a branch which elderly members are able to maintain, So it is in this branch that the main quarrels and struggles for production take place.

Here I refer again to an article by Labes quoted earlier. In this he said that the leaving of sons had not been detrimental to the village, a statement to which I suggest many of Kfar Hefer would not subscribe. The above situation shows, I believe, how analytically at least these views can be reconciled. The village as a whole has not suffered from the lack of second generation farmers in some farms, at least not economically. Their absence has enabled many other members to reach a higher standard of living. Those who have not benefited economically are the parents, and this as I said earlier has suddenly come into prominence in the village in the last few years. On the sale of their dairies these farmers have suddenly faced a drop in income and an increase in working time. This time they could now devote to increasing their poultry holdings to a level beyond that of 'women's work' and at the same time add to their income. In the past this difficulty of insufficient means of income has often been ameliorated by the farmer or his wife finding jobs in the village, in administration or in the village egg-grading station. A smaller number have found work outside the village in government or moshav agencies but these opportunities are limited so the majority of these farmers have to rely on agricultural production for their main income. This meeting described above was the first public omen of the discontent among these village members, and it portended a movement to rectify what they believed to be an unfair situation. In fact the village secretary was personally sympathetic to these members, but the existing system restricted his ability to ease their situation.

Citrus is the one agricultural branch in which everyone in Kfar Hefer is involved. In the year 1966/67 two members' groves did not yield any fruit because the whole grove was replanted after the severe frost of 1963 and the new trees have not yet borne fruit. For ten members in Kfar Hefer the sale of produce from their citrus groves is their only agricultural income: seven of these are elderly women living alone on the farm, and the other three are elderly married couples, who because of ill health are unable to engage in other production. The citrus groves of these families and of several other elderly couples are worked by hired labour. This labour is hired by the village as a whole and not by individual farmers; in this way some compromise is reached with the moshav's traditional ban on farmers hiring workers. The cost of hired labour is heavy, since wages take account of years, of seniority and of the size of the family of the worker. An experienced hired worker of several years seniority receives IL.25–IL.27 per day and in addition he receives several social benefits such as paid holidays and sick compensation, all of which have to be met by the farmer. On the farms which do not have hired labour citrus is considered to be a good branch because nearly all the income is net, as there are few expenses connected with production. For those families who do hire labour this is a big expense and considerably cuts down their net income from the branch. There is a professional member in the village who is responsible for the overall state of Kfar Hefer's *pardessim* (citrus groves) and he arranges the marketing and picking of the crop as well as advising farmers about the state of their groves. The coastal plain of Israel is the main citrus-growing area of the country, for the humidity and sandy soils favour these crops. In Kfar Hefer the main crops are Shamouti, Valencia and Clementinas: the first two are mainly for the export market and Clementinas provide for the home market. Crop yields from the several plots vary considerably, not always due to differences in the farmers' care. Small differences in soil or in exposure can result in big differences in yields. The possession of a good area or a poor area is largely due to chance, although an attempt has been made to overcome these differences by the granting of additional plots or the re-siting of plots for members who have very poor areas. Because of concern at poor yields and the slow development in newly planted groves, the village commissioned a survey of the citrus groves from the Ministry of Agriculture's extension service. In part these low yields were as a result of the severe frost in 1963, but even in areas less affected by frost the yields were very poor and in some cases the return did not cover the cost of production. The survey showed striking differences in production, notably in two areas of Shamouti: the plots between the river and the eastern highway had very low yields, but the area to the north of the road gave higher yields. Table 22 shows differences in production of the citrus crops. The Ministry of Agriculture consider 4–4½ tons per dunam a respectable yield. But in Kfar Hefer anything above 3½ tons is thought to be good.

Table 22 Citrus plots according to type and yield

	Shamouti	Valencia	Clementinas	Total
Age (years)	35	12	15/25	
Retarded Production				
Total dunams	72	15	75	**168**
Yield/dunam (tons)	2·5	1	2·5	
Low Yields				
Total dunams	170	50	130	**391**
Yield (tons)	2·5/3·5	1/2·5	2·5/3	
Average to good Yields				
Total dunams	126	20	205	**350**
Yield (tons)	3·5	2·5	3	
Total dunams	**368**	**85**	**410**	**919**

Table 23 shows 168 dunams of citrus which have a yield of 2½ tons per dunam with production of 3 tons per dunam, and of these 226 dunams are Shamouti and Valencia. These are very low yields and when one considers that there are expenses of IL.350–IL.400 per dunam, then there are 168 dunams which have a loss on production and 390 dunams which only cover costs. This means that almost 60 per cent of the fruit-bearing trees in Kfar Hefer are not profitable. In the future this will not be such a large percentage because over 700 dunams are planted with trees which have either only just begun to bear fruit or are shortly expected to do so. Notwithstanding this the immediate return on citrus gives cause for concern. In the area planted in 1955 yields, despite slow development, were at the expected level. In this area an experiment in irrigation was conducted by the extension service and they found a striking improvement in the areas where less water was used than was normally given. Other trees which were watered normally suffered from an excess of water. Here the farmers can easily take measures to improve their yield, but for others the difficulties are more serious. The oldest trees will probably continue to give fruit for another seven to ten years in good areas. It was suggested that inter-planting of new trees should be tried in the area to anticipate the loss of yields from old trees in the future. However, for others even this is not a practical possibility since the land on which the trees are planted is not suitable for citrus. These areas date from the time of the earliest plantation in the village, when members were not so well informed about citrus growing. In these areas the only answer is to uproot the trees and transfer to another crop. Government aid is available for farmers who replant citrus crops but many of those affected were elderly and did not want to go to this expense.

In a meeting of the village Executive and the committee for citrus in the village, at which the Ministry official gave his report, these factors were discussed. The official suggested the installation of thermometers in areas susceptible to frost and the purchase of a ventilator which causes air turbulence and disperses the cold air around the trees. He added that both these installations could be seen in Kfar Hefer's neighbour, a moshav shitufi that works all its lands as one unit.[1] Arad, a citrus committee member, objected that this ventilator would cost IL.20,000 and said: 'It is not for us.' Slowly and politely he told the official: 'Excuse me, but you don't know what a moshav is like. You can't compel farmers to do anything; if a member is satisfied with a yield of 2½ tons per dunam then he will continue with this.' Appealing to Dov, he queried: 'Imagine, telling our members that we are going to spend IL.20,000 on a ventilator,' and in explanation he addressed the official: 'It is not easy to plan joint ventures in Kfar Hefer, especially where they involve the spending of money.'

This problem of the conflict between individualism and the common good affected another aspect of citrus growing in the village, the marketing of produce. Here again the village is dependent upon the national situation: only high grades of fruit are taken for export and in years of surplus the government raises this standard so that some fruit is down-graded and lower prices are given. In 1966/67 the clementina crop of the village received good prices and on the whole the fruit was of good quality but the village had to send more fruit than expected to industry for processing. This fruit in normal conditions would have gone into the market but there were surpluses and also the fruit was damaged by high winds and heavy rains. There are sharp differences in the prices paid for the different grades of fruit. The best grade 'A-A' received IL.508 per ton in 1966 and the second grade 'A' received IL.412 per ton, while 'B' and 'C' received IL.333 per ton and IL.190 per ton respectively. In this year much fruit which normally would have sold for at the least IL.333 per ton drew only IL.190 per ton. Also in this year the fruit was in competition in the home market with fruit from the west bank of the Jordan and also with big crops of locally grown apples.

Marketing is arranged with the local packing house, situated near Kfar Hefer. This serves the settlements of the area and each receives a certain quota per day that it is allowed to market. Within the village picking is arranged by rota which is arranged according to the

[1] Labes (1962)

previous year's production. In 1966/67 there were 104 members on the ordinary rota of one picking per week, an extra 30 received an additional 50 per cent, and the remainder received a double rota, i.e. two pickings per week. At the beginning of the season there is a free period in which no restrictions are placed upon marketing. This is before the main citrus season and the fruit marketed at this time receives a good price because it enters the overseas markets early. However, it is difficult for farmers to take advantage of this, because save for those whose groves are anyway worked by hired labour, most farmers pick their own fruit. This is a family affair with the women and children of the family all taking part. Nevertheless other duties, especially fodder growing, are pressing at this period and the farmer finds it difficult to give time to fruit picking. In fact on the rota system members who have a lot of fruit cannot manage to market it all and they often have a rush to market their crop at the end of the season, and have to neglect other duties.

In 1966/67 severe difficulties arose in the marketing of clementinas. The village's marketing season began late because of heavy rains; and when the packing house announced the last date for the reception of fruit, much of Kfar Hefer's fruit was still on the trees. The village secretary, Dov, worked out a plan to deal with this situation which he presented to the village citrus committee for their consideration. He suggested that the village should concentrate on sending all their 'extra' grades, 'A-A' and 'A' to market in order to get the highest prices. The rest of the fruit, the 'B' and the 'C', should go to industry, though in normal years only 'C' is sent for industrial processing. The spokesman for the citrus committee was Arad and at a subsequent meeting he said after a lot of argument they had worked out a plan of action. They agreed that the 'extra' and the 'A' grades should be sent to market, and that then the remainder of the village's fruit should be treated as one unit but that the 'B' grade should receive a price above that normally paid by industry. They suggested a sum of IL.200 per ton, the extra amount to come from the accounts of the 'extra' and 'A' grades. Immediate objections were raised by Oren, a first generation member of the village Executive, who said that it was an unfair system. Arad interrupted Oren to say that he (Oren) did not understand the argument: grade 'B' should receive some compensation because normally it would have gone to market, and if they treated the village as one unit they could do this. On this last remark the village Executive laughingly accused Arad of showing his personal prejudices about Kfar Hefer; he would prefer it to be one unit. Ironically, they used almost the same words as Arad himself when he had explained to a Ministry of Agriculture

official that Kfar Hefer could not be seen as one holding (see above).
Oren explained his objection, saying it was not fair that those who
had little production should subsidise those who had more. As an
illustration he cited a hypothetical example of a man who had a
small production, but all 'extra' and 'A', while another big producer
had just as much 'extra' and 'A' but also a lot of 'B'. Was it equitable,
he asked, that the first producer should compensate the second? Arad
reiterated that Oren did not understand the heart of the matter:
grade 'B' must receive some compensation.

Here these two members are arguing the perpetual problem of
Kfar Hefer, the equating of individual rights with policies assuring
an equal distribution of benefits within the village as a co-operative,
a policy which conflicts with the fact that support of the best productive farms benefits the whole co-operative.

At this point, Ben, the village treasurer and external secretary,
asked how they had arrived at a figure of IL.200 per ton for grade
'B'. Ben is a professional member of the village, an ex-kibbuts
member who came to the post about seven years ago; normally he
does not take a part in policy discussions of the village Executive but
he does attend the meetings as an adviser. Arad answered that this
was felt to be a fair figure, even though it was below the market
price. Ben argued that if they were going to be compensated, this
should be at the market price. Dov announced that he did not agree
with any of these suggestions. He believed that everyone should pick
according to his rota and all grades should be sent to market and
later they could work out the prices. In support of his idea he pointed
out that Ilan, the professional member responsible for marketing,
often filled up the village quota with grade 'B' when there was not
enough 'extra' and 'A'. Everyone agreed with this remark but said
that it had no bearing on the problem under discussion. Ben,
apologising in advance for his directness, told Dov that he was
talking nonsense, it was far too complicated a system, members
would never receive accounts if his idea was adopted. Arad then said
that at last he had grasped what they were arguing about and went
on to say that as long as they were willing to pay some compensation, he would agree to any decision. Dov reasserted that he
still thought his idea was better than any of those put forward
and complained that they were not making an effort to understand
him.

The role and position of the village secretary is discussed in
another chapter together with a discussion of decision making. Here
I only comment that the pattern of this discussion was typical of the
meetings I attended in Kfar Hefer. Those at odds with each other

tended to restate and re-emphasise their own position, and no attempt was made to come to an accommodation between the disputants. In practice this meant that meetings dealing with important issues for the village tended to be very noisy affairs and served more as platforms for the statements of opinions than meeting grounds for the exchange of reasoned argument. Moreover, when decisions were reached, usually on a compromise proposed by someone other than the main contenders, the defeated parties often continued the fight outside the meeting in an attempt to get the decision changed.

In the present case, after the members present established that this was a decision they had to reach, the responsibility of informing members by a public notice devolved upon Ben, who strongly objected saying this was a 'political' and not an 'economic' decision. But he was overruled. Earlier I have referred to the use of 'marginal' men in village disputes: here again by a technical device the members at the meeting moved the problem from the sphere of internal village policy into the realm of economics. It should be stated that village notices are normally signed by the village secretary, Dov, or by the heads of committees concerned.

Even though the majority of the meeting had agreed upon the principle of compensation, the amount was still to be decided upon. Oren suggested that anything over five crates of 'B' should be compensated. In reply Dov said his own suggestion was the best because it mentioned no figure and afterwards on receipt of final returns they could decide upon a figure. Yoel, another member of the village Executive, said that the figure could be five or it could be eight: (sounding like Lord Melbourne) he said the number was unimportant as long as they all agreed. It was decided that five was a 'reasonable' number and the notice was drafted accordingly.

After the notice was displayed there was a series of letters in the village bulletin complaining about the system, and at the next General Meeting of the village the issue was heatedly discussed. The chief opponent was Cohen, a man who identified himself and was identified by others with the 'small' farmer of Kfar Hefer because of his lack of a dairy and the absence of a second generation continuation in his farm. At the meeting the majority was large producers who would be affected by the scheme. They objected to their 'B' grade being downgraded but accepted that the pressing situation demanded special measures, and they were concerned to raise the figure for which compensation would be paid. Dov put forward and argued in support of the scheme proposed by the village Executive; and it was accepted. But even after the decision was approved Cohen continued to write in the village bulletin that members had been 'robbed' by the Executive, and this was another triumph for might over right.

This chapter has dealt with the economic situation in Kfar Hefer in the years 1966–68. In the discussion I have been concerned to show the different farming patterns of various farmers, largely due to demographic differences within the family farms. Also I have shown how economic differences have developed from differences in farming, and the effects of these processes on village policies. I have shown how these differences are not simply related to the economic performance of the individual farmer; and in doing so I referred to the effect of both national and local village policies upon these trends. Within the village there has steadily emerged a category of farmers who because of the special characteristics of their farms (aged occupants and no second generation continuation) no longer play a full part in village production. A second category, comprising the majority of the village's farmers, are those who have the capacity to increase their production, but are limited by restrictions on village production. Finally there is a small number of farmers in Kfar Hefer, who because of historical reasons, and/or happy accidents, and/or hard work, are very big producers and are very successful financially. Reference has been made to the difficulties of the village administration, especially its elected members, in satisfying the demands of individual farmers particularly as an individual's interest often changes over time and from branch to branch. The next chapter deals with the developments in Kfar Hefer as they attempted to cope with the situation set out above.

V
Collaboration in farming

As early as 1955 a member of Kfar Hefer discussed the question of whether there should be mixed farming or specialised farming in the village.[1] He was a second generation farmer, and he stated that it was apparent that the development of agriculture would depend greatly upon economists and agricultural planners; therefore he asked whether in view of this the village should begin to specialise in one branch of agriculture. He wrote that socialist principles supported the idea of mixed farming and he would not wish, nor would he dare, to stand against these principles. When one spoke of socialism in agriculture, one meant co-operation; the importance of the principle that the moshav supply its own produce, with the remainder being marketed; the emphasis on small units of production; the decision by individuals, within the boundaries of competition that existed in the moshav, on his own production. However, those days had gone. Hence, he suggested that Kfar Heferites should re-appraise their situation and ask if the time had not come when they should specialise and concentrate their production. He added that he knew the standard complaint about one branch farming: what happened if there was a crop failure? Yet in the United States, which was far from being a socialist country, the government had agreed to buy 95 per cent of the produce at a good price and to lend money on credit in event of crop failure. If the Israeli government did not agree to be the guarantor then the various producers could form their own co-operative to carry the final responsibility. He urged members to consider this argument, especially in the light of the three problems which always faced the planner of a farm. These problems were: what to produce?, with the subsidiary question whether it is for the home market or for export?; how to produce?; and to whom the production is directed? He suggested that whatever were the answers to questions one and three, the answer to question two was always that the most efficient method of production was for the farm to concentrate on one product. The choice of product depended upon the availability of land, water and labour force, and upon market possibilities.

In the last chapter I described the effects on Kfar Heferites of government, market and local pressure to alter the pattern of agriculture in the moshav. Attempts to increase efficiency, to hasten

[1] *Tlamim* (1955)

specialisation, and to encourage the growing of new crops by the government have had limited success. From the last chapter it is seen that several factors mitigate against the adoption of these proposed solutions for economic difficulties. The moshav structure with its basic insistence on equality and co-operation restricts the possibility for a farmer to practise extensive farming and to benefit from economies of scale. Moreover, farmers are reluctant to concentrate on one branch of agriculture exclusively because of fears of sudden changes in government policy, which can quickly turn a profitable branch into a liability: the example of the dairy branch illustrated in the last chapter is a case in point. Similarly, fluctuations and changes in world markets add to the risks of specialised farming for export. Furthermore, as is apparent from the last chapter, farmers who perhaps would be willing to change production to the currently profitable export crops are unable to realise their existing investments in traditional farming. This is especially true of the efficient farmers, who have invested heavily, and now find it difficult to respond to changing conditions. There thus exists, as was illustrated in Chapter IV, a situation where members hold on to their existing production and attempt to improve their situation within this context. The result is a struggle for the limited resources of the moshav and the expressed complaints that the success of some members is achieved at the expense of others. It is true that some specialisation in agriculture did come about in Kfar Hefer but this was a result of processes wholly different from those advocated by the above writer and by the government. This specialisation resulted from demographic reasons and indeed exacerbated the struggle for resources in the moshav because of the differences in regard to income produced by the various agricultural branches. Out of the dissatisfaction with the existing system in Kfar Hefer and the failure of the government to provide alternative solutions, there developed within the village two distinct attempts by different groups of Kfar Heferites to repair their expressed economic ills.

Before discussing these two movements I should point out that in 1962 a 'co-operative' venture, outside the main three branches, had been set up in the village. This was the growing of pecan nuts in an area of land which had not been fully exploited by the village. In all 92 members of the village participated in this venture. The area cultivated formed a block of land but each farmer cared for his own individual plot: plots varied in size from 2½ dunams to 3 dunams. One member of the village was responsible for administering all the affairs of the venture, and, helped by the Ministry of Agriculture's extension service, advised members on the care of fields and crops.

During the time I was in the village the trees were giving only small yields, but the enterprise was regarded as a successful one, and had, I believe, an influence on two movements to be described below.

The first case to be discussed derived from the discontent felt by farmers who had given up dairy farming and transferred their lands to the village co-operative. I have, earlier, described this system, and the publication in the village bulletin of letters of complaint from these members. It will be remembered that the number of members in this category increased rapidly in the year 1968 and this greatly augmented the land available to others who were still actively farming. The secretary of the *va'adat ha'mesheq*, the committee for dealing with village land, wrote in the village bulletin of July 1967 that he had almost completed the list of members receiving additional plots of land and this would be posted in the near future. The secretary, Ron, is a young man, married, and is responsible for his family farm. His eldest sister lives in the village and is married to a son of Kfar Hefer who farms his own farm. The position of secretary of this committee is an elected one, and he serves with a committee of elected members, but his position is paid— a small amount monthly. Ron had in the past served on other committees in the village before being elected secretary of the *va' adat ha'mesheq*, and at this time he was in his second year of this office. In addition to the above notification Ron also wrote that it had been brought to his notice that some of those transferring land to the village were apprehensive about losing their rights in the land. He wrote that he wanted to emphasise that there was no intention on the part of the village institutions to deprive members of rights in land. Moreover he personally assured members that in the future there would not be such an intention. He stressed that a member giving land to the village could, whenever he wished, have the land returned to him for his own cultivation—a statement not without significance in the light of the following account.

Individual grumbles about this system were common in the village but at the Annual General Meeting of the village held in October 1967 there was for the first time an indication that the grumblers were joining forces. In a discussion about production quotas several of those without dairies clashed with the *va'adat ha'mesheq* in particular with Ron. One of these was Ben-David whom I have already described as an experienced battler in support of what he believed to be individual rights. Two of the others were Ben-Natan and Levine, who were to become the leaders of a coalition of 'non-farmers' in the village. The term 'non-farmers' will be explained fully below: here I use it as a shorthand term to describe those who

I

were engaged in some agricultural production but who had transferred most or even all of their land to the village co-operative for
the benefit of others.

The first to speak was Ben-Natan. He accused the *va'adat
ha'mesheq* of acting as informers, judge and jury in the village. He
criticised the system whereby they imposed 'fines' on village members
who did not farm their land. This was a reference to the sum of
IL.15 per dunam charged to all members who held land but did not
cultivate it. It is significant that this charge was seen as a penal
measure despite the village co-operative's justification for this
practice as a charge for the depreciation of installations and the first
payment for water which binds all members. Ben-Natan went on to
say that in no other village in Israel was there the situation where a
member who wished to work his land was not allowed to do so
because he did not have a dairy. Moreover in no other place was a
member deprived of his rights to enjoy the benefits of quotas
allocated to him. Here Ben-Natan touched upon the system of
internal allocations in the village whereby unused or unfilled quotas
were distributed among other producers.

In reply Ron reiterated that a member still retained his rights in
the land and it was for the member concerned to work out if it was
worthwhile to retain his land in view of the cost of upkeep and the
depreciation of equipment. Levine continued the discussion by
asking for a definition of 'working' the land. If a member ploughs his
land was this sufficient to be called working? He said that it was
incumbent upon the village to look after members who had given up
their dairies. Their land should be formed into a block and cultivated for them so that they could have some income from their
rights. Ben-David added that quotas were linked to the land and
water quota of the village, and members who had relinquished their
use of these resources should be compensated by comparable
additions in another branch of production. He argued that although
he appreciated that there were costs involved in water and land,
surely these were covered by the beneficiary of his land and of his
water?

These complaints covered wide aspects of village policy. On the
one hand, reference was made to the income of 'non-farmers': they
suffered a drop in income when they gave up their dairy. On the
other his criticism was directed against the system of dealing with
'rights' held by these members: they argued that they should be
compensated if others benefited from transfers of their land. No
reference was made to the payment of IL.5 per dunam received for
land transferred. Rather the complaint was more generally stated

with the implication that there should be some adjustments made between quotas for branches of agricultural production, as well as the existing adjustments which were made for quotas within the quotas for each branch. This type of adjustment has been referred to above in the discussion of poultry raising in the village, and undoubtedly poultry would be the branch most affected under such a scheme. Finally Levine had appealed to the moshav principle of mutual aid and mutual responsibility; like the big milk producers (see chapter IV) he argued that the village co-operative had a responsibility to ensure the welfare of all its members.

Both Ben-Natan and Levine had recently given up their dairies. Ben-Natan at this time was a man in his early sixties: he was recognised in the village as a hard-working farmer who, despite the handicap of having four daughters, had worked his land alone without hired help. He was one of the outspoken supporters of the moshav as a way of life and in the early days he was one of the first to refuse a loan from *Paza* when they had refused to give equal loans to all village members. He represented the village on several moshav organisations, and was also a delegate to *Tnuva*, where he sat as a member of the council. In the village, though he was a frequent candidate, he was seldom elected to office and at this time sat only in the 'constitutional' committee which only infrequently met. In the village he was regarded as somewhat unconventional because of his interest in, and devotion to, the study of history and philosophy. He was inclined to preface his remarks about village affairs with references to early Greece and Rome, references which most members at best found inapt and at worst irrelevant. Three of his daughters were married and living outside the village: the youngest had just left the army and was now a university student. It was considered unlikely that she would return to the village so Ben-Natan faced the situation where he had no continuation on the farm and no young labour to help him in production. In fact Ben-Natan delayed his decision to hand over his land for several months after selling his dairy herd and afterwards he spoke of this time of decision as a great 'personal crisis'. In all he transferred 13 dunams of land and for this he received an annual sum of IL.65. His main income now came from citrus groves and poultry. He had ten dunams of citrus and three dunams of pecan but for the moment he had little income from pecan. His citrus trees were on the whole old and declining in production, though he had three dunams which had been re-planted and now were coming into production. The main emphasis of his poultry was on turkeys which had given him a steady income. However, he had been handicapped by a shortage of labour on the farm, and also a lack of mechanisation. He cultivated his fields with hired equipment from the communal machinery store in the village which added to his expenses, and he was one of the few farmers still to own and use a horse and cart. In part this was an outcome of his ideological beliefs in the value of labour but also a reflection on the financial state of his farm: he had to provide for six people from his own labour. Similarly, his refusal to hire labour reflected these two facts; but he always stressed he had no ideological objection to the hiring of labour in case of need, he simply believed he should work his land for as long as possible.

After Levine gave up dairy production he was left with an income from agriculture only in the citrus branch; because of his wife's ill health he had no poultry holding. All his three children were married and lived outside the village; one son had made an attempt to stay in the village, working as an adviser especially for poultry, but he left soon afterwards. For a time Levine grew vegetables with the help of hired labour, but this proved exacting and expensive work and after he transferred his lands to the village he continued to grow vegetables only on the land around his house. In this he was helped by a young neighbour but only on a casual basis; and this young man told me that he received no payment for the work but was paid in kind by gifts of produce. Levine had only five dunams of citrus and a half dunam was not productive because of frost damage. In the past he had exchanged part of his citrus grove for land growing field crops but now he received only a small income from the sale of citrus. His income was supplemented by a pension and he had money in a village savings scheme which was a possible source of capital for him. I note that all members in the village had money in the savings scheme which was started in the 1950's, but the amounts are related to size of production. Every member is credited annually with two per cent of gross income. In the case of two-generation family farms, the amount is split after the son reaches the age of 35 years, with the father and son (or daughter) each receiving one half, i.e. 1 per cent of gross income. This fund is discussed in the chapter on co-operation in the village, but here it is important to note that the fund did provide a standby for those troubled farmers in case of need.

Ben-Natan followed up the criticisms expressed in the meeting by writing an article published in the village bulletin. The tone of this article was set in the opening sentence, which asked rhetorically if the younger generation of Kfar Hefer knew how to deal with the problems of a moshav and how to maintain its basic principles. He continued by stating that the second generation in a settlement must know how to maintain a good atmosphere in the village, to develop new branches, and to look after the village's economy and social life. At the Annual General Meeting one heard reports from committees but no-one touched upon the most important question: the future of the moshav. Land had already been taken away from some and given to others; soon there would be two levels in Kfar Hefer; already at this time a third of village members had given up land and some of them were alone and in difficulties. He asked why no arrangements were made for land to be worked on behalf of these members: did no-one care about their income? In many other settlements this was done; in Nahalal and other moshavim the village worked the land for such members and they received an income which gave satisfaction both to the member and his family. These villages did not take land from a farmer; in fact just the opposite was true, they gave all possible help to encourage the farmer to work his lands. In Kfar Hefer land which had been cultivated, watered and improved was taken away by force and under pressure. The article ended on a note of pathos and of hope. Ben-Natan wrote that the moshav was started by honourable men of conscience and they, the first generation of Kfar Hefer, had tried to emulate this high ideal. This had not been achieved without setbacks and disappointments but nevertheless they had ensured mutual aid and guarantees for Kfar Hefer's members. There were not many settlements like Kfar Hefer, and they had known how to look after the weak and those who were alone; now this responsibility lay in the hands of the second generation.

This was not an article which appealed to the second generation and in the next village bulletin there was a sharp reply by a young farmer. In this letter, which was unsigned, the writer asked why Ben-Natan should lecture the young of Kfar Hefer as if they were members of a primitive African tribe. He pointed out that the second generation of Kfar Hefer had done a lot for the village, and in three wars the first generation had relied upon the maligned second generation to defend them. He added that the 'old' of Kfar Hefer were habitually criticising the young for things which they, in their time, had not done; it was well known that not all the first generation were real moshavniks [members of a moshav].

Ben-Natan's article and the letter in reply contain the essence of the two extreme arguments in Kfar Hefer. The expressed view of those without land, of whom the great majority were also elderly and living alone on the farm, was an appeal to the ideals of moshav life, which they believed stressed the importance of care for all members, non-exploitation, and a minimum of differentiation. They looked upon the moshav as both a social and economic unit, the first of no less importance than the second. The view of young farmers, to whom the moshav is an accepted form of life, stressed the individual aspects of moshav life and while they were sympathetic to the position of those elder farmers they argued that economic necessity was responsible for changes in the way of life in the moshav. And like the young farmer cited above they pointed out that their parents had made compromises and changes in the moshav to suit their conditions. Moreover, they added, the situation of these farmers was a direct result of the lack of continuation in the family farm, which was a personal family problem and not that of the moshav. They, the younger farmers, contended that the village as a whole benefited from their own farming and gave as an example the minimum standard of living guaranteed to each family irrespective of their contribution to the village economy. Without the additional quota the younger generation would not be able to improve their efficiency and the village as a whole would suffer.

I examine now the background to these conflicting views of the generations.

In the year 1963/64, 87 farmers in Kfar Hefer received a supplement of land, and in the year 1966/67 the number had increased to 95 members.

The formal procedure for transferring lands to the village co-operative was that the farmer concerned notified the village secretary who, with the head of the land committee, acted as witnesses to his statement of transfer. Usually a letter was given to the farmer setting out the conditions of transfer. There was no standard form for these letters but it appears that each contained the four main provisions:

(1) the farmer gave the land to the village co-operative for the benefit of the village;

(2) the farmer gave his land for one year only, and if at the end of the year he wished to continue the arrangement another statement had to be drawn up;

(3) the farmer retained the rights in his land and could on reasonable notice claim it back at any time;

(4) the receiver of the land paid the donor IL.5 per dunam.

The donor could not choose the member who was to receive their land; this was a matter for the village committee. In one incident in the past a man giving up his land transferred it directly to his son-in-law, but the land was taken back by the village for redistribution. The village held that family attachments were irrelevant in agricultural production, and if special arrangements were made to suit families that this would be the first step to private financial arrangements with the consequent weakening of the village co-operative. At the end of 1967 there were rumours in the village that those without land were planning a move to improve their conditions. Ben-David, Levine and Ben-Natan all met from time to time informally and other non-farmers were approached. The general opinion was that they would ask for a rise in price per dunam paid by the person receiving the land. In the early days when members transferred land no payment had been made; only after objections and complaints had the sum of IL.5 per dunam been agreed upon. It was now felt that the members would again put pressure on the village Executive and the land committee to increase this sum. In anticipation of this one young farmer told one of those transferring land that, 'We can't afford to pay any more, it is not worth our while.' To which the donor of land replied, 'In that case don't take it, no-one asks you to'.

In January 1968, village members were surprised to hear that the 'non-farmers' intended to reclaim their lands and planned to start their own cultivation. Ben-Natan had sent a circular letter to all those who had transferred land to the village asking them if they were interested in joint cultivation. Those who were interested were invited to a meeting to be held shortly to discuss possible schemes. The initial reaction was surprise and amusement, and in the period after the announcement I was often told it would not come to anything. Joking references were made about Kfar Hefer's 'new, rejuvenated farmers'; and one young man was reported as saying: 'it won't work out, just look at them, there is not one under 60 years.' Some others wished the 'new farmers' success in their venture but added, 'if it comes to that.' Similar doubts, but in a less flippant fashion, were expressed by an elderly farmer still farming his lands. He explained that if they went ahead with the scheme they would be compelled to use hired labour which is very expensive, and the cost would be insuperable especially as most of those concerned already employed labour to work their citrus groves.

In a meeting of the village Executive, before the main business of the evening, the village secretary was asked what he thought about the development. He was more guarded in his comments than those reported above and merely replied that it was still early days and— 'We'll see what happens.' The editor of the village bulletin commented upon this development in the following edition of the paper. He said that one of the main reasons for this action was that the farmers concerned wished to find an additional income to supplement their small returns from farming. One of the difficulties of this scheme was that it planned to recover land from the owners of large dairy herds who were in need of it. Already the production from the big dairy men's fields was not enough to provide for large herds, and when the land was returned to its original holders this would even further reduce the area. He traced the consequences of this action; there would be a reduction in the quantity of milk and consequently in income. He believed the solution lay in the exploitation of new forms of production, not necessarily agricultural. When he canvassed members' opinions on this he reported that they told him they favoured joint enterprises. Among the suggestions he received were: to raise geese; to slaughter and prepare turkeys for market; to develop hothouse growing.

This last named project has very recently become popular in the country; the production was for export mainly for the winter market of Europe. A variety of crops are grown but the most profitable have been the growing of roses and strawberries. These enterprises need very heavy capital investments, up to IL.50,000; and the opinion in the village was that no individual would undertake it but that it was a possibility on a joint basis.

This editorial showed some of the thinking current in Kfar Hefer about possible solutions to their economic problems. But generally the farmers of Kfar Hefer concerned themselves with finding solutions within the already accepted means of production. Unlike many other settlements in the region, where individual farmers were developing hothouse growing and making a lot of money, Kfar Hefer, despite her historical position as the oldest settlement of the region and her reputation as a big producer, was taking no part in these enterprises. At the beginning of this chapter I analysed some of the reasons for this failure to respond to new agricultural crops. In addition to these reasons there is the further explanation that Kfar Hefer over time has been a large and strong producer, and that until recently this precluded her from breaking fresh ground into new agricultural branches. Only in recent years has the country suffered from excess of production in 'traditional' agriculture, and until this time Kfar Hefer, because of her large quotas, prospered. Other, newer settlements have not enjoyed these advantages, and so have been concerned to exploit new possibilities outside the traditional field of agriculture. The individual farmer in Kfar Hefer has been 'protected' against the full effect of national policies because he has been able to increase the scale of his farming as a result of the internal system of allocating production. Furthermore, the co-operative aspect of Kfar Hefer has been well organised; and I suggest (a suggestion which is developed more fully later) that this has made the individual farmer reluctant to take up production outside the sphere of the co-operative. In other settlements individual farmers have taken loans from the Ministry of Agriculture, but I believe the strength of Kfar Hefer's co-operative system which provides loans at a low rate of interest, and also acts as a guarantor on production, has inhibited similar processes in the village. If such developments do take place they probably will be a co-operative effort and I believe that this will not happen in Kfar Hefer until there are sufficient numbers of members who all feel a common bond which overrules, in this instance, all the differences between them. According to the evidence I have, it seems that in Kfar Hefer the time is now propitious for this to happen. Further, I believe it is not chance that the two developments in farming described below took place when they did. A set of factors (age of moshav, government policy, village policy, demographic and economic reasons) combined to produce numbers of farmers who felt a common bond sufficiently strongly to form coalitions within the village to press for their demands. I consider that neither of these two developments could have taken place earlier simply because there were not enough members sharing common interests to carry through the measures, which in the past may have been opposed.

Ben-Natan's first meeting took place on 1 January 1968. All those who did not farm their lands received an invitation to meet in one of the village halls. Not all of them turned up—later I was told by some of them that they were sceptical of the scheme and wanted to hear opinions from other members who did attend. In fact all they knew in advance about the scheme was what they learnt from the circular they received from Ben-Natan. Further discussion had taken place, but chiefly between Ben-Natan and Levine who had gone ahead with arrangements. In all, about 25 members came to the meeting, including Ron who had not been invited but who had heard about it from Dov, who had been informed about the meeting. Ron expressed his interest in attending the meeting and Ben-Natan invited him to stay. The meeting fell into two parts: the first, a talk by an official of the Ministry of Agriculture on the prospects of growing tomatoes for industry; the second, a discussion by the members present of the plan of campaign.

The Ministry official spoke at length about the possibilities of tomatoes as an industrial crop and stressed that there was a demand and a market for them. As an enterprise this had only been operating for three years in Israel, and therefore any information he gave should be interpreted in the light of this relatively short period of experience. He described the two varieties now being grown, and said that the type suited to the European market, and in his opinion to Kfar Hefer, could only be picked by hand and not cut mechanically. The available information suggested that growers could expect to make IL.140 per dunam on a season's work. These figures were immediately disputed by Ron, who pointed out that according to the figures given the actual profit was much lower, only about IL.55–IL.65 depending upon the yield per dunam. Furthermore, Ron added, the official was speaking about optimum conditions, and it could be reasonably expected that the actual returns would be smaller. Most of those present seemed nonplussed at this dispute, because they had not worked out the figures for themselves; and for a time the meeting became confused. Also, I suggest, those present were surprised at the form the meeting was taking: they had not expected to be confronted with information about crops before they had decided if they were going to take part in the scheme. Even though their presence evinced an interest in the idea of joint cultivation, they had not come to any firm decision, and Ben-Natan's action in inviting an official to speak to them anticipated a commitment they did not yet feel ready to make.

Ben-Natan cut short the interchange between Ron and the instructor by reminding Ron that the official was an expert in these matters and that he himself (Ben-Natan) had heard from the chief instructor of the Regional Office of the Ministry of Agriculture that there was a future in growing tomatoes for industry. The official then concluded by saying that in growing crops of this nature it was essential that there should be a strong organisation and that the land should be centralised into a single block. Ben-Natan assured him that all these arrangements were made, a statement which again took the members by surprise.

The end of the official's talk closed the 'public' nature of the meeting, and Ben-Natan turned to discuss the group's policy. The official left; but Ron remained until Ben-Natan reminded him that he had not been invited and these discussions were private. Ron's presence at the meeting indicated that he was holding a watching brief for the members who were possibly to lose land as a result of this movement. His challenging of the figures given by the official was an indication of their future strategy: to persuade the 'non-farmers' that it was not financially worthwhile to renew their farming activities.

Ben-Natan announced that he had arranged a meeting with the village secretary and the land committee to examine the possibility of getting a centralised block of land. But he felt that before he could go to the secretary he should be given authority to speak for the group. Therefore he suggested that they should elect a committee and he had drawn up a list of names which he considered suitable. He suggested that the committee be composed of four men: Ben-Natan, Levine, Amiram and Haim. The last two named were both young men in their thirties. Amiram bought his own farm in the village but has difficulties in running it. He has only a small dairy so his need for fodder is not very big, but the expenses of building up a farm have left him with a considerable debt to the village and so far this has only increased, not decreased. Haim is an agricultural member of the village and like Amiram he bought his own farm in the village. But for the greater part of his time in this farm he has not been engaged in full-time farming. Initially he worked as a driver for the village, and recently he has been appointed as the full-time head of the village store, supplying farmers with grain and feeding stuffs. This is a very responsible and demanding job and Haim can devote no time to working his fields. Haim had transferred all his lands to the village co-operative, but Amiram had not, and neither was present at this meeting. Ben-Natan's suggestion was greeted with silence: finally Levine remonstrated that it was for the meeting to decide who should represent it and he suggested that the members present should first of all have a chance to think things over before they decided about representation. This was agreed on and no vote was taken.

The direction of the meeting was then changed by Ish-Shalom who said that the enterprise, if it did develop, should be run by a manager and hired workers. He was not capable of working in the fields and he was sure the others present were also incapable of doing so. The question for him was to know if the enterprise could be economically profitable. Following on from this Michaeli (see page xxix) said his concern was to get an adequate income from his farm but the fault was neither his nor that of any of the others that they could not make an adequate income. The fault lay with Kfar Hefer and its system of so-called 'equality'. He felt that they were going about the problem in the wrong way: what they should do was to petition the village secretary and committees for real equality in Kfar Hefer. By this he meant that those farmers who had no dairy should be compensated by extra allocations of poultry.

In closing the meeting Ben-Natan said that he had much sympathy with Michaeli. One of the reasons he wanted the members to take back their lands was to teach the community a lesson. They were being exploited by the community and it should feel the penalty for behaving in such a manner. In answer to Ish-Shalom, Ben-Natan added that he agreed that the land should be worked by hired labour, both because of the difficulties of the members in performing physical work and because it was the most efficient way of planning the enterprise. Moreover, according to Karl Marx, it was permitted to take hired labour in case of need. Ish-Shalom interrupted him to say that he did not care what Marx had to say on the matter; all he wanted was that his lands should provide him with an income. On this remark the meeting ended; and Ben-Natan promised to keep members informed.

Throughout the meeting it was clear that the initiative lay with Ben-Natan. Even though Levine had been consulted, he was the lieutenant, the second-in-command. Ben-Natan had taken it upon himself to assume the leading role in the movement and he independently had done all the research and investigation for the meeting. When throughout the succeeding time that I remained in the village I enquired about the progress of the group, I was told: 'Oh, you'll have to ask Ben-Natan, we are all waiting for him.' In this way the other members of the group acquiesced; they were anxious to improve their situation and willing that Ben-Natan should do the preparatory work. He was more closely connected with agriculture than many of them because he had only recently given up his dairy. Also his known support for moshav principles, shown recently in the village bulletin, and his connections with moshav organisations, all fitted him for this position. But although those present were willing for him to act on their behalf in this sphere, they were not willing to give him *carte blanche* to plan their affairs. Their failure to ratify his plans for a committee signified that there were limits set to his taking of decisions. This objection pointed to another characteristic of the members present. They were not yet certain if they wished to be 'involved' in such a scheme. Ben-Natan's assumption that they already formed a 'group' was premature. They only formed a 'group' in a very minimal sense—that they had all shown enough interest in their common problem to attend the meeting. There were divisions amongst those present in their analyses of their situation and of possible solutions. Michaeli's remark showed that he was not really interested in farming: he was interested to form a group to put pressure on the village secretary in order to modify the quota system in the village. Ish-Shalom wanted to obtain sufficient livelihood from his land and he was not concerned how this was achieved. Others were still apprehensive about the viability of Ben-Natan's scheme, and Ben-Natan showed that in addition to all his other reasons he was interested in 'teaching the community a lesson'.

Ben-Natan's choice of committee was interesting, especially in the proposition that Amiram and Haim should serve. With the exception of Ron, all those present at the meeting were old men. Yet Ben-Natan suggested as their representatives two young men who did not even attend the meeting. Furthermore the circumstances of these young men were completely different from those of the members present. Haim had a full-time job in the employment of the village which was well paid; he had voluntarily given up the chance of farming because he preferred to work for the village. Amiram still farmed his fields, albeit not with great success. I consider that in proposing these two men Ben-Natan was widening the group and also altering its purpose as it had been understood: his suggestions transformed it from a movement of elderly men no longer in farming in the full sense but who were interested in re-asserting their rights *vis-à-vis* the village co-operative, into a straightforward co-operative farming enterprise. I believe the failure to ratify Ben-Natan's choice of committee was not only because of the members' right to choose their own representatives but also an objection to the 'dilution' of the group's purpose. But I can only guess at Ben-Natan's reason for proposing these two men. I think he may simply have been interested in increasing the numbers involved in the enterprise, though he may also have wished to diversify the basis of the group. In presenting the case of the non-farmers to the village secretary and Executive committee he may have wished to point to the association of two young men in order to counter the opinion already prevalent in the village, that this was simply a grievance committee of old men who could no longer farm and who were resentful of the success of others.

The next meeting was not called until the end of February 1968. In the meantime Ben-Natan met with the village secretary and with the land committee. Individual members also approached the secretary and Ron and made enquiries about their land and the possibility of having it returned to them. In some cases members did not know who was farming their lands, and in others because of re-arrangement of land (to be described later) they did not even know where their fields were: they only knew that they had rights to land. In the meantime the attitude of the farmers in the village and of the *va'adat ha'mesheq* underwent a change. They became concerned at the effects of having land withdrawn from them and urged Ron to do all possible to avert this. In his capacity as head of the land committee Ron wrote to each member who had given all or part of his land to the village for cultivation. This letter stated that after careful consideration by the land committee, he felt it incumbent upon him to advise members that the idea of co-operative farming as planned was neither economically profitable nor worthwhile.

When this letter was received by members it was considered to be

outrageous, an audacity on the part of Ron. Other members in Kfar
Hefer who were farming their lands also felt this letter to be a
mistake. They felt it would only strengthen the resolve of 'the old
men' to continue with the project. One farmer told me that he was
sure some agreement could have been made with them especially as
many were concerned about the cost of the venture and worried
about failure. On my evidence this was an accurate assessment. None
of those present at the meeting was firmly committed to the scheme,
which anyway could collapse because of overall insufficient support.
Further the 'new farmers' were divided in their aims, and by some
concessions the land committee and the village secretary could have
exploited these differences. By attacking one of the bonds which
made these members identify with one another, Ron strengthened
their common attachment. I suggest he blundered because he saw
these demands only in financial terms and he underestimated their
expressed feelings of injustice, which were increasingly directed
against him and Dov. After this letter a rumour went round the
village that the price per dunam paid by the receiver of the land was
to be increased from IL.5 to IL.15. No official ratification of this was
given, but the attitude of those transferring lands was summed up by
one old man who told me: 'Well, it is too late for that, they should
have treated us fairly before.'

The editor of the village bulletin added his comments upon the
situation. His article in the village bulletin began by citing para-
graph 10 of the village constitution which stated: the village is able
to compel a member who does not cultivate his land to transfer it to
the village Council and the Council will divide it between other
members, at a sum of money to be decided by the full village Council
[in practice it was the village secretary and the land committee who
actually divided the land, although these decisions had to be ratified
by the Council]. The editor suggested a hypothetical situation where
all 15 members of the Council might be big dairy farmers, each one
needing extra land; and he then asked whether these should be the
people who decided the amount to be paid to members? He also
asked about the position if some farmers increased their production
through the use of others' resources; should not they, as members
of a village with a tradition, as members of the *Histadrut* and as
socialists, adequately recompense the givers of these resources? He
urged that there should be some realistic thinking about these
problems.

The second meeting of Kfar Hefer's 'new farmers' was brief. In
addition to those present at the first meeting there were two young
farmers, Amiram (the young farmer proposed for the committee)

and Reuven. Reuven inherited the care of the family farm on the death of his father, but he was not a very enthusiastic farmer and a large part of the care of the farm fell upon his younger brother who was unmarried and still resident on the farm. Reuven supplemented his income by acting as a driver and carrier in the village.

Ben-Natan said the meeting was purely informative and he wished to pass on information about the prospects of growing alfalfa in the village. A nearby kibbuts had been growing this for over 12 years and it was very successful. The kibbuts produced for a processing plant which bore part of the cost of production and gave advice on growing. In addition to the income from alfalfa they could expect to make money from the sale of fodder. He told the members present that within the week he would call another meeting to give full details.

The third meeting, held the following week, was much more lively than the previous one. Ben-Natan opened the meeting by reading Ron's letter to the assembled group. He followed this by reading out a letter he had received from the land committee when he sold his dairy. He had asked the land committee whether the selling of his dairy compelled him to transfer his land to the village. The letter was as follows:

To the member Ben-Natan Josef.

(1) With reference to your enquiry I have to inform you that the plots of land registered on your name were at your disposal until summer 1966/67.

(2) In addition I draw your attention to a decision of the village Council 20.5.65; every member who does not cultivate the land he holds, even on a part-time basis (summer), will be compelled to contribute to the general expenses of the water installations at approximately IL.15 (fifteen pounds) for each dunam. This amount is necessary for the expenses of irrigation in heavy land and as a subscription to the J.N.F., a sum of IL.18.

After the reading of these two letters Ben-Natan announced that a man without land in the village was a man without recognition. Rather ingenuously he continued by saying he had believed that they would have received the maximum help from the village in their attempt to farm their lands. Unfortunately this was not forthcoming. However, he hoped to repair the situation of the moment in which almost a third of the village was no longer farming as it should. He then attacked the letter circulated by Ron, and said that Ron was 'interested' in seeing that 'we shall not receive our lands'. Rhetorically he asked: 'Do we live in a democratic village? This letter makes me doubt it.' But he assured those present that they would 'go forward' without help, even if some members of the village did mock them. This last remark was a reference to the village Purim party held a few days earlier. In a sketch a young farmer had parodied Ben-Natan, showing him planting tomatoes according to works of philosophy. Most of these stirring remarks were directed to Dov, the village secretary, who joined the meeting soon after its start. Still addressing Dov, Ben-Natan continued, by saying that the members assembled here had no wish to be the poor of the village; citrus groves and poultry did not bring in an income. When he, Ben-Natan, became a really old man he would write his autobiography and he would mention this bad time; 'this time of no co-operation from the village.' However, he added, 'We do not ask for help but only for no interference.'

Ben-Natan was cut short by Shwartz, who explained that Ben-Natan had no need to explain these things to them, they knew them only too well. He was more concerned about reports that some members were having difficulty in reclaiming their lands. These members, if they had foreseen the trouble they would experience, would never have relinquished their land. This point was taken up by another member who said that on applying for his land he was told he had no land. This was confirmed by Levine who said that he, too, had been told that there are members without land in the village. He found this impossible to believe but he had been assured that this was so.

Dov was asked to reply to these complaints. He said that he had not come here to exchange ideology with them. As far as he was concerned there seemed to be two approaches among those present. Firstly, there were those members who were able to get more economic benefits by working their own land rather than transferring it to the village. Secondly, there were those who were not interested in cultivating land. These people were claiming land with the sole purpose of annoying and they just wanted to make themselves known in the village. Dov added that those members who wanted their lands back would get them back even though it might not be convenient to others. Members in receipt of others' lands had already been notified of the situation. When pressed by the meeting to explain how some members were without land, he said that this was not true. The situation had arisen because the last time paths to the fields had been improved and the fields themselves laid with pipes and installed with water meters some members had objected. They complained that they did not wish to farm their lands and so they did not want to pay for installations. In a discussion, the village

Council of that time had decided that all members of the village were involved with the land and consequently the objectors were debited with their share of the costs. After the installations the land was re-allocated amongst members in order to rationalise land holding, but because some members had expressed a wish not to farm, they were not allocated separate plots of land. A block of land was set aside for all these farmers and they held rights to this land. The confusion had arisen because they did not have plots of land specifically in their names, but they would receive a plot of land. The land until now had been worked by other members of the village and it was possible that the members here present might be asked to compensate them for work and improvements made in the land. He continued to say that he, in his role of secretary, had a responsibility to warn farmers of possible difficulties. He urged them not to pin too much faith on the figures for production given to them; they all knew it was possible to draw up an account to prove anything. He also warned them that it might not be possible to have consolidated plots of land; to achieve this he would have to move other farmers, and he reminded Ben-Natan of his refusal to move when a neighbour wished to exchange land with him. Finally, he reminded them that if they went ahead with the plan they would be using hired labour. He did not have to remind them that in farming the border between profit and loss was very slight and he asked them to be realistic and not imaginative about their project. After finishing this lengthy speech Dov rose to leave the meeting; but he then turned, and added that, in spite of all, he admired their energy and hoped he would be the same when he reached their age.

Dov's departure caused the members to return to discussing their own affairs. Commenting on Dov's speech one member said he would cultivate his land even if he had a loss. Yet they should not forget their power, and pointing around the room he said: 'Here are 25 people all wanting their lands returned; this is power and we should use it.' In his opinion they themselves were also to blame; they should never have agreed to such an unfair system in the village. He believed that everything went to the dairy farmer; but conceivably there might be a time when the majority of the villagers were not dairy farmers; if 95 per cent of the villagers were not involved in dairying, would 5 per cent of the farmers control the land?

Shwartz confessed that he was worried that the reputed offer of more money per dunam might encourage some members to drop out of the scheme, and this would damage the prospects of all of the rest. He thought that all members should now sign a declaration that they were committed to the scheme. Ben-Natan said that he did not think this was necessary. Some young farmers who would lose land had suggested that they all talk things over, but before they would talk they wanted their lands returned. A pessimistic note was struck at this point by Meiri who dolefully remarked that he did not believe any of the estimates which had been given. He felt that they should all sign a document saying that they expected to make a loss and they accepted this loss. Only such a statement would show the strength of their resolution and armed with this document they should have no difficulty in getting back their lands. If they did not do this then the village on all kinds of pretexts would delay handing back their lands and because of this their plan would founder.

Levine then proposed that they elect a committee to represent them. Ben-Natan said that Amiram and Haim were unable to stand for election, and in their place he asked for nominations. Several names were proposed from the members present; as only Shwartz agreed to stand, Ben-Natan, Levine and Shwartz were appointed as representatives without a vote.

This meeting marked an important stage in the movement's development. The election of a committee can be seen as a sign that they now regarded themselves as a group. Although they had not signed any document committing themselves to become 'new farmers', they all did agree to make formal representation to the village for the return of their lands. I suggest that several reasons were responsible for the hardening of their collective resolution. After all, they were still not in possession of any firm information about crops they should grow nor could they be assured of the financial success of the scheme. Not least important among these reasons was the character of Ben-Natan's role in the proceedings. He assumed the task of organising the group and even in the absence of any support carried on with his plans. This, I believe, played an important part in the eventual formation of the group. For many years individuals in the village had grumbled about their conditions, but in recent years the increase in the category of 'non-farmers' created the basic conditions for some sort of joint protest. Nevertheless I consider that without the energy of Ben-Natan they would have remained as disaffected individuals. There were differences between the members in this category: some had never really been involved in farming and they had found jobs elsewhere, usually in village administration. Others had for a number of years been 'non-farmers' and had withdrawn from active participation in village affairs. In some spheres they were in competition with each other, for example in the acquiring of additional quotas of poultry. The ties between them were slight. None were related by family ties, either consanguinal or affinal. A few of them met from time to time at the synagogue, but synagogue attendance is not well developed in Kfar Hefer, and they usually met only at holiday times when the synagogue was crowded with members from Kfar Hefer and the surrounding settlements. Nor did they have any joint activities. Some met from time to time at the old people's club in the village, but despite their grumbling talk they never took any joint action. Ben-Natan, both because of his personal energy and because of his belief in the moshav way of life, succeeded in transforming them into a group. Although initially resented by some members involved, his action in providing them with possible schemes even before they were committed to the idea gave them a framework of thought and action. Also his greater knowledge of farming techniques and his contacts with other settlements gave them for the first time a belief in the possibility of effective action. The knowledge that others shared their feelings gave them hope of achieving something positive. Building upon this, the actions of the land committee and of farming members in the village and the views of Dov, all added to their determination. They believed Ron's letter to be high-handed and further proof that they could not rely upon village institutions for help in improving their position. They also interpreted the letter, together with a rumour of an increase in the price paid to them for their land, as signs that the village was worried by their actions and so they felt they were in a position to press home this advantage. The hesitations and contradictions about the availability of their lands added to their determination to find out what was happening in the village. Finally Dov's speech which was both threatening and cajoling confirmed their idea that they were unfairly treated. For many of those present the movement took on another aspect, that of a battle between the 'young' and the 'old'; and they were concerned to show that the 'old' were still a force to be reckoned with in Kfar Hefer. At this last meeting the verbal commitment given by some members to the scheme gave courage to the waverers who knew that the venture depended upon them if it was to start. They also knew that the force of moshav law was behind them and in case of failure to return lands, they could take action against the village institutions.

After this meeting the group did not meet again until late April, but from time to time Ben-Natan sent out circulars to inform them of progress, chiefly in deciding upon a crop to be grown. When I asked people concerned in the scheme they had no doubt that the project would develop. Their only concern was that Ben-Natan should, with all haste, make the necessary arrangements. Meanwhile discussion of the issue continued in the village. Members of the scheme wrote in the village bulletin explaining their action and the circumstances which they believed had brought about this action. The usual practice in the bulletin was for members to sign their articles, in some cases only with initials, while in others they used a nom-de-plume. If the intention was to conceal the identity of the writer, in practice members of the village could say with certainty who had written the article. The practice resulted in a good deal of personal accusation and acrimony amidst the general dispute. From time to time people objected that the village bulletin should be used as an organ for publicising personal quarrels, but in a situation where individuals were known to each other personalities invariably were involved. The new farmers felt that the village institutions and particular office holders, especially Ron, had behaved uncharitably towards them. This they saw as doubly wounding because those at fault were their 'own sons'. It is customary in Kfar Hefer, and apparently in other old-established settlements, to refer to the children born to members of a settlement as a son of the village; thus members spoke of a 'son of Kfar Hefer'. It was this nomenclature that the 'non-farmers' used in their complaints of the failings of 'their sons'. The term 'son of the village' is used as a term of identification: the known characteristics of a settlement are encapsulated into these words and attributed to individuals. This assumes that individuals in part can be understood in terms of their background and upbringing. It also assumes that the settlement is well known to the hearers, and in some cases, such as Kfar Hefer, this is true throughout the country. In a second sense the term also carries with it connotations of expected behaviour. Just as there are expectations about the behaviour of a child born to a family, in his role as child, so there are expectations about the behaviour of a 'son of the village'. In Kfar Hefer these are an extension of the expected behaviour towards natural parents, and chiefly involve obligations that the children concern themselves with the welfare of the older generation, and so of the community as a whole. In illustration of this point I relate an incident that took place in the village shortly after the third meeting of the 'new farmers'. Ben-Natan told a member of the 'new farmers' group how, to his surprise, he had heard one young farmer actually say that they should be given back their lands. The young man referred to, had married a 'daughter of Kfar Hefer', and was now farming his father-in-law's farm. The reaction of the hearer of the story was, 'Well, what do you think, that everyone is like our children?' The same expectations are not placed on individuals from outside Kfar Hefer, but when they are found to be fulfilled it is cause for surprised comment.

This usage was prevalent throughout Kfar Hefer even by the young themselves. But not in all cases was it interpreted in the same way. Not all the first generation farmers shared the same opinion of the young as those quoted above. Their expressed views were 'situational', a characteristic frequently described in anthropological literature,[1] and depended on the circumstances of the issue. Thus in a personal reply to one of the 'non-farmers'' complaints, a first generation farmer dismissed the complaint. This reply, signed with initials, came from a farmer still farming his lands with the help of his unmarried son. He wrote that the fault and the trouble of those members who had given over the land were personal and family problems. And in direct reference to the previous writer, mentioning him by name, he wrote that from the first day in the village this member had never worked his lands in a systematic fashion and for most of the time the lands lay fallow and uncultivated. It was the fault of no-one in the village that this member's farm remained at its low level. Moreover, he added, it was clear to the member concerned, when he entered co-operative farming, that the conditions were different from those of private farming.

This reply also indicates another point of difference between the 'farmers' and the 'non-farmers'. While the farmers accepted that some members of the village had insufficient agricultural income, they were concerned to analyse the reasons for this, and like the writer above pointed out that they came from personal and family difficulties and were not the responsibility of the village. The 'non-farmers' were not concerned with the reasons for their situation; they were concerned with its results which they argued were the concern of the whole village. In the absence of any action on the part of village institutions they decided to take the initiative themselves.

The new scheme was discussed in a meeting of the village Executive held in the first week in April. Ron was invited to the meeting to explain the position regarding lands. He reiterated the explanation given by Dov at his meeting with Ben-Natan and the others. But, he added, the situation was a good deal more complicated and serious than appeared at first sight. The desire of farmers for more land and the exchange of fields between farmers had resulted in complete confusion. This had reached a stage when farmers did not even know what was their land and what belonged to someone else. In support of this he cited the example of a farmer who was involved in a scheme to grow avocadoes (this scheme is discussed below). This man had in the past exchanged 3·6 dunams of land with another farmer to give him contiguous land. Now it came to light that the

[1] See 'Introduction' and 'Conclusion' to Gluckman (1964)

member who had exchanged the land had in fact rights over 2·2 dunams, for the remainder had been assigned to him by the village Executive and belonged to a third farmer. The present cultivator has farmed his land for many years and regarded it as his own. In an attempt to satisfy farmers' demands for land he, Ron, had made arrangements that were not 'legal'. In short, the village faced a situation in which there are only two plots free to be returned to their owners. Further, these plots were on the border of Kfar Hefer's lands and were of poor quality. The block set aside after the last reorganisation of the lands has been steadily encroached upon until none remained. Dov agreed that the situation was very worrying. The demand for the return of lands could do a good deal of harm to those farmers who had come to rely upon the use of extra land. The problem of demands for land was one of the most serious the village had to face and he had just received a complaint from the Regional Council that the village had extended on to land beyond the village boundaries. He said that some solution had to be found, because even if these members did not actually take back their fields they were now interested in the state of their lands. He had even been asked about lands by members not connected with the scheme.

A member of the village Executive suggested a possible way out of the difficulty. He said that since not all those people who had transferred land to the village were asking for it to be returned, then the Executive could transfer the land between them. By this he meant that they could give the lands of those not requesting their land to those who were. When asked what he would do if both were to demand their land, he answered: 'Well, you will just have to take it from yet another.' Ron refused to listen to this suggestion, saying he had already had more than enough problems. He gave an example of one woman, a widow, who fortunately was not asking for her land to be returned. The fields assigned to this woman were in fact public land, situated in the middle of the village. While freely admitting that this was wrong he said that it was an example of the lengths he had gone in order to satisfy the demands for land. He added that they had inherited from past committees a land situation which at the best was unclear, and now, because of the pressure of economics, was chaotic. He suggested that the village buy one of the farms which stood empty and use the land to divide amongst members. Dov replied that such a suggestion was untenable; the village would never agree. He could only suggest that Ron study the situation again and report to them at a later date. Ron agreed but protested that he would have to bear the brunt of the complaints and he implored the Executive to come to an early decision. Later it was rumoured that Ron had resigned his position as the head of the land committee because of disputes with the internal secretary. This was never confirmed, and he did stay in office.

Meanwhile those in possession of extra land held from the 'non-farmers' were officially informed that they might be required to give up part of their lands, and were advised to make their plans accordingly. This was a confusing piece of advice because the recipients of this letter did not know if they would be affected or to what extent. When I asked farmers how they thought they would be affected by the withdrawal of part of the lands they were using I received various answers. Some were reluctant to believe that it would ever happen because of a disbelief that the 'old men' would ever set up as farmers. When pressed to give an answer, they agreed that it could be difficult but seemed to imply that the village would find some solution for them. In answer to further questioning they said that either other land would be obtained from somewhere else, possibly from the Regional Council, or they would buy fodder through the village or even come to some agreement with the 'old men' that they should produce for them. Certainly they were concerned about the matter but the accepted attitude seemed to be that the village would come to some arrangement on their behalf. This was probably not an unrealistic assumption, for those concerned were among Kfar Hefer's biggest producers and the village had an interest in their continued success.

In May the 'new farmers' decided to grow alfalfa. They had been offered good terms by the firm in the area that processed alfalfa. They received an estimate which gave the cost and revenue for a 100 dunam area, on which the profit would be IL.102 per dunam. The expected total of area of the new farmers was greater than this but it was not all in one place, although they did anticipate having blocks of land of 25 dunams and above. The enterprise was willing to accept these areas, so at a meeting called in May it was decided to accept the offer and to go ahead with plans. At this point a definite commitment to the scheme was asked for by Ben-Natan who had to give details to the firm. In all 23 members signed that they were willing to undertake the scheme. Among these members were those mentioned previously—Ish-Shalom, Haim, Meiri, Cohen, Reuven, Shwartz, Ben-Natan, Ben-David, Levine, Zioni and Amiram. Two members dropped out of the scheme, Ben-David and Haim's father, both of whom felt unable to involve themselves in the scheme because of doubts about its success. In fact, later, Amiram also left the scheme to join a more profitable venture described below. It will be remembered that he had not transferred his land to the village, and when this second venture recruited members he preferred to use his land in association with them. Of the 20 members remaining in the scheme, two were young men, Reuven and Haim, and Reuven also joined the second scheme. For Haim this scheme gave him the possibility of increasing his revenue from his land in addition to his salary from paid work, and it did not involve him in any hard physical work. Similarly, this scheme gave Reuven more income than he had received from the village and also allowed him to devote time to interests outside farming. The remaining 18 were all elderly 'non-farmers' and included one woman. At the meetings in the village there had, typically, been some 25 to 27 members present. So in addition to those who had withdrawn from the scheme there were three or four members who, despite their interest, never joined the project. In one case, the man died, and his widow decided not to continue with the idea. In another case, the member transferred to the second scheme. A third member used the scheme to find out about his lands; although he claimed them back from the village he did not farm them and he transferred them back to the village. This member had a grandson soon to come out of the army and it was said that he wished to transfer the farm to him and so wanted to ensure that all the necessary land was attached to the farm. Nevertheless, half of those who had transferred all or part of their lands to the village showed no interest in the scheme. Several of these were widows living alone in the farm and they took no active part in agriculture. In other cases some members joined the second scheme. Some of the first generation members still kept part of their fields for a small dairy and did not want to be involved in more farming especially as they doubted its profitability. In two other cases, both families were earning large incomes from outside the farm: in one, the man was a member of the *Knesset*, and in the other both the husband and wife, who were first generation, worked part-time in the village and their son worked full-time outside the village.

I suggest that the figures support my earlier contention that a concerted move by 'non-farmers' could not have taken place in the past. The decisive factor enabling it to take place now was the sudden increase in 'non-farmers' in the immediate past. These farmers were not able to make other financial arrangements as earlier 'non-farmers' had done: jobs in the village were filled, and they were unlikely to receive work outside the village at their age. This state of affairs was aggravated by the effect of national policy which had a double effect on the village. It encouraged small dairy farmers to go out of production, and encouraged stronger dairy farmers to extend their holdings.

Land was returned to those reclaiming it, but not as promptly as they wished. I had left the village when the alfalfa growing started: it had been planned for April, 1968, and it was not until several months later that the scheme got under way. In part this was due to the uncertainties on the side of the 'non-farmers' but in the majority of cases these delays happened because the recipients of land did not vacate it when required to do so. The farmers of extra land knew that according to moshav law they had no alternative to returning the land but they tried in various ways to 'persuade' the non-farmers not to take back the land. I have earlier described some of this persuasion, such as the offer of more money per dunam and the letter from Ron in his role as the head of the land committee. In the event these proved unsuccessful so the farmers used another strategy, that of delaying tactics. They hoped for either of two results from delay: either the non-farmers might lose interest; or they could delay the start of the scheme in which case the commitment of the non-farmers would have to be sustained for a longer period, when even the withdrawal of one or two might have endangered the whole scheme. The effect on the farmers of Kfar Hefer was not as serious as initially feared. The number actually reclaiming lands was smaller than expected and the loss per person was not very big. In addition the village cleared a piece of land which had been covered with thorn bushes and this became available to farmers. A more serious result was the use of water by the new farmers. Previously they had used little of their water quota and this had been available for others. Although the variety of alfalfa grown by the non-farmers needed less water than other varieties, it was expected that each of the 20 members would use about 4,500 m^3 in addition to the water they had previously used. This meant that the water available to others was considerably cut, and the village urged all farmers to use water more efficiently than they had done in the past.

Even after the 'non-farmers' had taken the decision to become 'new-farmers' discussion of the issue still continued in the village. As he had done in the past, the editor of the village bulletin played a part in keeping the discussion going. He asked why the village, which, he added, was said to be socialist and co-operative, did not help those without a dairy to find another alternative income from agriculture within the village? He added that it would be a sorry day for Kfar Hefer if it took over the Indian belief that the cow was sacred, and those who did not possess it were less than sacred. In conclusion he reminded the members of Kfar Hefer that no one wanted to be the victim of another's profits. This article provoked several letters in reply, including one from Dov which said that there was not, nor would there ever be, a situation where the possibilities of those who did not have dairies were cut down; everyone could work his land as he felt fit. Other letters warned the new farmers that they would find cultivation a costly business and also cast doubts about the success of joint enterprises which, they argued, village experience had shown to be a failure. This ignored the apparent success of the pecan plantation, probably because it was not yet bringing in much return. Others reiterated earlier objections to the scheme, that this was a personal and not a village problem. This view was put very forcefully by a first generation farmer who now farms with his son-in-law. He wrote: 'Who are those in the village without a dairy? They are the farmers where only the parents are on the farm. These parents have given up their dairy to make life easier for themselves . . . no one persuades them to give up their dairy.'

Many of these letters attacked the editor personally, accusing him of stirring up trouble in the village and criticising him for talking about things he did not understand. He was also told that he should concentrate on his work outside the village which apparently did not adequately occupy his time. This is very much like Frankenberg's description of a Welsh village where members despite their quarrels asserted that, 'We would be happy if foreigners did not make trouble.' [1] Here some members asserted that there was nothing wrong with the moshav as a system if the editor did not make trouble. They attributed complaining members' difficulties to their own personal problems and not the problems of the moshav.

Part of the difficulty may be a result of processes described by Talmon-Garber[2] when she writes that one of the problems in collective communities is that there is no pattern for aging, no defined rights in the community for those who are old and unable to work fully in the community. I consider that this applies clearly to Kfar Hefer: the blueprint of the moshav delineates individual work in farming with the alternative of working as a public worker in the community. The moshav scheme is an 'ideal type' assuming continuation in farming from generation to generation. No account is taken of 'abnormal' factors, such as a farm being occupied by an elderly couple unable to engage in farming. Such provisions are believed to be covered in the 'mutual aid' clause of the moshav constitution. But, as I have shown, this is a term open to many interpretations. This is not to deny that there was a genuine problem of young and old in the village: the fears of the old that they would not have sufficient livelihood; the complaints of the young that they had to support an aging population. On farms where there was the con-

[1] See Gluckman's 'Foreword' to Frankenberg (1957)   [2] Talmon-Garber

tinuation of the second generation then this dispute was a private, family matter; only in the farms where there was no continuation did the matter become public, and for this reason I contend that the dispute was more than a difference between generations.

Another effect of the moshav scheme of things is arbitrarily to divide farmers into 'young' and 'old', a tendency which is sharpened because of the narrow age band of the first generation. I have shown how the dispute was believed by many in the village to be a dispute between the two age groups. I myself argue that these were in fact two categories with different social characteristics. The nature of agricultural production, with its emphasis on physical labour, is suited to young people, but many of those who had given up dairy farming were not 'old', in the sense that in other jobs they would still be working and earning a living. This formed a big part of the 'non-farmers'' complaints; their expressed feeling was that simply because they did not farm their lands, they were dismissed as 'old' and no heed was paid to them.

The second movement was far less spectacular and caused much less fuss in the village. This was a decision on the part of some farmers to start growing avocadoes, a new enterprise in the village. Recently the growing of this crop for the export market had been increased in Israel and large profits were made. Several young farmers in the village got together and suggested that they approach the Ministry of Agriculture for details of production. The initial group had as its nucleus a group of young farmers who had either bought their own farm in Kfar Hefer, or had taken over control of the family farm which had not been fully developed. One of these young men had no dairy, and the others had only small dairies. Like the 'non-farmers' described above they, despite their farming, felt that the traditional branches of agriculture in the village did not give them sufficient income. In poultry and in citrus they had little chance of extending production; their main hope was in the dairy branch. However, to develop this branch quickly and adequately involved heavy expenses, which they knew they would not be allowed as loans from the village co-operative. Furthermore the situation in dairy farming was uncertain and under the village system an increase in production resulted in a smaller personal quota, at a time when the economics of production demanded larger production. They decided upon avocado growing because they had an area of land which they believed to be suitable, and they were attracted by its profits. They approached other members whom they believed to be in a similar position to themselves and altogether collected the names of 20 members who were interested. These 20 included several farmers who came in the 'continuation doubtful' category of second generation continuity (see chapter III). In some ways their situation was like that of the young members despite the difference in ages. These farmers typically had small dairies which were marginally profitable, and they saw that this situation was likely to deteriorate in the future. It therefore seemed possible that in the immediate future they would relinquish their dairy branch, but they were still able physically to work in agriculture, and neither physically nor economically did they wish to be tied to citrus and poultry. One of these farmers was Videtsky (account 4, chapter IV) and at a meeting of the group he was appointed chairman, with the responsibility of getting information and passing it on to members. The group's representatives met with the land committee to find a suitable area and then afterwards applied to the village Executive. At this meeting Videtsky and two other members of the proposed scheme discussed plans with the Executive. Although the scheme was to go ahead with loans from the Ministry of Agriculture, it still depended on the village co-operative. Loans covered the cost of plants and certain advances in anticipation of production, but the preparation of the land and the cost of care was the responsibility of the individual farmer. Nevertheless in practice this meant the village co-operative, because none of those involved were able to finance such a scheme and all had to rely on credit from the village. Therefore the village Executive had the power to veto any member to whom they did not want to extend credit.

When the list of 20 names was read aloud, doubts were expressed by Dov about three of those named. Two of these were farmers in their late twenties who had bought their own farms in the village and had large debts to the co-operative because of initial expenses of investment. The other was a first generation farmer who also had a large debt and was working his farm with only occasional help from his son who was in the army. Dov said he would speak to these three members and discuss with them the state of their farms. The delegation left after this and said that they would now go ahead with the ordering of plants. Dov answered that they did not know how many would be involved, since the Executive might refuse aid to these three members, to which Videtsky answered that two more or less did not make a lot of difference. They planned to plant about 80 dunams so they would order on that basis. In fact, I suggest the group was confident that the members would be allowed to participate in the scheme. This feeling was confirmed by Yoel, a member of the Executive after the departure of the delegation. He said that there was no point in refusing permission to any of them, because if they did refuse this week they would only agree the following week. The village Executive often did refuse applications from individuals for loans to buy equipment, but as Yoel pointed out, the conditions of a group application were different. To refuse the application of one farmer while agreeing to others was to leave the Executive open to accusations of discrimination and favouritism. Also the scheme needed a certain number of participants to ensure economies of scale, for the initial preparation was to be joint with the individual afterwards working his own area. Dov did speak to the two young farmers and agreed to their participation, while the older member withdrew even before this because he misunderstood the scheme and thought that like the alfalfa scheme the whole process of cultivation was to be joint. The final number of those planting avocado was 27, because other members, including Dov, joined the scheme. Planting was delayed to accommodate them all. The scheme was also delayed because of re-arrangements in land resulting from the alfalfa scheme. Three of those concerned Reuven, Zioni and Shwartz also took part in the alfalfa scheme. Of the total number of those involved, six were 'first generation' farmers who were farming alone.

Although these two schemes caused different reactions in the village they were both a response to the agricultural and economic situation in Kfar Hefer. In some ways the stated reasons of members of both groups for their participation in the schemes were at odds with each other. The alfalfa group stated that everything went to the dairy farmer in Kfar Hefer who was becoming rich at their expense, while the avocado group said that despite their participation in all agricultural branches they had a hard time to make farming profitable. The reconciliation of these points of view can be seen in the context of the economic conditions in Israel and in Kfar Hefer described in the last chapter. It was true that some farmers in Kfar Hefer were big and successful producers and they had benefited from increased quotas, but there were farms where other social factors played a part. For historical reasons, or because there was a large labour force in the home, or because a farmer possessed money from outside farming production, these farms had enjoyed favourable conditions for development. Those taking part in the avocado scheme, with one 'exception, did not fall into any of these categories. Their production in all cases was profitable, but only just so, and they could see no prospects of increasing this within the traditional branches of Kfar Hefer. The one exception was Shimoni in Case 5 referred to in the previous chapter; his biggest income came from turkey production and not from working the land or maintaining a dairy.

The presentation of the arguments for the two schemes also differed. The alfalfa group expressed feelings of injustice and appealed to moshav law and principles; the second group spoke solely in economic terms. In fact both were a result of internal and external circumstances. Even though the internal re-arrangements and re-adjustments absorbed and alleviated these results, I consider that the two movements show the effects of direct national intervention in both social and economic life in co-operative settlements, and the 'revolution' in agriculture referred to by Ron (see chapter IV). The initiation of these schemes reflects the farmers' awareness of the problems, and that joint schemes with a pooling of resources are a possible alternative to the need for individuals to specialise and to increase the scale of operations in modern farming.

VI
Village administration

The structure of village committees remains the same as in the early days of the village. Election to the Council of fifteen members is by secret ballot. Nominations are accepted by an 'election committee' set up for the purpose of organising the elections. It is sufficient for one sponsor to nominate a candidate but the consent of the nominee must be obtained. The list of candidates is drawn up and published in the village bulletin; on the election day ballot boxes are set up in the dairy and inside the village store, and professional workers or residents are appointed as returning officers. Each agricultural member of the village, including young people over the age of 18 years who have signed that they wish to be members of the village, is allowed one vote. Arrangements are made for people serving in the army to return their votes by post. Strictly, each member should register his vote personally but the practice is often that one member of the family votes for all the other members. When remonstrations were raised in a village meeting about this practice, which it was said was illegal, the attitude of those present was that it may be illegal but it worked. For a time after this meeting efforts were made to ensure that each member voted separately and that where one member voted for another the written permission of the absentee should be given. But this practice fell into abeyance, since one of the returning officers said at the meeting it was very unpleasant and tiresome for him to argue with every member who came along to vote, especially as members became very offended when doubts were cast upon their honesty. He said that it was no use pointing to the legal backing for the argument because members took all expostulations personally and said that it was 'their' committee that was being elected and they would choose how this was to be done. These members argued that since each farm is considered to be a unit, then inevitably the interests of the members of that farm were the same. Elections from the Council to the Executive committee were made in the Council itself.

Other committees in the village were elected from the village meeting on a show of hands and the appropriate number for each committee was elected from those receiving the highest number of votes.

The results of the election to the Council were published in the village bulletin. A list of the successful candidates for all committees was published at the same time, but no voting figures were given.

Fifteen members are elected to the Council and each serves for two years, but each year seven or eight of the members retire; there is thus every year a combination of new members and members with experience in the Council. Theoretically any member of the village can stand for the Council but an examination of Council members over the years shows that there is a recurring membership. In some cases this dates back to the early days of the village and members of the Council thirty years ago serve as present-day members of the Council. Among the second generation there seems to be a pattern of gaining membership of committees for specific topics (education, land, poultry, etc.) before seeking election to the Council. And according to the evidence of the last five years it appears that a member who has not served upon another committee in Kfar Hefer is unlikely to be elected to the Council.

Women have equal rights with men in election but no woman has ever been elected to the village Executive committee although from time to time they have served on the Council. There are certain committees which are believed to be especially appropriate to women, chiefly the recent committee set up for studying the problems of the village store and the education and cultural committee. However, even though women have served on these committees they have never been the heads of their committees. This is bemoaned from time to time in the village bulletin, by male members of the village who point out the equal rights of membership of women both on the family farms and in the village co-operative. In the election for the Council 1966/67 two women stood as candidates but one was persuaded to stand down because it was felt that two women candidates would split the vote and a single candidate stood a better chance of election; the woman was elected. The Council represents farming interests and as men do most of the farming work the women are less likely to stand for election and also less likely to be elected. Women in their role as housewives and mothers are not intimately involved in the work of the farm but in their care of the farm's poultry they do play a complementary role to that of their husband's work in the dairy and fields. This situation is often modified in the two family farms where there tends to be a division of labour between two women, mother and daughter or daughter-in-law. Usually the older woman, health permitting, is responsible for the poultry and the younger woman is concerned with care of children. And as the children grow the presence of grandmother on the farm often allows the younger woman to take on paid employment either in the village or outside. It sometimes happens that the woman's work takes her into a wider social field than that experienced by her husband who stays in the village, and her interest in village affairs is accordingly diminished.

In the year 1945/46 two 'youth representatives', one woman and one man, were co-opted without election to the village Council. This practice was continued in the following year, but after this the young of the village stood for candidature of the Council in the normal way. After this time at least one young person was elected to the Council, but not until 1951/52 did a second generation member sit on the Executive, David Shauli who is now a *Knesset* member. The representation of the second generation continued to grow until in 1963/64 half the members of the village Council were second generation, and after 1964/65 they have consistently formed a majority in the Council.

In the two elections for members of the Council which took place during my stay in the village, in the year 1966/67, nine of the fifteen Council members were second generation, and in the year 1967/68 ten served as members of the Council. Five second generation members and one first generation member retired at the end of 1966/67, and in their place six second generation members were elected. In both elections the two candidates not elected were second generation members. The secretary of the village is ensured a place on the Council and in the Executive and his position did not come up for re-election.

All the first generation members had been active in village affairs from the beginning of settlement and several had served on the village Council and in the Executive Committee, while the others had been members of the village committees.

The one woman is Dora, a 'daughter of Kfar Hefer' who is married to a 'son of Kfar Hefer'. After their marriage, her husband, the eldest of three sons, moved into her family farm and on the death of both her parents they together run the farm. Dora is one of the few of the 'elder' second-generation to have continued schooling to matriculation level. After she completed the village school she went to Tel Aviv to take the matriculation examination but returned to the village. Her mother was politically active in the *Mapai*[1] party and worked in its Central Committee in Tel Aviv for many years. Dora is recognised in the village to be an intelligent and able person who has for many years taken an interest in village affairs and served on committees. At this time she also sat on the editorial board of the village bulletin and she was a frequent contributor. I was told that

---

[1] The leading socialist party in Israel

L

at one time the sons-in-law of Kfar Hefer, those who had married a Kfar Hefer girl and stayed on her family farm, felt that they did not get a fair representation. This complaint is usually illustrated by the story of one of these young men who one night attended the village Council offices where committee meetings are held. He opened the door of each room where the meetings were being held, looked inside and remarked to each of the assembled groups: 'Yet another meeting without one son-in-law.' If this was true the son-in-law could have no complaints about the Councils of the years 1966–68. In the first Council there were three sons-in-law and in the second a further two. Two of these young men were not employed in farming, both having full-time jobs, one in the Moshav Movement and one in the Ministry of Agriculture. It may have been true that the village was interested in having these representatives of outside organisations in the Council because of the information they held, and also as informal representatives of the village to these bodies, but both were popular figures in the village and took a part in the village affairs.

None of the Council members had the highest level of production in the village, although the second generation farmers were on the whole from the good farmers of the village, those with well-developed and efficient farms. This bears out the findings of Talmon-Garber in a study of old-established farming communities where she wrote: 'Leading office holders were in the middle and upper middle economic range.'[1] This also applied to the first generation farmers with the exception of Oren who had given up dairy farming and was the only one without second generation continuation. But he had been a leading figure in the village affairs from the days before the union of the two original groups to form Kfar Hefer and was also valued for his special knowledge of tax problems, on which subject he was the village's expert.

The village Executive (*ha'hanala*) is composed of five members, one of whom is the village's internal secretary. In 1966/67 this was composed of Dov, the village's internal secretary; Yoel, a 'son-in-law of Kfar Hefer', a man in his middle forties with teenage children; Oren; Marks, a first generation farmer who worked with his son in the farm and has over the years been consistently involved in village affairs; and Ori, a 'son of Kfar Hefer', a man in his late thirties, who farmed his wife's family farm. In 1967/68 Yoel retired from the Executive on completion of his two years service and was replaced by Dani, another 'son-in-law' who farms his father-in-law's farm.

Dov the village secretary was in his middle thirties, and was married to a girl from another old-established moshav. He lived with his

[1] Talmon-Garber (1952)

parents in the family farm and until his appointment to the position of secretary farmed with his father. His family have a close association with moshav life and with moshav administration. Dov served as an instructor in a new moshav after the foundation of the State, his sisters are all married to farmers and live in other moshavim, his father has been prominent in village life and actually preceded Dov in his appointment as village secretary. The circumstances surrounding this are described more fully later in this chapter, here it is sufficient to say that the village in 1963/64 appointed an 'outsider' as internal secretary. This man had no connections with Kfar Hefer and was appointed because of his specialist economic and administrative knowledge. The appointment was not a success and the following year in the middle of the village year he resigned from office and Dov's father was appointed to finish the year. At the beginning of the year 1965/66 Dov was appointed to the position and at the time I came to Kfar Hefer he was in his second year of office. Dov had previously served as a Council member and was recognised to be a good farmer. I cannot with certainty say why he was chosen, but his previous experience, his family's connections with administration, and the fact that his father was still able to work in the farm, all contributed. From conversations with members and from my own observations it seems it is difficult for a young farmer to take on this position and few farms can afford to spare the labour force of a young man. On taking office Dov sold part of his dairy, leaving only an amount his father and he could manage in their spare time. He entered into an agreement with the village that on his leaving office they would restore his dairy to a size and composition comparable with that he had sold. This stipulation and the village's acceptance reflect some of the difficulties involved in the filling of the post.

A new development in the village is that Kfar Hefer now has a full-time external secretary who came from outside the village. I have earlier referred to Ben, the holder of this office (see chapter V). He has been the external secretary since 1961/62. Previously there had been a member of the Executive committee who acted as representative to external bodies and dealt with village financing, but the real development of this role came after Ben's appointment. The national situation (see chapter IV) required that the village have a full-time representative to deal with their affairs; and perhaps because of some of the difficulties described above, Ben, and not an agriculturalist member of Kfar Hefer, was chosen.

The General Meeting of village members represents the ultimate deciding body in village affairs. The relationships between the various committees and councils are laid down in the village constitution.

The village Executive is required to meet at least once a week to discuss the running of the village, and the village secretary should attend a village Council meeting once a month to report to them; if necessary he should call an additional meeting to discuss urgent business. In the event of a failure on the part of the Council to agree, they should report to a special General Meeting of village members. The Council is empowered to refer any important business to a village General Meeting. The decision of the General Meeting is the decisive voice and is binding on village members and on village institutions. If a member feels that he has been unfairly treated by the village Executive or by the Council he can, on application to the Council, apply for the issue to be discussed at a General Meeting. Members who feel that an issue has not been fully covered in a General Meeting may again raise the issue at another General Meeting.

One of the first public indications of disputes concerning the working of this system arose over the appointment of Haim to the post of head of the village agricultural stores. A lot of disagreement was engendered about this appointment which was made by the village Executive, agreed to by the Council, and ratified in a General Meeting. Aside from the personal issues in this dispute, it also raised the question of action open to members who did not agree to village decisions. A petition was raised and signatures collected against this appointment and application was made to the village Executive asking for the ratification and the appointment to be cancelled. The organisers of the petition, who never identified themselves publicly, argued that the collection of 30 signatures opposing a village decision should be enough to re-open an issue for debate. Dov refused to do this, and so one of the organisers asked to appear before the village Executive who also refused the petition. Dov followed up his refusal by inserting a notice in the village bulletin which stated that neither in the moshav constitution nor in the internal decisions of the village was there any such precedent. In no instance have the members the right to call a general meeting to enquire into the decisions of the Executive committee. He concluded that the only way he knew to protect the public good was for members to elect delegates whom they knew would act in accordance with the public good. This was followed by Dora who wrote an article in the same edition of the village bulletin. She pointed out that in the general meeting of the village the presentation of signatures to re-open an issue had been discussed and rejected. At the general meeting to discuss Haim's appointment the general meeting had decided by 37 votes to 16 to accept the appointment and not to enquire into it.

Despite this, she added, the very next day a notice had appeared on the village notice board outside the store asking for signatures to re-open the issue. This behaviour, she declared, was flouting both the authority of the General Meeting and of those who took part in it. She suggested that those signing the notice should be called to order by the General Meeting or this would set a precedent for the future, and decisions would not be decisions but rather points for debate. The constitutional order was that members could raise questions at the next general meeting, but until then the decision must be accepted by all members without exception. And firmly, she added that people who voted within a certain framework must accept decisions even if they did not like them. Finally, she wrote that the village Executive must not succumb to these demands and if they did, they should resign.

This issue raised many points which were to re-appear several times during the period I spent in the village. Doubts were cast on the powers to make decisions, and on the authority and power of the general meeting; and questions were raised about the constitutional position of dissidents who refused to conform to decisions of the general meeting. These doubts were expressed in different ways. Those directed against the Executive were expressed in personal terms, chiefly against the internal secretary. Nothing was felt to be wrong with the system and difficulties were attributed to personal characteristics of office holders. The attitude to the General Meeting was different: here the whole suitability and validity of the meeting was challenged.

A third interesting point to be taken up later is that both Dov and Dora referred to 'precedent' in the village. This point recurred consistently in the village whenever issues were discussed. Most of the points raised, like this case, were not covered by the moshav constitution. But during the history of the village certain decisions had been made and certain patterns of behaviour had been laid down, and these had assumed the significance of 'customary law'. It was to this that reference was made in cases of difficulty and indecision. In practice this was often a difficult business because records of decisions and minutes of meetings were kept in a very imprecise manner, and even though the intention may have been clear to the individuals concerned, later readers were allowed a good deal of latitude in interpretation.

In the Executive meeting, the position of the internal secretary was 'primus inter pares', although in his role as village internal secretary he was seen differently. It was recognised that his job involved him in wider spheres than those of the village Executive and as such it was accepted that he was usually better informed on affairs concerning the village and the wider environment. In this the role of the external secretary and his relationship with the internal secretary played a significant part.

Ben, the external secretary, came to the village at a time when agricultural production in Israel and Kfar Hefer was undergoing a series of changes. The role of external secretary, whose responsibility is to handle the village's relationships with outside bodies, underwent a change both in response to these changes and due to Ben's direction. Seven years earlier the role of external secretary was not well developed, and was secondary to that of the internal secretary. The external secretary did not sit as a member of the Executive, nor was he involved in village planning. Ben had previous experience in communal settlements and he brought his experience to Kfar Hefer. Now, the external secretary has the responsibility for the financial affairs of the village and is closely involved with internal village planning. He sits in the Executive and the Council meetings, and although he has no voting rights he does exert a considerable influence on decisions. Much of his work takes him out of the village in connection with his duties as treasurer and as the village representative to many semi-government and moshav organisations. This gave rise to the comment in Kfar Hefer that he did not work very hard; as one first generation member told me, 'All he does is talk on the telephone.' 'Working hard' in Kfar Hefer is usually defined by physical work, and although the value and importance of administrative duties is recognised this is not 'hard work'. This attitude is often expressed against Gavish, Kfar Hefer's neighbouring moshav shitufi, where, as a young Kfar Hefer farmer told me, 'They don't know what it is to work, they are all managers.'

As a result of national planning Kfar Hefer has become increasingly involved with government planning agencies and the importance of outside contacts which are influential in policymaking has increased. Ben represented the village to the Central Poultry Agency, in the Moshav Movement he sat on the central policy-making board and he also headed the Moshav Movement's fruit marketing and milk delegations to the national boards. Kfar Hefer's success in achieving the most favourable production quotas and terms is to a great extent dependent upon him. The positions he held are a result of both his personal ability and Kfar Hefer's reputation in the Moshav Movement; and they are very important as arenas in which Kfar Hefer can present her interests in relation to those of other moshavim. The increasing influence of national policies on settlement production, and the need for expertise in financial and economic planning within the individual settlement, have increased the authority and power of the external secretary in Kfar Hefer.

Although Ben is not an economist he has undergone specialised training and his years of experience in administrative work have resulted in his taking over much of the administration of the village. He also has held office continuously while in the same period the village has had four internal secretaries. It takes time for a member to learn the duties of internal secretary and even though some have had previous experience, new tasks have arisen to meet the changing situation. Meanwhile administration of village affairs has to continue; and here Ben and the office staff of Kfar Hefer have taken over the running of the village. But Dov, the internal secretary, and Ben share a room in the village offices which means that they are in constant touch with each other's work and are able to discuss village affairs.

Ben has few duties which bring him into contact with the individual members of Kfar Hefer, the most important being that he sees members who wish to withdraw more money from their account than is customarily allowed to them. Each family in Kfar Hefer is allowed a minimum sum monthly which is awarded according to family size and conditions. The state of the family farm is also taken into consideration, but the minimum sum is guaranteed without regard to the member's affairs. It is usually the women as the managers of household affairs who collect this money and they approach Ben if they wish to withdraw more than this sum. In some cases, where the family is in credit in the co-operative, this procedure is not necessary, but the majority of families in the village are indebted to the co-operative. Until the middle of the year 1967/68 Ben had the right to refuse or agree to the granting of extra money, after this time the village Executive decided that the consent of the internal secretary must be given and he became the final arbiter. Dov, therefore, added to his dealings with individual members and Ben became further removed from them, adding to the uncertainty about his actual job in the village. He seldom attended village general meetings and only once a year, at the Annual General Meeting, did he present a report; but anyway these meetings were only sparsely attended. In the Executive meetings and in the Council he sat as an adviser and explained the workings of the government and semi-government agencies, but he took no part in debates except to explain to members the financial consequences of policies. Yet despite his 'shadowy' presence to most village members, he did play a big part in forming village policies, both internally and externally. Unlike Dov, who was clearly involved with individual members and who was recognised by them to have both responsibilities to individuals and to the village as a whole, Ben's influence on internal policies was masked by the conventions of village policy which made the internal secretary directly responsible for village affairs. Much discussion in anthropological literature[1] has been given to individuals who hold positions which are 'intercalary' or 'articulating' or 'inter-hierarchical' roles, i.e. those who occupy positions which bring them into direct contact with two levels in an ordered hierarchy and whose duty it is both to represent and to try to enforce the demands of both sets of relationships. In Kfar Hefer the division between 'internal' and 'external' secretary was an attempt clearly to separate and distinguish these functions, but as I have shown the two tasks were intimately involved. The effect of partial knowledge on the part of villagers and their day-to-day involvement with the internal secretary led to the identification of both roles in his person, and he bore the brunt of village reaction.

It is the internal secretary's duty to inform members of the Executive of decisions he has taken and to inform and consult them about the running of the village. He prepares the agenda for the Executive meetings and only on rare occasions during the time I attended the meetings did other members of the Executive raise topics for discussion.

These obligations are set down in general terms and there are no defined rules about issues which the internal secretary has to refer to the Executive committee; the area of discretion left to him is fairly wide. Members can and do present their problems to the internal secretary at any time during his working day and not infrequently outside the hours. Much of this is dealt with by the internal secretary himself, without reference to the Executive, although a member can demand the right to appear before the Executive committee if he is dissatisfied with the results of his enquiry. A case already referred to in Chapter IV, illustrates the secretary's initiative in his dealings with members. In this case the appellant applied for an extra quota of turkeys saying that that already given to him was insufficient. On Dov's refusal he claimed his right to appear before the village Council. In the discussions in the Executive and in the Council, Dov admitted that he had already granted him an extra allocation without consulting the Executive committee; and he was censured by both bodies for failing to refer to them. In some situations it is to the individual's benefit that he can consult the internal secretary without reference to the Executive for he may be reluctant to discuss personal or family problems before a wider body.

[1] See especially Gluckman (1963b)

During the period I attended village Executive meetings, from January 1967 until May 1968, both individual cases and village policy were discussed. Typically, individual cases concerned the financial demands of members for loans to buy personal consumer goods or agricultural machinery and also the unceasing and ubiquitous requests for additional quotas of agricultural produce. Cases involving disputes between members are not referred to the internal secretary or to the Executive: these go to a special committee dealing with personal difficulties between members. Usually the issues listed above went no further than the Executive, the one exception being the case about the quota for turkeys already cited. Questions involving village policy were passed on to the Council. These were initiated from several sources: from members' complaints; from village committees; and from Dov and Ben. There seemed to be the feeling that discussion of individual cases was not appropriate in the village Council and only on the insistence of the member concerned were individual circumstances discussed in this body.

Individual applications for loans were usually dealt with by reference to the account of the member in the co-operative although in the case of new farmers special help was given to enable them to build up their farm. Issues involving village responsibility towards members and village policy in the light of national policies were more keenly debated in the Executive. There was little members could do to change government policy and village efforts were directed to achieving the best possible terms for the village through her connections with outside bodies. The main attention was paid to the administration of its results, which was a twofold problem, both social and economic. It is in the discussion of these issues that the differing effects of the role of village secretary and of the role of other members are revealed. As a result of his involvement in village administration, the secretary is anxious to keep to a minimum the responsibility and guarantees by the village to the individual member. This view is not shared by the individual members themselves. In this discussion the question of precedent is of central interest: the internal secretary is concerned not to introduce new measures which might in the future be used as precedents for the strengthening of the position of individuals against that of the co-operative. The actual balance achieved between these two conflicting views is an outcome of both economic and social factors, and I cite two cases which illustrate this process.

The first case involves the responsibility of village institutions for the agricultural production of a member. The member concerned is a second generation farmer, Josef, who farms with his father and unmarried brother, and the issue involved an allocation of citrus trees bought by the head of the citrus plantation on his behalf. Josef appeared before Dov personally and broached the question of the trees which had not developed properly and had only stunted growth. He asked that Dov recommend compensation for the trees, to be paid by the village. Dov answered that this was not an individual problem but involved a question of village principle and he invited Josef to a meeting of the village Executive. Josef appeared before the next meeting of the Executive and explained what had happened. The new plants had been ordered two years earlier by his father to replace citrus affected by frost; in all 200 new trees were delivered. At the time when the trees were delivered his father was in hospital and he and his brother accepted the consignment. Two weeks later on his father's return from hospital he visited the citrus groves and told his sons that they should never have accepted delivery of such poor specimens. They consulted Ilan who was responsible for the citrus plantation, and who had bought the trees, and asked his advice. He said that they were not the best trees in the world but they would develop. After a year the trees had only grown a little, and it was decided by Ilan to replace half the trees at the charge of the village. The remaining trees were examined by an instructor from the Ministry of Agriculture's extension service and he advised certain changes in the care of the trees. Now another year had passed and these trees had not developed, so Josef had decided to apply to the Executive for some recompense for the initial cost of the trees and for the care he had given them. Josef presented his case quietly and in reasoned terms and said that he asked the Executive to consider his application.

The discussion of an application does not take place in the presence of the member concerned so Josef left. The timing of the discussion is left to Dov; sometimes it took place immediately after the presentation of a case, in others, all the cases were presented and only afterwards did discussion take place. There appeared to be no pattern to this, but Dov often explained that when there were several people waiting to appear before the Executive he did not want to keep them waiting. Whatever the reason for this practice, it did have a marked effect upon the discussion that took place. When the issues were fresh in the minds of the Executive then a more detailed analysis of the problem at hand ensued, whereas if time had elapsed, members talked about the broad outlines and implications of the case. This was further affected by the fact that members were tired and wished to reach a decision quickly. Executive meetings seldom started before 9 o'clock in the evening and usually ended after midnight. In the latter type of discussions Dov, who because of his prior knowledge was better informed, often succeeded in persuading the Executive to accept his ideas. Where there was a difference of opinion, the decision was usually referred to the Council. This happened in the case of Josef, the discussion of which was delayed until after the hearing of several other matters, and then it was inconclusive. Dov maintained that it was the individual's duty to accept responsibility after he had accepted the consignment. He argued that if the Executive agreed to Josef's request this would involve the co-operative in costly future demands on the part of members. This would set a precedent, not only in citrus, but also in other branches, for members to demand reparations for their ills, however caused. This view was supported by Yoel who was known in the village for his policy of advocating individual rights and obligations against the demands of the co-operative principle. The other three did not share this view. Marks, a long-time member of village institutions, argued that the member had rights in the co-operative and in this case the co-operative's obligation had been recognised in the replanting of 100 trees at its expense. Oren supported this view and added that there could be no co-operative if the rights of individuals were not acknowledged. Ori was hesitant about the issue, and he expressed the view that the individual should be able to claim against the village but the question was the limits to which this could be allowed. Marks told him that this was not the problem; they did not have to decide future cases, they had to reach a decision in this case.

This statement raises a point often discussed in legal proceedings where judgments are reached not by precisely delimiting the areas within which the case falls, but by using the concept of 'reasonableness' and deciding that the particular case is reasonable in terms of broad principles. The concern is not to legislate for all future cases but to decide if the case at hand falls 'on the right side of any reasonable line that could be drawn' (Lord Coleridge). Thus, in addition to the question of the rights of the individual *vis-à-vis* the co-operative, another question is raised, that of the application of general principles to specific cases. Dov was attempting to circumscribe and delimit the area of village responsibility, while Oren and Marks were concerned with the 'spirit' of customary procedure.

Similar points were raised in the meeting of the Council at which Josef appeared. After the presentation of his case he left the meeting, even though this assembly is open to the public. Once again the discussion was postponed until the rest of the business had been heard. Dov opened the debate by saying that this was an issue of general importance for the village, involving as it did the whole accountability of the village institutions to individual members. Ilan and Arad had been invited to the meeting to answer questions from the Council members and Marks opened the questioning by asking Ilan if he had noticed that the plants were defective. Ilan answered that they were ordinary plants, not particularly good and not particularly bad. He added that another member had received a consignment of trees from the same batch and these had developed normally. In answer to further questioning he said that the trees which had replaced the uprooted trees were developing well but the other trees were of noticeably poor quality. Dov reiterated that this was not the point: he maintained that the village's responsibility ended when Josef received and accepted the trees. This was supported by Almagor who said that if this principle were to be accepted then the village owed him thousands of pounds. Many years ago he had bought, through the village, a young heifer which had died the following day. But he had accepted this as part of the hazards of farming and it never occurred to him to claim against the village. Dora argued that the village already had accepted responsibility for production in other agricultural branches, since there were now insurance schemes run by the village for members in the dairy and poultry branches, and the village should now accept its responsibility in the citrus branch. Objections were raised to this by several members who said that the premiums were paid by the members themselves and it was only an administrative convenience that it was organised co-operatively. The argument was countered by Dora who said that all the co-operative aspects of a moshav were a 'convenience' for its members, but that this had no meaning if the co-operative did not act as guarantor on its services. At this point a different argument was raised by Shulman, a first generation farmer, who said that the cooperative in the person of Ilan had only acted as agent in the transaction and the claim, if any, should be made against the supplier. Pursuing this thought he said that if he bought a bottle of oil which was contaminated, from the village store, he would take it back to the store and they would claim against the manufacturers; why then should not Josef claim against the suppliers? Shlomo, a second generation member, farming his own farm, answered by saying that the enterprise was different. The village co-operative was not an economic venture like a shop, but in performing services for its members it must also bear the responsibility; if it did not do so then the individual member would be justified in opting out of the cooperative framework and acting on his own behalf. And he added that this would mean the end of Kfar Hefer. Dora seconded this point and summed up the question for the Council as, 'Are there guarantees in Kfar Hefer or are there not?' Dov disputed this presentation and said the question was the danger of setting a precedent which others would exploit to the detriment of the co-operative.

The Council voted by eleven votes to four in favour of compensation for Josef. Dov, Almagor, Schulman and Yoel opposed the motion. In announcing the result Dov said that it was a bad decision and would cause a lot of trouble in the future. Shlomo argued that nothing had been decided about future cases, and each would be examined and decided on its merits. The question of the amount of compensation remained; and when Shlomo proposed an amount equal to the cost of the plants, this was agreed without a vote. In the next edition of the village bulletin Dov announced that compensation had been awarded to Josef, but added that no blame attached to Ilan for his part in the transaction.

This case was significant in showing the varying attitudes of village members to the village as a co-operative unit. And it also explicates the interpretation, over time, given to the role of the co-operative in the life of the village. As Almagor reminded the Council, the idea of the co-operative compensating individuals for mishaps had never arisen in the early days of settlement. This new development reflects the growing formalisation of agricultural production and economic affairs. In the past individual difficulties were helped by mutual or reciprocal aid on a personal basis between members, but increasingly this has been replaced by agencies and formal ties. This also reflected the changing nature of Kfar Hefer's production: the original settlers proposed a system of self-sufficiency in agriculture and on this the system of mixed farming was built. This has now changed to an emphasis on production for the market and now a farmer's livelihood comes in cash and not in kind. The decision was in line with these developments. But Dov saw this as another added burden on village administration and activities. In all important social characteristics Dov belonged to the group that was pressing for these changes but in his job as secretary he was conscious of the effects upon his tasks, and hence he opposed the motion.

The second case also concerns the village co-operative in its role as the guarantor of members' interests. This issue was raised by Ben in consultation with Dov. At a meeting of the Executive Dov announced the issue and said that Ben would explain it. Ben explained that the financial situation in Israel was that banks were no longer encouraging deposits. The rate of interest paid to depositors had fallen to 7 per cent and the rate to borrowers had fallen to 13 or 14 per cent. They in Kfar Hefer were now receiving a smaller amount of interest on their investments, but on money held in the village they were paying a high rate of 9 or 10 per cent, and they were charging 13 per cent on loans. He suggested that the village rates be brought into line with those of outside bodies. He proposed that they charge 11 per cent on loans and give 7 per cent on deposits. But difficulties would arise in operating the new rates because in some cases they had guaranteed the original returns to members for two years, and there were also some outsiders who had invested in the village. Dov then took up the argument and said that he did not think that they were bound by this agreement; after all the money situation had changed and the banks were now making re-adjustments. He did not think that the village could be accused of defaulting on its obligations. This proposal affected many members in the village; apart from those members who were in credit and kept their money in the village, most members were contributing to the savings fund which gave loans to the co-operative. Yoel, who was involved in the savings fund, objected, and said that it would be considered a default; the co-operative had made a decision and must stick by it. Oren agreed with this, as did Marks and Ori. Only Dov argued in favour of the scheme and in face of determined opposition he said that he would refer the matter to the Council.

At the next Council meeting Dov explained the matter to the assembled members, and then called upon Ben to elaborate the situation. After he had finished speaking Oren said that he had been thinking about the matter, and he thought they should hold the rates as they were for those who had given one-year loans, but reduce them for those people who had given two-year loans. They should inform all the outside holders of money who could decide whether they wished to withdraw from their agreements. This proposal was seconded by Yoel. Marks objected and said that an agreement was an agreement and the village should have the courage to stick by it. The word of the co-operative would be worthless if they changed their policies every moment. Dora also argued in favour of this point of view; she said that the co-operative had a duty to its members who held their money in the village and did not invest it outside as well they could have done. A vote was taken and the compromise solution of Oren and Yoel was accepted.

The three cases described in this chapter all deal with the internal secretary's relationship with individual members, with the Executive and with the Council In dealing with individual members the internal secretary can and does take action independently of these elected bodies, although he is accountable to them for his actions. I have shown how in the question involving the internal rights of members both the Council and the Executive overruled Dov; but how in the last case which involved the system 'external' to Kfar Hefer a compromise was reached.

The significance of this was seen in much of the village debate that went on concerning the Executive, the Council and the General Meeting. The Executive's relationship to the village was seen in the relationship between it and the *va'adat ha'bikoret* which was elected in the village in 1966/67. The duties of the *va'adat ha'bikoret* are to examine and scrutinise village administration, to see that decisions of the General Meeting are implemented and to act as a sort of ombudsman for village members who had grievances against the administration. Literally, the words *va'adat ha'bikoret* may be translated as 'criticising committee' but in the text I refer to it as a 'scrutinising committee'. The decision to set up this committee was of long standing; more than 30 years ago members had decided that such a committee should be established. Apparently abortive attempts had been made to introduce the committee but all these committees had failed to perform their duties, chiefly it was said because of the opposition of the Executive. On 31 October 1967, at the Annual General Meeting of the village, it was decided that a scrutinising committee should be elected and that this should be of three members. It was further decided that the members should be elected by ordinary vote from the assembly of the General Meeting, and each member should sit for two years. In a discussion about the functions of the committee it was laid down that the following five duties were to be performed by the members elected:

(1) The committee shall examine written decisions accepted in the General Meeting of the village members and those of the Council and the Executive;

(2) To examine, as they deem necessary, accounts, all aspects of financial affairs, the economics and administration of all village institutions;

(3) To examine the cash in hand of the Executive, the village store and the cultural committees;

(4) To check stocks in all the village supply stores;

(5) To report on their work in the village bulletin.

The following conditions were laid down for the work of the committee, requiring the Executive of the village:

(1) To write the decisions of the General Meeting and of Council in special separate books;

(2) To ensure that all village buildings, those standing and those to be built in the future, are available for stocks to be inspected;

(3) To give the committee, a financial budget, equal to an amount of half a day's work, for work done in inspection.

The meeting concluded by deciding that if the Executive debated any part of the findings of the scrutinising committee the decision must be passed on to the Council and on to the General Meeting. Finally, in 'special cases' in which discussions of Council discussions were examined, the scrutinising committee was empowered to call a General Meeting.

The same General Meeting also laid down precise conditions for the writing of minutes and the recording of meetings. At this General Meeting Dov's father complained that decisions which were made at one General Meeting were never carried out and at the next Annual General Meeting the same decisions were taken again. He was speaking in support of the scrutinising committee. Dov spoke against the formation of such a committee which he said was unnecessary in the village, and he denied that General Meeting decisions were not carried out. At this his father gave him as an example, a decision taken the previous year to examine stocks in the village supplies store, a decision which had just been passed again.

The three members elected to the scrutinising committee were Doron, now no longer involved in farming; Sonia Marks, the wife of Marks of the Executive committee; and Guy, a 'Kfar Hefer son-in-law', a former member of the Council and a farmer. Dov pledged his help to the committee in their activities.

From the beginning the scrutinising committee was beset with difficulties. Even though they had been given an outline of work by the General Meeting, they were unsure how to approach their enquiries, and at the beginning they spent much of their time enquiring how the system worked in other settlements who used it. At the end of December Doron reported to a General Meeting that in conjunction with several of the village committees they were engaged in studies of the village store, and the agricultural supply store. Moreover, he added, that they had decided that it was a *mitzva*, a point of honour, not to inquire into the Executive. This last remark caused a storm of protest from the assembly, for many of whom the whole point of a scrutinising committee was to act as a check on the Executive. Doron said that he thought they were merely quarrelling over words; the Executive was elected from a secret ballot of all members while the scrutinising committee was not elected in the same way and he did not think the scrutinising committee had any right to examine the Executive. But he concluded that this was a question for the village to decide and he did not want to interfere because of *shlom bait*, literally, 'peace in the house'. Jonathan, a second generation farmer who was known as a vociferous critic of administration and of office holders, said that the scrutinising committee was not simply a question of checking papers but he believed that they should also check decisions. Marks supported this and said that he believed that everything should be checked. He continued that the Executive was not sacred; indeed he thought that the scrutinising committee should begin its work by checking the Executive, the most influential body in village affairs. Doron announced that they had put up a notice asking anyone who had complaints about the running of village affairs to contact them, but no-one had come forward.

This is a characteristic feature of the village's life and other studies have shown it to be true in other communities.[1] Everyone 'knew' that 'things were wrong' in the village but were unwilling to come forward openly to identify themselves. Discussion usually went on informally among people who met socially or in the course of their work, and in meetings individuals did state their comments, but only if they knew that they had the backing of others. Similarly, even though articles in the village bulletin were written by individuals, the writers were careful to point out that their view was shared by others. It seems that in a life which is administratively defined as 'co-operative' and in which members themselves feel they should form a 'community', one member alone is unwilling to fight a battle. The few incidents known to me in the village of men pursuing objections alone have all concerned people who were 'marginal' to the village, in that they were non-farmers or only part-time farmers. There is, of course, sound reasoning behind this custom: it is easier for those attacked simply to dismiss a one-man grievance as self-interest or the pursuit of personal quarrels in a public sphere, a practice which is negatively sanctioned by moshav principles.

At the General Meeting I am reporting Doron announced that from their preliminary investigations, they already had some questions to ask Dov about the village store, and about the question of recording decisions, some of which were known to have been taken, but of which there were no records.

At a meeting of the village Executive Dov read out a letter which Doron had sent to him. This set out some of the above complaints but also referred to the decision of the General Meeting that the affairs of the internal secretary and the Executive should be examined. After finishing the letter, Dov said that he was not prepared to accept this. He had the Executive to keep him in order; the Executive had the Council; and there was a General Meeting, so they did not need the interference of another committee. Yoel agreed and said that

[1] See Frankenberg (1957) and Williams (1956)

M

it was not their job. Only Marks supported the view that the Executive should be open to scrutiny. But Yoel told him he was confusing two issues: no-one disputed the right to examine whether or not decisions were carried out, but no-one could question if decisions taken were the correct ones. This indeed was the crux of the matter. Dov explained it by saying that it would be impossible to work if every decision taken by the Executive was to be examined by the scrutinising committee. Sometimes decisions had to be reached quickly. In other cases they took decisions when not all the circumstances were known to them, and these only later came to light. Nothing would ever be achieved if they had to wait for an examination. Moreover, he said, it was not the right of the scrutinising committee to check decisions; only a general meeting of all members could do this. Marks then asked Dov what he was going to do about it and he answered that he would wait to see what happened; if Doron pursued the matter then he would tell him of his disagreement and if Doron wished he could take the issue to the Council and to a general meeting.

Doron did none of these things, and Dov did not press the issue. Failure to take action on specific issues, or the avoidance of action, is part of the strategy that the internal secretary uses to maintain his control and power in the village. In fact the imprecision of village records and indeed the failure to record certain decisions enable him to do this. He is helped by the facts that the collective memory is short in Kfar Hefer, and also that so few members attend the general meetings that many of the village are unaware that any decision has been taken. It is only when a new specific issue has been brought into prominence that past incidents are recalled and the actions of the Executive and the internal secretary are called into question. And in this case an appeal is made to village records which, as I have remarked, are usually open to many interpretations. In the case of the disagreement between Dov and his father, Dov interpreted a written record as being a 'suggestion' and not a binding decision.

The scrutinising committee itself was internally divided about its approach to the job, and Doron appeared before a General Meeting to ask for two more members to be elected to the committee so it could do its job efficiently. He suggested that Johnathan and Hadar, both young farmers, should be co-opted to the committee. This was accepted. Hadar was one of the organisers of the avocado scheme and was a Council member, and Jonathan was an outspoken critic of village affairs. He was chosen because Doron worked on the principle that the best way to disarm one's critics was to incorporate them into the scheme of things. This, however, proved to be a theory of doubtful validity; and at a General Meeting held in April 1968, Dov announced that Doron had resigned from the committee. Questions were asked about his reasons for leaving but Dov said that he had no information; Hadar was present at the meeting so members could ask him. Hadar replied that they should ask Doron. A member of the meeting called out that Doron had been appointed by the General Meeting and he should appear before a meeting to give his reasons for resignation. At this point Hadar gave Dov a letter that Doron had written to the scrutinising committee tendering his resignation. The text of the letter was that Doron apologised for not attending the committee meeting but he felt he could not be upset by any more disputes and he did not want anyone to leave the committee because of him and so he had no alternative but to resign. Shimoni spoke from the hall to say that obviously there were lots of things underfoot in the committee and they should not choose anyone else to fill Doron's place until they had received a full explanation. Hadar said that this was not necessary; Doron had resigned and that was that. On a vote, by a big majority, it was decided to invite Doron to a future meeting.

The following week Doron reluctantly appeared at the meeting. All the week he had been telling members that he would not appear and in fact an elderly non-farmer went to his house before the meeting to accompany him to the meeting. In his explanation Doron said that he did not feel happy in the committee especially as the Executive in Kfar Hefer did not look favourably upon the scrutinising committee. As an example he cited the committee's suggestion to the accounts department that all receipts should be stamped, according to accepted legal procedure. The chief accountant had agreed and had stamped the receipts; but Dov saw the stamps and, with scissors, had removed them all. Within the committee itself there had been a quarrel about the writing of the minutes. He wrote the minutes of the meetings after the meeting had finished and then sent each member a copy before the next meeting. Jonathan had objected to this and demanded that Doron be called to order at the next meeting. He could not stand any more disputes so he had offered his resignation.

Ben-Natan was the first to speak and he urged Doron to retract his resignation. Jonathan said that his dispute with Doron was personal and should not be subjected to enquiry. Dov said he was still doubtful of the value of the scrutinising committee in Kfar Hefer, but he was in no doubt of the importance of minutes in a meeting, and he felt Jonathan was justified in his actions. Doron replied by saying the real quarrel between him and Jonathan concerned the relationships between the scrutinising committee and the

Executive; he believed the scrutinising committee could only put pressure on the Executive, not interfere in its making of decisions as Jonathan and Hadar urged. Hadar said that this trouble had started even before Jonathan joined the committee so he was not to blame. Shimoni then proposed that even if Doron persisted in his resignation they should not elect anyone in his place. The motion was then put to the assembly, saying that Doron's resignation was accepted. By 34 votes to 7 this was rejected.

This incident showed a series of surprising alliances and tactics on the part of those involved. Dov's part in the affair showed, I believe, that while he could not openly refuse to co-operate with the scrutinising committee he could influence its functionings and direct its interest away from the Executive. In part he did this by direct interference: the removal of the stamps was in defiance of the committee, but it was in a sphere not involved with his functions. I suggest that by this action he attempted to employ the efforts of the committee solely on administrative duties and keep them away from the decision-making arena. In line with his policy he also actively co-operated with the committee and encouraged their examination of village stores and even suggested further lines of enquiry for them. In an Executive meeting, referred to earlier, he remarked that as long as the scrutinising committee kept to issues of stamps it was all right, and added humorously, that there are far worse things happening in Kfar Hefer than that. In view of this policy why did he then support Jonathan and Hadar (who were trying to investigate Executive affairs) in their attempt to oust Doron? I suggest two reasons for this. Firstly, I believe Dov saw Doron had been chosen as head of this committee because he was no longer closely involved in village affairs. As a secretary in the early days of Kfar Hefer he had been recognised as a just, if firm, administrator. Also in his work outside the village, both in the moshav movement and in his present job with an export board, he had gained knowledge of administration. Probably more than anyone else in the village he possessed the skills to investigate the Executive and the necessary social characteristics for his judgment to be accepted. Secondly, by his support of Jonathan and Hadar, Dov created a debt of obligation on their part. If this was not sufficient to curtail their stated aims of investigating his sphere of influence, they were more vulnerable to accusation of personal ambition and the pursuit of personal interests than was Doron. I have already referred to Jonathan as a known critic of Dov and the Executive. So the use of this line of attack, or defence, by Dov was likely to be sanctioned by the General Meeting. The attitude of the General Meeting supported the idea of a scrutinising committee, denounced the principle of pursuing personal quarrels, and upheld the communal principle. The report given by Doron, Jonathan and Hadar, of the meetings of the scrutinising committee shows that the meeting was seriously divided on its idea of its role. The question of the minutes was only a technical means of ousting Doron without acknowledging these differences.

The incident of the scrutinising committee reflected the concern and uneasiness about decision making and democratic processes that was felt in Kfar Hefer. If, as Walter Bagehot said, the English are born with a belief in 12 men, each with a pen and blotter, sitting around a table, in Kfar Hefer this belief took on the form of three or five moshavniks, spruce and tidy after work, sitting in committee. One of the noticeable features of Kfar Hefer's life during the period I spent in the village was the proliferation of committees. Almost every issue raised in the General Meetings was greeted with demands for a special committee to be set up, to investigate the affair thoroughly. At the time when I left the village there were some 28 committees which functioned regularly in addition to various ad-hoc committees which were not expected to continue. In part this was a desire to involve as many people as possible in the democratic process in Kfar Hefer, but I believe it reflected equally the doubts of Kfar Hefer's population about the suitability of existing frameworks of the moshav's government. Much of this doubt was directed against the Executive, and the setting up of a special committee to investigate the recommendations of the Executive not only challenged the power of the Executive, it served also to delay any decision. I shall argue that wherever disputes arose out of the conflict between different principles contained in moshav law, conflicts which members were reluctant to admit, there was a tendency to set up a special committee. It sometimes happened that the committee's findings came only after the issue had long ceased to be an issue in the village; here the appeal to democratic principles serve to legitimise the postponement of decision making.

In this chapter I have been concerned to show that various attempts were made to make the Executive accountable to the general public. Different interests have emerged in the village. These have been greatly influenced by trends to differential production, and factors 'external' to the village, notably the country's agricultural situation, have reinforced these trends. For most members the only way open for them to express their opinion is through the village bulletin or through the General Meeting of the village. But grave doubts were expressed about the General Meeting as an effective instrument of public opinion.

The most common complaint about the General Meeting was that few attended. In legislation for co-operative settlements laid down in the time of the British Mandate, the quorum for meetings is 50 members. If, at the first meeting, there is no quorum, then a notice must be posted to this effect prior to a second meeting, at which any number of members is legally empowered to take and to enforce decisions. It was only the exceptional meeting in Kfar Hefer that attracted more than 50 members. After I had been a regular attender at these meetings for several months even I was counted, jokingly, amongst those present, though not as a whole person. Initially I was counted as a 'half': then after protestations on my behalf that I was among the most regular attenders, my standing was increased to 'three-quarters'. But even with this most meetings were far from reaching a quorum.

Most meetings which were intended to be of an informatory nature did take place despite the lack of quorum. More important meetings at which village policy was discussed were many times postponed because of the small attendance. One, concerning village taxes, was delayed three times because, despite the legal basis for the second meeting, those present felt that such an important decision should be made by more than the 19 members present.

Another feature of village General Meetings was that they almost never started promptly. Meetings were generally scheduled to start at 9 p.m. but seldom got under way until 20 minutes later. Much of the time was spent waiting for members to arrive. Even if it was felt that a satisfactory number were present, there was no guarantee that the number would remain until the end of the meeting; there was a good deal of coming and going during most meetings. The one occasion during my stay in the village when a meeting, which involved an outside speaker, did start on time, caused cries of complaint from late arrivals who said that they should have been informed that the meeting was going to start at nine o'clock as announced. Unpunctuality is not an essential characteristic of Kfar Hefer, since Executive meetings always started promptly, but it is indicative of an attitude towards the General Meeting. This was expressed in an article written by a first generation woman in the village bulletin. She wrote that on her way home from a meeting which had failed to take place because too few had attended, she met a group of young people and asked why they had not been at the meeting. She reported them as replying: 'Whom does it interest, who needs it?' Complaints about village apathy, especially of the 'young', in regard to the General Meeting were commonplace in Kfar Hefer. In the village bulletin many first generation members pointed out the curious situation that the most regular attenders at meetings were first generation members, many of whom were no longer active in farming.

In the article referred to above the writer continued by saying that no-one disagreed with the fact that the General Meeting is the highest instrument of the village both in making and abolishing decisions. However, she added, if the General Meeting had only as many members attending as those who attend the Council, then the General Meeting had even less value than the Council, because this body was at least chosen by members to take decisions.

The same issue of the bulletin contained an editorial on the subject. The editor said that the number attending village meetings was only about 10 per cent of those eligible. He cited the case of the meeting to discuss taxes and dismissed the voting on this issue, as, 'like the result of a girls' basketball match, of the lowest level'. Those members who did come to meetings, he said, were the ones who had grown accustomed to spending their Saturday evenings in the community hall. Furthermore, he added, very many important decisions were taken by 'accident'; a motion could be passed by a few interested people while the rest remained apathetic and 'let it go'. 'The village meeting in our village has gone bankrupt and a new alternative, both efficient and democratic is needed.' He suggested in place of the General Meeting a body which he called the 'representative' committee. This council should be composed of 20–30 members who would, 'discuss, decide and direct the Executive committee' and provide a balance in the democratic structure of the village. Support was given to this scheme by Dov, in a formal interview with the editor, reported in the village bulletin. He agreed that decisions taken in the General Meeting were the most democratic, and the most desirable. Yet, he pointed out that, save for one or two meetings a year, the General Meeting had ceased to exist. Not all members shared this view and at a General Meeting which proposed to move the Annual General Meeting from the beginning of the Jewish year (around September) to December, strong opposition was expressed by several elderly members. They said that the General Meeting had always been at New Year. But it was not only the traditionalists who opposed the move; others pointed out that whenever General Meetings were held, members simply did not come. Therefore they argued, the reason for apathy lay deeper than the timing of meetings. Opponents of the move to abolish the General Meeting wrote that this was one of the most important ways in which a member attending General Meetings exercised his right to express an opinion and to question actions taken in the village. Others agreed that the number attending General Meetings was small but argued that the village could not deprive those who wish to exercise their rights simply because most people did not.

It was often said, as a joke, among those waiting for a quorum in order to start a meeting that this was a good sign. They interpreted lack of interest in the General Meeting as a lack of problems on the part of members, and said they would soon come back if they had any objections. This, I believe, was an over-optimistic view. This and the previous chapter have shown that there were a good many people in Kfar Hefer who were disturbed both about their personal situation and about the situation in the village. The nostalgic memories of the first generation about the packed general meetings of past years, overlooked the shift in power, which had moved from the General Meeting to the two secretaries and the Executive, and from the village to the central bureaucratic bodies. The descriptions in this chapter have shown that the information which was retained in the persons of the secretaries and of the Executive was of greater significance than that which filtered down to the General Meeting. This was the context in which the disputes about the scrutinising committee took place. The General Meeting was designed to formulate policy for the village, but policy-making could not take place in a vacuum. It was linked to the wider environment in which Kfar Hefer was set. The roles of the internal and external secretary which were the formal articulating offices with this wider system played the decisive part in fixing a balance between these two sets of relationships. The discussions in Chapter V have shown how this was achieved in the economic sphere: a system of internal differentiation enabled the village, as a whole, to withstand the effects of external policy. I consider that in the legislative and executive sphere this was achieved by the decline in influence of the General Meeting and a corresponding gain by the formally designated 'Executive'. Of course there existed a series of 'checks and balances' against this process, but here the General Meeting played only a small part. The development of a series of different interest groups within the village, many of whom held contradictory views about desirable village policies again contributed to the decline of the General Meeting as an effective forum. And I suggest that the development of the two schemes described in Chapter VI can be seen not only as an economic protest but also as a political protest: the only way these members could make their views felt in the village was in the economic sphere.

Apart from the administrative checks on the Executive by the Council and by the Executive on the internal secretary, most of the other 'checks and balances' were personal efforts by individual members. Here I think that it is significant that the overwhelming view of the village was that the village secretary should be selected from village members. In his interview with the editor of the village bulletin Dov firmly stated his belief that the secretary must be someone from the village. And he added that three to four years is the best time for a person to serve in the appointment. His reasons for this statement were that it takes time for an individual to learn the duties of an internal secretary, but that to remain longer in the role would make it a 'job' and an occupant of the role would forget his links with the village. (Here the word 'job' probably has a special Israeli connotation, derived from the army. A 'job' is an easy task, with the implication that the holder of the job is shirking service.) I consider that the evidence from Kfar Hefer shows that it is very difficult for an internal secretary to 'forget' his links with the village. It is the constant reminders by the village members that serve as the most influential check upon the performance of his duties. The nature of the role which brings him constantly into contact with village members, both personally and in the taking of decisions which affect their lives, reminds him that he is one of the village, a little different perhaps, but none the less one of the village. In a similar way members of the village expressed the same opinion in the village bulletin. Arad wrote, 'It is easier to find a Prime Minister or a member of the *Knesset* in Kfar Hefer than it is to find a good internal secretary.'[1] The demands and the expectations of an internal secretary held by the village members make the above opinion a masterly understatement. One member wrote that the internal secretary must pay heed to all the differing views and approaches to village events and come to a decision satisfying all. This is in addition to his tasks of consulting village committees, administering village affairs, dealing with outside organisations, and ensuring the welfare of all Kfar Hefer's members. In an earlier chapter I have reported the differences between the 'social' and the 'economic' committees in the early days of settlement. Now the village has vested all these tasks in a single person and expect him to carry them all out efficiently. Thus, the internal secretary has to deal with two problems. Firstly, there is the problem of the large amount of work involved in the task. Secondly, in this work the secretary is expected to satisfy the impossible demands of the village members (the requirement that he should satisfy all).

In the recent past two attempts have been made to employ a village internal secretary from outside Kfar Hefer. Both have failed. In one case the holder of the office was dismissed; in the second case he

[1] Kfar Hefer village bulletin, August 1968

resigned despite a vote of confidence by the General Meeting. When I asked members why these men had failed to hold office, two replies were given. One said that an outsider cannot understand Kfar Hefer, the other said that the 'young' of the village had 'got him out'. I think that these comments can be understood by the nature of the pressures that are applied by members on an internal secretary. These were described in the following way, '. . . there are times when the members of the village behave towards the secretary in a way that members of the village understand but would be difficult for others to bear'.[1]

The greater part of the working life and social life of Kfar Hefer's first generation has been spent together. The nature of the moshav demands a minimum consensus on co-operation and mutual aid. Those who remained in Kfar Hefer were to a large extent a self-selected group, since those who opposed the ideals or could not reach a compromise left the village. The second generation remaining in Kfar Hefer have shared together similar experiences: their education and their social life were spent together. Members shared a common culture and experience; individual idiosyncrasies and past lives were shared as 'common property' by all members. An individual's life was lived not only within his own family but also within the village. The consequence of many relationships—kinship ties, economic ties, leisure activities, shared education—all reinforce the idea held in Kfar Hefer that the village is a 'community'. These multifarious ties have grown up and operate within the administratively defined areas of co-operation in the moshav. This is both the strength and weakness of village members; and this may be seen in the role of internal secretary. Individual demands or requests to the internal secretary were seldom single-stranded: they involved incidents from the past of shared experiences or tried to exploit personal attributes or characteristics. An internal secretary who has grown up in this culture and in his everyday life is part of these numerous sets of relationships, is subjected to the pressures and obligations that these involve. Rarely are these obligations made explicit; it is enough for the suitor or complainant merely to indicate his thoughts and the knowledge that these references are part of the secretary's life experience is enough for them to be effective. Indeed to state them bluntly would be to nullify their effect, for this then falls under the rubric of 'personal interest' which, as I have shown, is denounced both by the moshav constitution and by the members of Kfar Hefer. In some ways this resembles the pattern of 'joking relationships' described for other societies;[2] and as long as members 'play the game' then a solution

[1] Kfar Hefer village bulletin, August 1968   [2] Colson (1953)

may be found. A person external to Kfar Hefer is not and cannot be involved in this process; and even though he may be willing and anxious to carry out his job successfully he is cut off from one of the essential tools of success. This I believe may explain the failure of both 'outside' secretaries in Kfar Hefer. In the absence of these relationships he can only use the formal lines of administration and his technical skills. But these are crude and inefficient tools compared with the delicate skills of using social relationships.

In addition an 'outsider' is unable to use these relationships, and does not have the flexibility of multifarious ties. For it is part of the strength of an inside secretary that he too can use his experience and knowledge of village members to pursue his policies. I do not know the detailed circumstances concerning the two 'outside' secretaries in Kfar Hefer, but I tentatively suggest that they failed in their jobs because they could work only in economic terms with village members. It was said that the 'young' of Kfar Hefer were responsible for the departure of one man. The use of the 'young' to defend and re-affirm values in a community has been described elsewhere.[1] The young are the transmitters in some situations of community culture learnt from the old and in this case because the 'outsider' was a young man, it was appropriate that the 'young' should be the ones to oppose him. Although I have shown that there were disputes between the 'young' and the 'old' of Kfar Hefer concerning their different interpretations of their shared culture, certain tenets are held, without dissension by all village members. Amongst these is the ideal of village democracy, the accountability of village office holders to the general public, and the equality of all members. In this case the accusations of the 'young' which alleged favouritism on the part of the internal secretary and failure to consult village opinion, rested on the above list of unimpeachable values of Kfar Hefer.

Dov's relationship to members showed all these characteristics and perhaps explains his remarks to me that: 'Specialists [economists and advisers] are all right for giving advice but they never solve anything.' I have already described how criticisms of the internal secretary were expressed in personal terms. This, I argue, was the natural outcome of the content of the individual's relationships to the office of internal secretary. The complaint was often expressed that, 'those who know how to bang on the table' are the ones who are successful in gaining benefits within the village. I suggest a rephrasing of this, to say that those who knew how to mobilise and manipulate personal relationships in the context of a shared heritage

[1] Rees, *Life in a Welsh Countryside* (1951)

and culture did not have to bang on the table; those without this ability had to resort to this.

The ties are suitable for individual dealings but in a group context they lose their effectiveness. I consider that this is what roused the concern of Kfar Hefer: that as individuals they could control the Executive, but in groups, where issues had to be stated in broad terms of principle, they lost this control. Furthermore I suggest that the increasing pressure of external events upon Kfar Hefer also circumscribed the use of these controls. The internal secretary's area of discretion was impinged upon by the imposition of government control on the internal affairs of the village. This may also explain Ben's success in his role; he had little contact with village members who did not see revealed the effects of his decisions on policy making and he was not subjected to the same demands as the former 'outside' village secretaries.

In this chapter I have attempted to show the workings of village administration in Kfar Hefer. Many members were disturbed by the power which was vested in the Executive and their lack of control over affairs. I have argued that this disturbance of mind resulted from several processes: the division of interests among the members of Kfar Hefer; the increasing importance of factors 'external' to Kfar Hefer for its internal policy; and with this the diminishing applicability of 'individual' control over the Executive. The decision to set up the scrutinising committee was a result of these processes. The disputes both within and outside this committee reflect this theme. But in itself the committee could only deal with the 'symptoms' and not the cause of these processes; the establishment of a 'scrutinising committee' could not reverse the process of increasing outside control on the village.

VII

Politics, government and administration

Previous chapters have been concerned with relationships inside
Kfar Hefer, and the wider 'external' system has only been incorporated selectively into that discussion. This chapter attempts to
place Kfar Hefer in its wider context, and to analyse village links
with government, municipal and moshav organisations. Some of
these links are purely economic in content; others, like those with
the Moshav Movement and the Regional Council, involve social
and cultural activities.

I have earlier referred to the determination of overall agricultural
policy in Israel. Many agencies and departments are involved in
making this policy and producers can exert influence and pressure
on them in many ways. The Ministry of Agriculture is involved in
all phases of taking decisions and in regulating prices. The Minister
of Agriculture and the Head of Central Planning (a position once
occupied by a son of Kfar Hefer) participate in top-level discussions. Representatives of the various moshav and kibbuts federations
and private farming are consulted. The marketing boards for agricultural production, *Tnuva* (marketing), and regional associations
also take part in discussions.

In the past and in the present Kfar Hefer has been represented in
many of these organisations. This representation takes several forms,
including the straightforward sending of delegates to represent the
village in organisations, the holding of important positions by delegates in influential committees, and the occupation by some members
of Kfar Hefer of key roles in organisations as full-time employees
of the organisations.

The first of these, the sending of delegates to organisations, is
open to any settlement, but it is the holding of important political
and administrative positions that is desired by Kfar Hefer. In part
this is because they wish to present their opinions and press for
the action most favourable to the village. But 'having a man in
the right place' is more than this: the power and influence residing
in an office holder can often save the village much time and expense in other fields. Simply knowing whom to approach about
problems can ease difficulties; and in the labyrinth of committees
and offices involved in agricultural and economic policy, spheres of
responsibility are often unclear. Thus these positions are favoured
both for their potential use in propounding the village's interest, and
for the information vested in them. In the case of full-time employees

in certain organisations the village is concerned that the links with the village are not allowed to lapse so the office-holder does not disregard his ties to the village. The village did not try actively, in all cases, to get Kfar Hefer members into positions of influence. In some cases the initiative came from the organisation, which invited applications. It frequently happened that the initiative was taken by the individual. Many of Kfar Hefer's representatives in the recent past have been members of the first generation whose sons have taken over the farm, enabling their elders to seek work outside the village. The early founding of Kfar Hefer gave them an advantage, for often these members had been active in village and national affairs, and had had previous contact with outside bodies. An example of this is Reuven's father (see Chapter V) who until his death was one of the chief executives in *Tnuva* in Tel Aviv. He had served the village in the Executive as the member responsible for external affairs. When eventually he failed to be re-elected, he took the job with *Tnuva*. Doron now works for an export board in a town close to Kfar Hefer: he had formerly many outside connections, especially in his work connected with the Moshav Movement. When his son took over full-time running of the farm Doron took a job outside the village. In another case a member whose only son died took on a job outside the village with the Ministry of Agriculture.

Strictly speaking it is forbidden for moshav members to take on outside work, but jobs with government agencies or occupations linked to moshavim are felt to be qualitatively different from other work outside the village. Even if the member did not take on the job as a delegate of Kfar Hefer, he is expected to act as such by village members. It is considered natural that he should be concerned to promote the village's interests. These expectations are not always, if ever, fulfilled. In discussing an appointment to the Regional Council Dov complained that none of their members in full-time employment in outside agencies had done anything for the village. Nevertheless it is considered to the village's advantage that both delegates and 'outside' workers should occupy influential positions, as potential, if not actual, representatives of Kfar Hefer.

In an earlier chapter I have described Kfar Hefer's involvement in 'national' organisations both before and after the State was established, and its influential role in determining public and national policy. In more recent years the village's range of influence has diminished. This is partly due to the growth of other forces in national life which have superseded past considerations. The growth of professionalism and technical skills in government and administration have lessened the part that unqualified advisers can play in deciding affairs. Factors external to Israel, political and economic, have caused an internal re-adjustment of structures of power: thus the individual moshav is affected not only by local policy but it is also involved in the context of world markets. Changes within Kfar Hefer have also affected the village's representations in outside bodies. Young farmers who have the main task of providing for both the family of origin and the family of procreation on a farm cannot afford the time to devote to outside bodies. Elderly farmers whose sons work the farm may be appointed as village representatives but are not likely to be employed by outside bodies. The increase and the variety of interests that have developed since Statehood within government and moshav agencies have also affected the role which Kfar Hefer plays in these movements. The Moshav Movement to which Kfar Hefer is affiliated is now overwhelmingly composed of 'young' (post-state) settlements whose interests are different from those of old-established settlements. Kfar Hefer is not only in competition with other types of settlement in promoting her interests; there is also more competition between moshavim.

Ben, the external secretary, and Dov, the internal secretary, are most commonly the delegates to outside bodies. The choice of others is said to be in the hand of the General Meeting but usually they are chosen by the Executive. This causes complaints in the village, and members argue that sometimes the delegates chosen do not represent village opinion. Later in this chapter I refer to a case based on this accusation. When I came to the village in 1966 the village had full-time employees in *Tnuva* and in the Ministry of Agriculture as representatives of the moshavim. Both these members have died and the positions have not been filled from Kfar Hefer. Apart from these two individuals, the village had members working in the Ministry of Agriculture, in the Moshav Movement, and in the export section of *Tnuva*. The village had a member of *Knesset*, formerly a representative of Rafi[1], now of the new alignment Labour Party. Village sons now no longer living in the village are counted by the village as 'their men' in office. In this, one 'son of Kfar Hefer' is regarded as especially important: in the past he worked for the Moshav Movement, then he moved to the Ministry of Agriculture, and now he is an important figure in the *Histadrut* as the representative of the new Labour Party.

As a result of her history and importance in pre-state affairs Kfar Hefer's members have associations with many members of collective settlements and their sons. These ties may be very tenuous, but they

[1] Rafi: A breakaway party from *Mapai*, now recently united in a new labour party with *Mapai*, *Achdut Avoda* and aligned with *Mapam*

are potential points of pressure. The secession of *Rafi* from *Mapai* took place before I came to Kfar Hefer, but the alignment took place during the time I was in the village. Before the secession the village was overwhelmingly *Mapai*, and party subscriptions were automatically deducted from each member's account in the co-operative. The villagers are members of the Moshav Movement which was associated with *Mapai*, and villagers are members of the Mapai-controlled *Histadrut*. Much of their economic life is associated with *Mapai*-dominated marketing agencies and boards. I was told that when the secession of *Rafi* took place this was expected to have severe repercussions in the village. Zioni, the head of the Regional Council, and a member of Kfar Hefer, supported *Rafi*; and one of the leaders of *Mapai* in the village was reported as saying that they would have to ensure his removal. Zioni stayed on in the job and the rift in the party was afterwards described as having 'made no difference in Kfar Hefer'. Sometimes it was acknowledged that 'perhaps some people are less friendly with each other' but this was said to be minimal. Sixty-four of the families in Kfar Hefer had at least one member of *Rafi*, but this does not mean that the remaining families were *Mapai*. In fact in the one election held after the party split, the voting in the village was almost equal, with *Mapai* just having the edge. *Rafi* members had to make a definite statement that they supported the party and did not want to pay subscriptions to *Mapai*. The *Mapai* list works on the assumption that all Kfar members are *Mapai* unless they specifically state that they are not. In some cases this means that the *Mapai* list contains *Rafi* sympathisers who do not want publically to show their support and politically apathetic members who may not support *Mapai*. There were one or two members in Kfar Hefer who worked in *Mapai*-controlled agencies and departments at the time of the split, for example in the Jewish Agency, and they did not want publicly to announce their support for *Rafi*. In another case a man's wife worked for a *Mapai*-controlled women's organisation: he told me he was a *Rafi* sympathiser but did not want to acknowledge this because of his wife's job. Doron solved the problem by paying subscriptions to both parties, and on the election day lent his car to both parties equally. I believe that initially people were uncertain about the effect of the split on the village but as control in the country remained with *Mapai*, the main party in the government coalition, they felt little change in their lives.

Dov and his father were both *Mapai* supporters and the father organised the *Mapai* campaign in the village for the election. His membership may have affected Dov's dealings with *Mapai*-controlled agencies and boards, and this may have been a factor in his election to the position of internal secretary. Ben also was a listed supporter of *Mapai*, so both the main agents of Kfar Hefer's links to the wider sphere were members of the country's dominant party. In elections for internal committees and the Council of Kfar Hefer I can find no evidence that party membership played a part in election. But in the village's relationships with outside bodies this did play a part. After the formation of the new Labour Party Dov remarked that he believed that it would be easier for Kfar Hefer to fill positions outside the village now the political differences were over. Dov was speaking about his concern that Kfar Hefer's members no longer played an active part in outside bodies. He referred to the two positions, in *Tnuva* and in the Ministry of Agriculture, formerly filled by Kfar Hefer members, and said that even though the village had been approached to find substitutes they had not been successful. Indeed after the reunion of *Rafi* and *Mapai* in the new party, a village member who worked in the Moshav Movement was promoted to be head of planning in the Movement. This young man was a known supporter of *Rafi* and it was felt in the village that it was not coincidental that his promotion came immediately after the formation of the new party.

Kfar Hefer conceived of most of her outside ties in purely economic terms. Ben's positions in the Moshav Movement and in the marketing boards were means whereby moshavim in general and Kfar Hefer in particular could get the best terms for production. But the village could not rely upon membership in one organisation to achieve this, and Kfar Hefer is connected with several organisations. The structure of decision-making in Israel is, as I have shown, open to pressure and influence at many points. The variety of interests in any one association formed as a pressure group may result in the interests of some members being overruled by those of others. Kfar Hefer tried to guard against this by having a multiplicity of ties with several associations, many of which might seem to serve the same general purpose. Thus the village was a member of the Moshav Movement, member of an association of local moshavim, member of the Regional Council, member of marketing boards, and member of marketing associations. From time to time at meetings, village members questioned the membership of all these organisations and said that they were not necessary because Kfar Hefer got nothing out of them. I consider that the multiplicity of ties served to reinforce pressures made by the village. If in one area the village failed in its demands there remained other associations through which the same demands, but with a different emphasis, could be made. In locally based associations Kfar Hefer, because of her historical predomi-

N

nance and greater productivity, nominally took the lead. In the Moshav Movement, these two factors also played an important part, but in this arena Kfar Hefer was handicapped because the 'new' moshavim greatly outnumbered the 'old'. Until very recently the 'young' and the 'old' moshavim saw themselves in opposition. The 'old' moshavim were the big producers who were trying to expand even further, while 'young' moshavim were trying to make a living from insufficient means of production. This picture was modified slightly because some of the 'young' moshavim have now become big producers. Yet there still remained a division expressed to me by Ben as, 'the big producers feel they subsidise the rest; the rest feel that they are downtrodden'. In part this was competition for quotas but also until very recently this was the division between creditors and debtors. The Moshav Movement ran a system of loans from the financially secure moshavim to those in difficulty. These loans were at very favourable rates of interest, but moshavim like Kfar Hefer could have used this capital to gain higher interest rates elsewhere. In this instance membership in the Moshav Movement was not selective and Kfar Hefer needed the Movement as a pressure group, but they tried to keep their participation in the loan scheme to a minimum. Another facet of the different interests within the movement was that Kfar Hefer's interests often had more in common with settlements outside the Movement than those within. As a big producer Kfar Hefer's interests were linked with those of other big producers, notably kibbutsim, and not with the majority of their fellow moshavim. An official of the movement in a talk given in Kfar Hefer acknowledged that probably the Moshav Movement needed a new structure. He suggested a union of all farmers; but existing federations are based on national party lines and it is difficult to alter the set-up.

In some cases this indebtedness by virtue of membership in large organisations caused disputes within Kfar Hefer. This happened when the individual farmer was personally indebted to the organisation. An illustration of this is the village's relationship with *Tnuva*, the dairy marketing board. *Tnuva* is the biggest marketing agency in the country and takes all Kfar Hefer's milk production. The individual producer paid a 'forced loan' every year to the organisation to cover administrative costs. The size of the loan depended upon the amount of produce marketed, and Kfar Hefer's members as big producers were big contributors. This loan was paid regardless of the individual's financial state and so it frequently happened that members in the village were paying interest on the loan they gave to *Tnuva*. This caused considerable complaints within the village, and from time to time members urged the Executive to take action to remedy this. However, Kfar Hefer was dependent upon the services of *Tnuva* and therefore was compelled to accede to its demands. For the individual member this grievance is aggravated because *Tnuva* does not pay back these loans to individuals. Only if the whole village leaves the organisation is the sum repaid. The village can always employ the threat of withdrawing from these organisations, but as *Tnuva* is a subsidiary of the Histadrut thus leaving *Tnuva* means more than changing the marketing organisation, and so there is little that the village can do.

In the marketing of turkeys the village does not belong to any organisation. This is organised by the village Executive, especially by Ben, the external secretary. Kfar Hefer as I have pointed out is a relative newcomer to this branch and the 'numbers' involved are relatively small. As a small producer in organisations the village would have to accept and not determine conditions, and so the village preferred to deal with this herself rather than be involved in the obligations inherent in group membership.

Similarly, in the marketing of cattle for slaughter Kfar Hefer preferred to join a 'private', though government-supported, agency, rather than accept the conditions offered by regional boards or by *Tnuva*. Village discussion of this project brings to light the views of individual members and of the Executive committee in their relationships with marketing agencies. This agency, *Marbek*, was originally intended to serve settlements in the southern region of Israel. Each would hold shares in it and they would gain a return according to the numbers of shares held. The venture did not work out as planned because salesmen operating individually in this area offered better terms to settlements than those offered by *Marbek*. So the venture decided to market the produce of all settlements joining the scheme. Kfar Hefer joined the scheme because as a recent and small producer she felt she did not get favourable terms from the regional agency. When the village joined the scheme each member paid a contribution at the rate of IL.30 per cow per farm; later *Marbek* demanded increased donations from those using the services. *Marbek* never had enough investment to cover its costs and they applied for a bank loan from the Bank of Israel. This was agreed to, but on the condition that the agency became at least 25 per cent self-financing. Therefore *Marbek* applied to its subscribers to raise the sum of money paid into the scheme. This could be paid over a number of years, but interest would be paid on the debt by the debtor. Dov reported that he as the village's delegate proposed that the amount should be raised to only IL.50 per cow but he had been overruled.

When this issue was discussed in the village Executive the point in debate was the length of time that Kfar Hefer should take to pay off the investment. Dov proposed a period of 12 years, but Ben and Marks wanted to pay it off quickly in five years. Eventually a compromise was reached of seven to eight years. However, when this was reported to the General Meeting the debate took a completely different line. Here members disputed the increase in donations. One first generation member stated flatly that he was opposed to any increase of investment in *Marbek*. The village should tell the agency that they would continue to market according to the shares they already held, and if *Marbek* did not agree then the village should withdraw from the scheme. This man said that he wanted the maximum return on his cattle and he was not sure that *Marbek* gave it. Jonathan supported him and argued that Kfar Hefer is a 'strong moshav' and they could put pressure on *Marbek* to accept their terms. He went on to criticise the joining of *Marbek* and said that the majority of the village were opposed. He said that agreement had been given because a member of the Executive had given them information that indicated they would get better terms. This evidence had proved to be inaccurate. He failed to see why Kfar Hefer should help *Marbek* out of a difficult situation; they did not want to build 'another *Tnuva*'. Emanuel, a farmer with a large dairy and cattle holding, took up this criticism of the Executive. Speaking to Dov, he said that it was natural that when one sat on the board of an organisation one did not see its faults. He urged that there should be no additional payment. Kfar Hefer already had IL.27,000 invested in *Marbek* and they could negotiate from this. Dov rose to say that the extra dues would automatically be deducted by *Marbek*, starting at the beginning of the next month. Shimoni also opposed the increase in investment in *Marbek* and said that the village should deal with salesmen as they did in the marketing of turkeys. He added that none of the surrounding settlements were in *Marbek* or in other organisations, and they organised their sales with agents. Yoel answered that *Marbek* gave good service to Kfar Hefer, especially as the cattle they sent for slaughter were not of good quality. Emanuel then proposed that they set up a committee to investigate the affair. Marks objected and said that they should come to a decision there and then: the majority of settlements in *Marbek* were opposed to Kfar Hefer and Dov had to know the line he had to take. When it was put to the vote it was decided to postpone the decision and to elect a committee. Three members, Emanuel, Yoel and one other young farmer, were chosen to form the committee.

Much of the above discussion can be interpreted in the terms suggested in the last chapter, the struggle by members to control Executive action, expressed by Emanuel when he reminded Dov that his most important duties were to the village. Aside from these points the discussion showed both the village members' and the Executive's attitude to outside bodies. Both expressed the belief that Kfar Hefer as a big producer and a financially stable moshav should be able to get better terms from organisations. They supported co-operative ventures outside the village as long as these gave favourable conditions to the village, and the individual farmer was more concerned with his immediate price than the support of co-operative ventures. The launching of co-operative ventures was viewed by members in the short-term, an attitude expressed to me by Ben as: 'All Kfar Hefer are interested in is getting a few more agorot per kilo than Gavish.' I do not think that this attitude was due to a lack of foresight on the part of Kfar Hefer's farmers, nor a lack of understanding of financing. They were concerned with the short-term because events in the present showed that long-term planning on the national level was a chancy and unreliable procedure. They had been encouraged to increase dairy and poultry production but within a couple of years they were now suffering penalties on this production because of the changed national situation. Dov and Ben had the task of ensuring good returns for the members and of establishing security for production. This difficulty showed up most clearly in organisations like *Marbek* where Kfar Hefer was a new member and could not persuade from strength. In associations where the village was established and held a big share of the market the situation was easier, but here again the village was concerned to keep her co-operative financing to a minimum. In this the assets held by the village played an important part. These had been built up over the years in various associations, including banks, and this enabled the village to maintain a certain independence from the pressure of any one organisation.

Kfar Hefer's pursuit of independent action within all co-operative frameworks outside the village is revealed in her attitude to the Moshav Movement. This organisation is conceived by its officers as not simply a pressure group for the interests of moshavim, but also as a social and cultural entity, dealing with the affiliated settlements. The aim is to extend the tenets of individual moshav life to an inter-moshav level. Within the Movement there are departments dealing with moshav law, culture and education, and with the conditions of employment for moshav workers. The 'committee for law' in the Moshav Movement is concerned with national laws covering co-operative settlements but also is empowered to settle disputes between moshavim and between individuals and their moshav. Kfar

Hefer in the past was involved in a lengthy dispute with this committee concerning the rights of 'agricultural members' who also worked in public administration as hired workers. The outcome of the 'trial' has affected both the position of these members in the co-operative and the attitude of Kfar Hefer towards activities of the Movement in non-economic spheres.

The members concerned fell between the two main categories of 'agricultural members' and 'professional members'. The salaries of professional members are laid down by the Histadrut and there is also a union '*Otsem*',[1] for workers in moshavim. The village cannot change salary rates for these workers and must abide by laws of compensation, sick benefits and holiday times. The position of hired workers who are also agricultural members is not so clear: they are members of the co-operative and do not have membership in *Otsem*. The rights of these workers came under discussion when one of those concerned learnt that they were paid less than workers in other settlements. He appeared before the Executive but the internal secretary, himself a hired worker, said he could not deal with the problem because he would be accused of personal interest. The issue went before the Council which appointed two members to investigate the complaint. In November 1956, on the report of these two men, it was decided to pay an additional IL.25 per month to all hired workers. In January 1957, a farmer in Kfar Hefer called a General Meeting to discuss the situation, by which, he alleged, these hired workers were making more than farmers. After a discussion it was decided to withdraw the supplement which had been received for three months. In March the workers applied for an enquiry, but this was refused, though it was agreed that the issue again be returned to a General Meeting.

At the Annual General Meeting held in September 1958, the whole issue of the position of hired workers was discussed. Those in favour of the increase said that the agricultural members employed by the village were paying more per day to the hired labour who worked their fields than they were receiving. The hired workers argued that while professional members, as members of *Otsem*, received increases, members of the co-operative employed in similar work did not. This sometimes resulted in the anomaly that the manager of a store, an agricultural member, received less than the worker members of *Otsem*. The opponents argued that agricultural members also had an income from agriculture and they expressed a view which implicitly stated the primacy of agriculture in the village. They argued that

[1] '*Otsem*' is derived from the initial letters in Hebrew of 'Public Workers in a Moshav'

membership in the co-operative more than compensated for lower earnings. In the early days of settlement this attitude was prevalent towards professional members of the moshav. Willner sees the moshav's belief that 'losses of income would be more than compensated by the advantages of membership' as, 'an indication of the naïvete of moshav members and planners and ideologists in regard to differences of interests inherent in the division of labour in the moshav situation'.[1] This was the attitude of the workers' opponents, while the workers argued that they should be paid the rate for the job.

The debate in the Annual General Meeting was inconclusive and the question was referred back to the Council. In December 1958, the Council decided that workers should be paid a graded salary on *Histadrut* rates, according to the rate for a bachelor. The management committee was given the responsibility of deciding the grades, but when its suggestion was considered in the Council, the decision was to down-grade the workers. In 1962 a national special enquiry commission recommended that salaries should be paid to these workers according to the type of work, not inclusive of seniority payments and family allowances. They should receive at least 14 days holiday per year, 7 of which were to be paid. Cost-of-living allowances were to be automatic and contributions to the savings fund should be paid from salaries, in addition to those paid from income earned in agriculture. This was recommended for acceptance in Kfar Hefer but the Council voted against it by seven votes to six. In July 1962, the workers concerned decided to refer the whole question to the Moshav Movement and to have a moshav 'trial' under the auspices of the movement.

This decision brought the dispute openly into the public sphere. But within the Moshav Movement there were differences in opinion and the case dragged on for several years. Then in 1965, Allon, as Minister of Labour, was instrumental in passing a law giving compensation to hired workers dismissed from their jobs. Kfar Hefer became alarmed that they would have to pay compensation to hired workers, and also to those who were agricultural members. The Moshav Movement informed each settlement that they should come to an agreement with their workers in lieu of compensation. If they failed to reach an agreement they should go to a 'trial' in the Moshav Movement. The movement would have to give a decision within three months of the completion of the case.

Concurrently with the trial in the Moshav Movement discussions also went on inside the village. The members received a letter for

[1] Willner (1960)

signature from the Executive saying that their salaries included social benefits and they did not demand compensation. The workers refused to sign this letter which they pointed out was untrue, and they received a notice of dismissal from the Executive.

At the trial the village was represented by a member of the Council and Haim represented the workers. The spokesman for the village said they had tried to reach an agreement with the workers but all attempts had been unsuccessful. Speaking of the members involved, he said that some were 'social cases', unable to work elsewhere, while others had income from their farms. Representing the workers, Haim said that they all worked, and if they did not perform the tasks the village would have to employ others. He argued that the village did not enquire into additional sources of income enjoyed by members of *Otsem*, so why should they take into consideration the agricultural income of hired workers?

The village had a permanent representative in the committee for law in the Moshav Movement, Eden, already referred to in a previous chapter. For a time the village did not hear any decision, and after more than three months had elapsed, they approached Eden to ask what was happening. He replied that there were so many cases in the movement that a decision had not yet been reached. In fact one of the workers heard from a friend in the Movement who alleged that a decision had been reached but Eden was holding it back because he did not approve. The truth of this allegation was not ascertained but both parties in the dispute expressed their lack of belief in the Movement as an effective body for disputes of this kind. Eventually a decision was agreed upon: the Movement recommended that the workers should receive salaries according to the *Histadrut* rates and there should be individual contracts between the individual and the co-operative. When the village received this reply they did not understand it and sent it back to the Movement, asking for an explanation. On clarification the village reached an agreement with the workers that they should pay 3 per cent of social benefits into the savings fund for workers in lieu of compensation.

This protracted dispute reinforced the village's scepticism and disillusionment with the Moshav Movement in its role as legal arbiter. Those opposed to the workers believed that the Movement was failing in its duty to the moshav principles by deciding in favour of the workers. The workers objected that they had not been treated fairly because the acknowledgment of equal rates for jobs had not been agreed upon. Both sides blamed the Movement; and although both parties continued to express dissatisfaction about the outcome of the dispute they were unanimous in their condemnation of the part played by the Movement. The outcome of the affair also reflects the increasingly limited influence of purely political power as exercised through the Moshav Movement, in face of the growing administrative and organisational power of the Ministry of Agriculture and the Marketing Boards.

This case is well remembered in Kfar Hefer. When, during the time I was there, an application was made by Eden for the village to go to the Movement in a dispute it was having with the member of another moshav, the village refused. The case concerned a member of a nearby moshav who had bought baby chicks from the village's incubator. The village alleged that he had not paid for them. After a year passed the village Executive decided that they would sue him for repayment through the civil courts. Oren in a later discussion of this issue said that they had talked with the man but to no avail and they would have been willing to settle for half the amount due just to close the affair. The village informed the man of the action they proposed to take, and he contacted Eden. Eden saw Dov and said that the man had complaints about the quality of the chicks sold to him and he wished to go to the Moshav Movement for a clarification of the issue. Dov refused and said that the man could make his defence in court; the Executive had already decided to take civil action. Eden then applied to appear before the Council to explain the issue.

On his appearance before the Council, Eden said that the question of payment was not the issue. The point was that a member of another moshav had a complaint about Kfar Hefer and the appropriate place for this to be heard was in the Moshav Movement. He added that he did not understand Dov's objection. People began to ask questions, but Dov said that Eden should be allowed to finish. He was surprised when Eden said that he had finished. The questions concerned the objections about quality—whether they had been made before or after the announcement of civil action. Eden answered that he did not know, but the point was irrelevant. Dora then said that citizens live in a State which has laws for dealing with these cases and one must use these laws. Almagor asked about the respective standing of the two courts: could they go to both courts or would they have to drop the civil action? Dov answered that he believed they could pursue only one course of action, but Oren assured him that both could be followed. Here Dov said that, in this case, the man concerned could go to the Movement after the court case. The floor was then given to Eden and Dov asked him what he had to say. Eden replied that it was difficult to begin when one had to start from 'A,B,C'. At this there was a general murmur of, 'and it is not worthwhile'. Eden seemed unaware of this response and merely said that the question was very simple. There was a dispute between the members of Kfar Hefer and a member of another moshav. This member had applied to go to the court of the moshavim. He thought that this was a justifiable request and he did not see why Kfar Hefer did not agree. He began to raise his voice and spoke with vehemence, perhaps in response to the mood of the meeting; the members of the Council were not listening to him and were talking among themselves. Eden reasserted that the case had to go to the Moshav Movement because that is why it existed. Here Dov added, sotto voce, that they had nothing else to do. Eden continued to say that in the history of the movement disputes had always gone to the moshavim court and wherever interests of moshavim were concerned it always should. He cited cases where judges in other courts had recommended that disputants should go to the Moshav Movement. He did not see the point of paying thousands of pounds for a civil action when they could go to the Movement. Dov, throughout the hearing, save for his murmured comments, behaved to Eden with courtesy and politeness, in marked contrast with the others present. He thanked Eden for his explanation and said the Council would decide on the issue. The Council refused Eden's request. Again this refusal reflects the Moshav Movement's 'lack of power of persuasion'; the Movement has few resources and so is not acceptable as a mediator in a dispute.

It was not until two months later that Eden again raised the issue, this time in a General Meeting. He explained the circumstances of the case to those present and accused Dov of 'dismissing' his complaints. Someone in the meeting called out to Eden and asked him what was his interest in the affair. Eden replied that he was interested because he was a member of Kfar Hefer. He expressed his concern at the way events were going in Kfar Hefer, and said that they were losing their Jewish identity. He believed that members should not work on the Sabbath. At this remark there was a burst of laughter from the village and cries that no-one had worked more on the Sabbath than Eden both by day and by night. Eden acknowledged this but said he had made a mistake. He then began to speak about the scrutinising committee in the village but again cries from the hall told him that this was not under discussion and he sat down.

Two weeks later at another General Meeting Eden again put forward his plea for action in the Moshav Movement. At this meeting he received scant attention and barely concealed impatience. Even before he began to speak someone proposed that the motion be taken off the agenda. The young man who proposed this was rebuked by his father and Eden began to speak. He was constantly interrupted by both young and old: one member stated that he had sat for many years in the committee of the Movement and he knew their decisions were worth nothing. Eden again reiterated that this attitude was detrimental to the village and it was 'against the honour' of the village not to go to the Movement. On a vote it was decided that the Executive has the power to decide when issues should go to the Movement.

These two incidents show some of the thinking in Kfar Hefer about relationships with outside bodies. Membership in the Moshav Movement implied more than economic interests, but Kfar Hefer does not feel bound by their conventions. As in economic relationships there is a selective approach. The village keeps open her option to use her connections but in unfavourable circumstances asserts her independence. Eden was careful to express his interest in the case in terms of his membership in the village, but the lack of concern about his views showed that the village viewed his interest as that of the Moshav Movement.

The same situation arose in the village's relationship with the Regional Council. At the end of 1967 Zioni announced that he wished to retire from his position as head of the Regional Council. Announcing this in the Executive committee, Dov said that it was in the village's interests that they should have someone from Kfar Hefer to replace him. The trouble was, he added, that there was no-one suitable. Young farmers could not spare the time. Dov then suggested several names as possibilities: all these were from farms where there was sufficient labour. Marks said that if that was the best they could do then they had better forget it. Dov retorted that they were no worse than any of the others already serving, to which Marks replied, 'and no better'. The village was concerned to have the position filled by one of its members even though they took a poor view of the organisation. One of the Executive said the Regional Council had never been any use to Kfar Hefer. All that happened to them was that they lost IL.36,000 in an economic venture planned by the Regional Council.

The Regional Council represents all the settlements in the area, kibbutsim and moshavim, and members from Kfar Hefer said it was difficult to make this an effective body because of the differential membership. In fact the Regional Council did serve the village, both by the granting of loans, and by the loan of land. And the village as the founding member was obliged to donate to the factory set up by the Regional Council for sons of moshavim who could not stay in the farms. Ben described this as a 'Zionistic' venture and said that

Kfar Hefer's donation was also 'Zionistic'. He said that they had no trouble with their sons, 'they had a university 35 minutes away' from them.

The siting of the Regional Council's headquarters in Kfar Hefer and the chairmanship of Zioni did bring advantages to the village, in the provision of small personal services and in the provision of employment. Several of Kfar Hefer's women worked in the offices and the village also had teachers in the Regional High School. Because of her leading position in the Council, Kfar Hefer played a leading part in the screening of candidates to be chairman. It was said that the moshavim, who were in the majority in the Council, would not accept a chairman from a kibbuts; and if Kfar Hefer could not provide the new chairman, she was interested that the replacement was 'suitable'. In the event they persuaded Zioni to continue in office for another two years. In this they were helped by other settlements who were anxious that the unsuccessful factory, which was rapidly losing money, should be put on a firm footing and urged that Zioni as the initiator of the idea should be the one to repair the damage.

Throughout this chapter I have been concerned to show that Kfar Hefer judged outside links primarily in terms of economic interests. There is the apparent paradox that internally the Executive is concerned to ensure unity in the co-operative while outside the village emphasis is put on a diversity of ties. In the past I believe that these two processes have worked hand-in-hand, and Kfar Hefer's success in her outside links has been directly related to the strength of her internal co-operation. This relationship is not static; and as I have indicated in earlier chapters, differentiation within the village has been accentuated by the effects of demographic processes and by national economic policies. This has had an effect on the village's external ties. In the traditional areas of participation the village has held a strong position because of historical and economic reasons, but this is now being modified by the growth of other settlements. In new areas of production the village cannot rely upon these factors working to her advantage and the village has gone outside the usual organisational frameworks. In this the importance of a wider network of ties has increased and the village has been concerned at her lack of representation in outside bodies. Representation has been handicapped by labour problems within the farms and by political differences. Even though the villagers may express indifference to certain organisations with which they are associated, they are concerned that they should not only be represented but also play an important role. Kfar Hefer is concerned to maintain independent action within the framework of growing national impingement on internal policies. And in these the existence of a variety of potential links is significant. Hence, despite her expressed indifference, the village is now actively engaged in forging new ties, especially in attempting to place individuals in influential offices. Chapter V has shown how categories of people within the village have used outside connections to set up their own new ventures within the co-operative. The alfalfa group tried to work within the co-operative framework to press their demands but finally went outside; the avocado group from the beginning consulted bodies outside the village. This is, I believe, consonant both with moshav principles and with the conventions of Kfar Hefer. The Executive is seen as serving individual members but initiative lies with the member. In the past, when the numerical size of different interest groups was smaller, the village Executive could assume unity within the village and this helped it in establishing itself as a power in outside associations. The growth in the size of interest groups has led to a by-passing of the Executive and a feeling that the co-operative in its role as a consolidator of village strength is unable to cope with the demands of new interest groups. This trend has been accelerated by shifts of power: firstly, from the village to outside agencies; secondly, within these agencies there has been a differential shift of power from the purely political organisations to administrative agencies and organisations. Thus the village while retaining its political connections now seeks influence in these new agencies.

VIII
Social control and social sanctions

When I was in Kfar Hefer I was told repeatedly by villagers that it was important for me to understand the 'atmosphere' of Kfar Hefer. Sometimes after conversations with villagers I would be told that I could not understand Kfar Hefer by collecting information and asking questions. Mostly people were kind enough to add that this was not a personal failing on my part and presumably to console me they said that 'No outsider can understand Kfar Hefer.' In an effort to track down this elusive quality of 'atmosphere', I asked people to define it for me. Usually the answer was, 'It is our way of life in a moshav.' When I pointed out to them the variety of types of life in settlements which are formally designated 'moshavim' I was told: 'They are not really moshavim; Kfar Hefer is a real moshav.' While acknowledging the expressed opinion of Kfar Hefer's population that it is impossible to define 'atmosphere', I believe that this quality can be perceived in the operation of social control and social sanctions within the village. These processes indicate how Kfar Hefer perceived herself and was perceived by others. In this analysis I describe both the 'formal' controls of the village bodies, the Executive, the Council and the General Meeting, and the 'informal' controls exercised through gossip. This analysis takes as its starting point an article by Gluckman in which he states that, '. . . gossip, and even scandal, have important positive virtues. Clearly they maintain the unity, morals and values of social groups. Beyond this, they enable these groups to control the competing cliques and aspiring individuals of which all groups are composed.'[1]

Kfar Hefer believed herself to be 'a special place'. In an earlier chapter I have described the high status achieved by members of collective settlements in the *Yishuv* and even today in the Israeli State. The settlement of many ideologically uncommitted immigrants into the moshav framework, and the rise of alternative statuses in Israel, have affected the standing of the moshav in national values. Kfar Hefer takes a pride in the fact that despite all these changes she is 'still a real moshav' and is concerned to show that in the new rankings of the State Kfar Hefer is, as one young man described it to me, 'still a good address'. Therefore I suggest, social controls and sanctions, gossip and scandal, are concerned not simply with the unity of the group but also in maintaining status in the wider com-

[1] Gluckman (1963a)

munity. This bears similarity to Colson's study of Makah Indians where Gluckman points out that since, '. . . gossip and scandal involve the criticism and assessment of people against the traditional values of Makah society, it maintains the tribe as Indians against whites and as Makah against other Indians'.[1] In Kfar Hefer the gossip maintains the village against the wider Israeli society and against other moshavim. And as Gluckman points out, 'To be a Makah, you must be able to scandalise skilfully. This entails that you know the individual histories of your fellows, for the knowledgeable can hit at you through your ancestry, and you must be able to retort in kind. You have also got to have some knowledge of the old ways of the Makah tribe.'[2]

Thus I was often told by members in Kfar Hefer that in spite of my residence in the village and my increasing knowledge of Hebrew, 'You'll never understand us until you know Yiddish.' Each achievement in conforming to the values of the group brought a new hurdle to be surmounted before one could be 'in' the group. The knowledge of Yiddish was not merely the language, but the shared culture and common experience of Kfar Hefer. I, as a non-Israeli, non-Jew, could never expect to understand and participate in this. Indeed much of the first generation's criticism of their children was that they had never learned, or had forgotten or disregarded, this culture. But being a 'stranger' or 'outsider'[3] also meant that the expectations upon one were less. I have referred to the importance of the idea of a 'son (or daughter) of Kfar Hefer' and that the expectations towards a 'son-in-law or daughter-in-law' were not the same, and caused surprise and favourable comment when they were fulfilled.

Again like the Makah, Kfar Hefer's members seek to maintain the principle of equality between 'all members'. This is sanctioned by moshav law which states equality as one of its basic principles. Differences may exist between members and between and within families, but all are equal in the light of the moshav. It will be remembered that a large part of the discontent of the 'alfalfa group' (see Chapter V) was that they were considered less than full members of the moshav because they no longer farmed their lands. Reference has also been made to the apparent failure of professionally qualified sons to stay in the village. Similarly the difficulty of the 'outside' internal secretaries can be seen in terms of their lack of the social tools—social manipulation, shared culture, gossip, necessary for them in their dealings with members. And I have shown how Dov in his relationships with individual members used and had used

[1] Colson (1953), quoted in Gluckman (1963a) [2] Colson (1953)
[3] See Frankenberg (1957)

against him the myriad of social relationships, past and present. Part of Ben's success in maintaining his role may have been his relative isolation from village members.

This attitude is extended to members who have found influential positions outside the village. David Shauli, the *Knesset* member, was careful to maintain his ties with the village, and worked his farm during the time he was in the village. Members pointed this out and commented that despite his status in the national arena, 'he is no different from us'. The mother of a son, no longer in the village, but who holds a very powerful position in national politics, complained that the village preferred Shauli to her son, 'because Shauli is a gossip and my son is not'. Eden's views and opinions were disregarded by village members because he was no longer in the village: his farm was run by his son, he lived for most of the week outside the village, and he had lost touch with village affairs. Members could not gossip with him about village life and the failure to gossip showed that he was no longer 'in the village'.

In their attitude to national leaders, Kfar Hefer's members expressed much the same views. This was brought home to me very forcibly in a conversation with a person, not a member of Kfar Hefer, but who knew the village well. I made some disparaging remark about a national leader to which I received the reply: 'You sound just like Kfar Hefer.' National figures are put in their perspective by Kfar Hefer members, who in reference to established figures are apt to remark that they cleared swamps with them in Nahalal, or they worked together in the kitchen in Balfouria. In the case of younger figures, the young of Kfar Hefer remark that they were in the army together or in the same youth group. This is not just the claiming of relationships with important figures but also a statement that 'they are no different from us'. An important figure in the national scene is seen in a new light when it is known that he too was a labourer or an insignificant figure in a youth group.

Paine taking up a point made by Gluckman,[1] developed the 'information-management' aspect of gossip, and commented, 'gossip is, first a genre of informal communication and second a device intended to forward and protect individual interests'. Gossip in Kfar Hefer subscribes to both these definitions, and I show later in the chapter how farmers who are in competition for increased quotas of production in Kfar Hefer, where competition is maintained within certain limits imposed by the moshav constitution and customary practice, use gossip to promote their interests. However most of the

---

[1] Paine (1967) and Gluckman (1963a). All references in this chapter, unless otherwise stated, are to these articles

gossip which Paine designates as 'exchange of information' is directed against non-farmers (including professional workers) in the village and against other settlements. Relationships with the neighbouring moshav shitufi of Gavish, and with other old-established moshavim and kibbutsim in Israel, exhibit this characteristic. Members were keenly interested in developments within these settlements, especially in the economic field and reviewed their own actions in the light of the information they gained. The interests of these various settlements are often the same, and they form a united pressure group in the national bargaining for favourable quotas. But they are also in competition with each other in the division of these quotas and in the terms they receive from national and other agencies. Thus, in Kfar Hefer great interest was shown in the prices received for produce, and change in policy within these settlements. It was noticeable that the village showed no interest in events in settlements which were geographically close but economically less well developed than Kfar Hefer.

The gossip in Kfar Hefer amongst farming members was really what Paine would call 'scandal', 'they talk to discredit (not to learn)'. Of course the distinction between 'discrediting' and 'learning' is seldom as clear as the quotation might suggest. And gossip amongst members of Kfar Hefer displayed both these traits. However, as Gluckman points out, the gossip was set in, and against, the context of norms and values held by the community. Competition in farming between individuals in Kfar Hefer is regulated, and competition for office is the main sphere in which individuals are seen to be in competition. However, office in village institutions is not eagerly sought by members, and rather than occupy the arduous and time consuming jobs of policymaking and administration they prefer to seek to control office holders and hence to ensure the fulfilment of their interests. Jonathan who was a known gossip about office holders in the village, never sought election to village committees. When, after his repeated criticisms of village policy, he was invited to join the scrutinising committee, this brought about a breach in the committee which led to his own exclusion and the strengthening of the position of the chairman, whom he had tried to oust from office. This bears out the point made by Paine that gossip (and scandal) is informal communication although not informal information. And this raises the question of the effectiveness of gossip as a means for change. The evidence from Kfar Hefer would seem to suggest, as I pointed out in an earlier chapter, that gossip is effective in person-to-person relationships. But in institutional relationships, which subsume wider sets of relationships, including those of power and authority,

o

then gossip (and scandal) are relatively ineffective as agents of change. Paine has criticised former analyses of gossips as putting the emphasis on the community and not on the individual: this I believe points to the limitation of gossip as a social tool. In Kfar Hefer it has been effective in changing office holders but not in changing the structure of power and authority in the village. Paine states that gossip is a catalyst of social process: later in this chapter I cite several types of gossip in the village and examine their consequences for individuals and the village.

Gossiping is an art and is not simply used to establish who is in the group and who is outside. It is also a device whereby group identification can be tested; to be in the group one has to be able to gossip, but to gossip too much or to reveal more than it is considered appropriate that one should know, involves censure. In a conversation between good personal friends, one a member of Gavish Shitufi and the other of Kfar Hefer, the Gavish member laughingly criticised Kfar Hefer's 'individual collectivism' which he said was a wasteful and inefficient system. The Kfar Hefer member replied: 'This is our affair, after all what do you know about hard work?' In this reply the Kfar Hefer member imposed the boundary of gossip; his friend had presumed too much and trespassed beyond his rights. Also the rebuke was placed in the context of the value given to physical work which Kfar Hefer's members accused Gavish of not practising, in spite of their claims to be a moshav.

Although gossip is a pleasurable activity, to be known as a persistent gossip is very undesirable. A friend reported to me a conversation she had with a woman in Kfar Hefer who recounted to her the detailed events of another's life. She was surprised to hear that the woman knew such intimate information and asked how she got to know all those things. The woman replied, 'What do you mean, how do I know? I ask.' Retelling this story to me my friend expressed her disapproval of such behaviour, but I found more interesting the fact that people are prepared to tell others so much about their private lives. I think the answer is that few relationships are 'private' in Kfar Hefer, they are shared with others. To refuse to share would be to refuse to belong to the community. Belonging to the community entrusts one with a store of gossip and each member of the 'gossip group' is a custodian of this gossip, freely exchanging it with others but open to censure if it is allowed to pass outside the group. In addition, perhaps one is under pressure to provide some information about oneself.

Both men and women are engaged in the gathering and passing of information. Unlike many rural communities, where wives are relatively isolated from other women,[1] the women of Kfar Hefer meet often in the village store, in the school, and informally in one another's houses. The men meet at work, in the dairy, or in the agricultural machinery store. Men and women also meet in the village, and villagers meet together at the cinema and at plays in the village hall. There are also many societies, mainly cultural, such as the choir, the bible class and a dramatic group, in which members meet. In leisure time and at work the members of Kfar Hefer are constantly in touch with one another.

Much of the gossip they exchange is specific and involves only sections of the population. Amongst the older women of the village, gossip is common about young wives who are criticised for failing to fulfil their duties. To be a 'good wife' in Kfar Hefer means helping one's husband: amongst older women this is stated in terms of helping on the farm. Young women who do not help with the care of the poultry or leave this to the older women in the farm are criticised for failing to help their husbands. The necessity for a woman's work in the farm, if it is to be strong, is re-affirmed by this gossip.

Amongst younger women gossip centres on the woman's style of life. Unsuitable clothes, or the acquiring of expensive articles for the home, are gossiped about, for these are felt to be out of place in the village.

Men criticise one another's work performance: neglect of a farm or dislike of physical work are both reproved. Performance in official positions is also criticised, and allegations of incompetence or favouritism are not uncommon. It will be remembered that Ben-Natan and the alfalfa group bitterly criticised both Dov and Ron and accused them of favouring dairy farmers against the interests of others in the village. Conversely hard physical work and high standards achieved in farming are widely praised in the village. Office holders are seldom, if ever, praised for the performance of their duties; it is expected that they should make the correct decisions, and the impossibility of satisfying all, makes unfavourable criticism the usual reaction to these men.

It is common amongst the older generation to accuse the young of being the gossips and the scandalmongers. In contrast they speak of their harmonious days when mutual aid and support were dominant, but presumably this is seen through a golden glow. But in the incidents of the two outside secretaries it was said that the youth of the village was responsible for their resignation.

Other studies have shown how the young are the transmitters of certain values in a community and this is tacitly approved by the

[1] See Rees (1951)

old, who can then deny their participation in the affair. In one such study of a Welsh parish the 'youth group' contains boys in their late teens and unmarried men into the thirties,[1] but the 'youth' of Kfar Hefer is typically in the middle twenties or early thirties and married. These are the young who have committed themselves to staying on in the village, but even though they are involved in farming usually they share this work with their parents. Although they have the status of married men with their own families they are not independent farmers. Their assumption of the role of social arbiters in the village expresses their involvement in the community, but as they are 'young' and not, at least nominally, in charge of farms, they are permitted a licence in behaviour which would be considered inappropriate in the old.

This granting of licence to the young is also positively sanctioned in the wider Israeli society. The immigrants of the early part of the century were concerned to establish a new Jewish way of life free from the constraints of Jewish life in the diaspora. They believed that the fulfilment of this aim would come through their children, those born in Palestine or Israel. A special pride is felt in, and value ascribed to, these young people who are said to be characterised by self-confidence and freedom from the traditional Jewish life outside '*Eretz Israel*'.[2]

The young were recently involved in the one case where a member was compelled to leave the village. This involved a young man, married to a Kfar Hefer girl, who was accused by the police of attacking a girl in the village, only for the charge to be dropped. This happened several years before I came to the village but in the recounting of this tale to me I was always told that it was the 'young' who made him leave. They did this by sending the man to Coventry, and by sabotaging his farming. Eventually the man approached the Executive who bought his farm from him, at a good price, and sold it later at a loss. Here the young acted against the young and even though the first generation in the village attributed the man's leaving the village to the young, they did not criticise the outcome. By this action the youth demonstrated the ability of village's young people to punish someone whom they suspected of a gross offence, a breach of the norm that women are not to be molested, even though the police for whatsoever reason could not sustain a charge. The suspect happened to be an 'outsider'. I cannot say what would have happened had he been a son of Kfar Hefer.

[1] See Rees (1951)
[2] Literally 'land of Israel', used in pre-state days to describe the biblical land of Israel

Usually social sanctioning and criticism of members do not reach such formal levels. In the village bulletin members sometimes criticised one another by name. This practice was always roundly condemned by other members of the village and the writer of the article was denounced for his ill-mannered behaviour. After a series of articles in the bulletin in which certain members were attacked specifically, Dov inserted a notice saying that the practice of personal criticism was against all the rules of the moshav life and individuals must refrain from this. However, I suggest that there was a purpose behind the deliberate 'naming of names'. The use of formal social control and gossip can be very effective in certain spheres of social relationships, as where the young farmer who allegedly attacked the girl was forced to leave the village. But in other cases while it may cause the target of the gossip a certain embarrassment, as long as the gossip is in general terms he can continue to meet people and to work with them. Moreover with the increased differential production in the village, some members are not intimately involved with others in their working lives. Once an accusation is made publicly, then the whole village is involved in the dispute; and the accuser runs the risk of being repudiated for his accusations. Therefore I suggest that public statements of this kind are only made when the accuser is assured of a substantial backing for his argument and when the issue is one that cannot be solved by 'normal' channels of gossip. It signifies that a number of members are not satisfied that unity in the village should be maintained and wish to establish a new pattern of relationships. A case in point, illustrating this process, involves Haim's appointment as manager of the supply store in the village.

This appointment was a controversial one. The previous manager of the store was not an agricultural member of the village and on his death the position remained vacant for several months. Haim was put forward as a replacement by the Executive: he was a young man suited to the physical work involved in the job; he had been employed for many years by the village as a driver; he was an agricultural member of the village, so the co-operative would not have to pay him severance money in the event of his dismissal. The announcement caused a stir in the village and there was a strong body of opinion against the appointment. Some argued that they needed a professional: this was an important job and they needed someone who knew about stock control and could run things smoothly. Amidst all the argument about whether there should be a professional man or a villager, personal recriminations against Haim were expressed. People remembered his part in the agricultural workers' dispute and said that he had betrayed the village by acting as spokesman for the dissidents against the village. In addition to Kfar Hefer's scepticism about the Moshav Movement as an agent for settling disputes, there is also the feeling that village disputes should be settled in the village without recourse to outside bodies. Kfar Hefer has a reputation amongst moshavim for adherence to moshav principles, and some said that Haim was endangering this by airing internal difficulties to 'outsiders'. However, the Executive decided he should be appointed. The meeting at which this was announced was very noisy and the next day a petition was started to annul the appointment. Again the promoters were the young of the village. In attempts to gain support for their action they gossiped and scandalised about Haim, in his public and his private life. Gossip as idle chatter, albeit with the effect of asserting 'how things should be done', is different from scandal, the attempt to shock others. Through their scandalmongering the youth were not only attacking Haim, but also the Executive: they put forward a view of the kind of people who should serve them and also denied the power of the Executive to take this decision on behalf of the village. This attempt failed and Haim continued in office.

It appears that within Kfar Hefer gossip and scandal are successful in challenging individuals in possession of office, but are not sufficient to attack the role itself. Gossip may change the individuals holding office but it is not strong enough to change the structure of offices within the village. The attack on the Executive failed because the criticism was a public display of private gossip. The village to maintain its unity must denounce this publicity; and in denouncing it the Executive must stand by its decision, for to waver or to compromise would be to undermine the values which unite individuals into a community.

There exist within the village certain procedures for dealing with breaches of 'communal law'. The Executive deals with offenders, who may, on appeal, appear before the Council. The most common offences are in economic affairs. Individuals who attempt to market privately, outside the co-operative, or who disobey Executive orders, are called before the Executive. The usual penalty is an economic one, or generally the imposition of a fine. Persistent offenders also incur social penalties, which in the village are considered to be more damaging. One case which occurred while I was in the village involved a young man who was twice in a short space of time accused of operating outside the co-operative framework. The first time he was said to have bought turkeys from outside the village, to have reared them with food bought from the village, and then to have attempted to market them privately. This was discovered by chance when Dov noticed the turkeys on the farm and knew that he should not have them. When he was questioned about this, Yuval, the young man, said he had permission to take them from outside the village. In some cases where there are not enough supplies from the village incubator or when the market allows, members are permitted to buy from outside but the marketing must be done through the co-operative. There was no record of a decision to allow Yuval to buy from outside the village and Dov said that he would certainly not have allowed him to take birds because the market was already overcrowded and prices were falling. Yuval was summoned to the Executive and a fine of IL.150 was imposed upon him. The issue went no further and Yuval paid the fine. Private marketing is not only an economic misdemeanour by the individual against the co-operative, but it also affects other members in the village whose produce often receives a reduced price in the market because of unscheduled production and the willingness of private marketeers to accept a lower price than normal for ready cash.

Several months later Yuval was again accused of private marketing. This second incident was also discovered by chance because a telephone call intended to reach Yuval was taken by Ben. The call came through late one evening to the village offices, where Ben took the message which was to tell Yuval that he could not market his turkeys that night, and the collection would be delayed. Ben did not pass on the message that night: he said Yuval lived at the other end of the village and he did not want to go out of his way. But the next morning he told Dov and together they went to Yuval's farm where the birds were crated and awaiting transport. Dov asked Yuval about them and he said that Dov had given him permission. Dov denied this and asked him to appear before the next Executive meeting.

At the meeting Yuval repeated his assertion that Dov had given him permission, and accused Ben of setting a trap for him. Other members of the Executive asked him why, if Dov had given him permission, was he marketing the turkeys privately, and why was there all the secrecy about it? Yuval said that there was no secret about it; after all, he said, the telephone call to the village offices proved that. The Executive was unconvinced by his explanation and after his departure discussed the appropriate action to be taken against him. The suggestion was that he should be heavily fined as this was the second incident in a few months. Dov said that a fine was not enough. This was no discouragement for the future, as they had seen. He proposed that the village should stop supplying him with foodstuff, but others said this would not work, since his friends would get it for him. Yoel added that Yuval was anxious to build up the poultry section which was his main concern in the farm. Yuval was the second son of the family, and his parents and his older married brother all worked on the farm. The farm had too many hands for the production available to them; they could not become 'big farmers' in the sense of extending their land, nor could they increase their quotas within the village. Hence the only way open to Yuval was to go outside the co-operative framework. Dov said family details were unimportant: what mattered was the principle that there should be no private marketing. Dov proposed that he should be fined IL.200; that the incident should be published in the village bulletin; that Yuval should never again represent the village; that he should have no more supplies until the end of the year. Marks objected to this saying that if Yuval paid for his mistake they, the village, could not punish him for the future. He was overruled and it was decided that Dov should inform Yuval of the decision.

On hearing the decision Yuval appealed to the Council. He retold his story to the Council and said that Dov knew all the circumstances of the purchase from outside the village. After presenting his case he left the meeting and Dov was asked if he had given permission. He said that he had not. Marks then said that Ben had not acted properly; he was not a policeman whose duty it was to apprehend law breakers. He believed the village had acted incorrectly in the affair and the fine should be dropped. The point was taken up by others who, without criticising Ben directly, said that it was inappropriate in a 'community' that individuals should act as guards and overseers. They agreed that Yuval must be punished but said that economic measures by villagers against villagers were inappropriate. On a vote Dov's proposals were defeated by 11 votes to 4, only Dov, Oren, Yoel and Ori (all members of the Executive) voting for the motion.

It was decided that Yuval be fined IL.100 and the incident should be reported in the bulletin, but that there should be no withholding of supplies and no decision could be made about Yuval's future representation of the village.

This decision was in line with a development I described earlier: the emphasis by the Executive and especially Dov on delimiting areas of control by the Executive and within these to work according to strictly laid down procedure. The Council were concerned to maintain flexibility in making decisions, and gave primacy to the circumstances of individual cases and did not work with a fixed idea of Executive control.

But, this case shows more: it raised the question of formal sanctions and control within the village. When Dov argued that the breach was clear, the Council agreed, but it objected that in community relationships it is impossible to work according to 'law'. Unlike Dov they did not draw a difference between the 'co-operative' as an economic unit and as a social entity. Their concern was that between members, who are designated as equals, the imposition of fines is inappropriate. They believed the recourse to economic measures defined the misdemeanour as an economic one, while they considered that it was a breach of the 'co-operative' principle involving social as well as economic issues. The part played by Ben in the affair was also criticised: he was an employee of the village and though he was a professional member, it was felt that it was not his business to become concerned in issues involving agricultural members. I suggest, but cannot substantiate, that if Ben's action had been taken by an agricultural member then the opposition would have been less. The Council acknowledged that there must be penalties against those who disregarded moshav principles but the problem was the type of control to use. In the end a compromise was reached, on a diminished economic measure and a lesser social one, but there remained many in the village who were opposed to the use of formal sanctions against members.

I have shown that as a unit the village was not slow to use formal legal procedures against outsiders, but within the village there was a conflict of principle about measures to be taken against defaulting members. The peccadilloes of village members can be dealt with by gossip, which reaffirm village values. But the individual might if he chose, be able to ignore gossip and surface relationships remained unchanged. Scandals are more disruptive; and when they are public they demand retribution to restate the 'proper behaviour' in the community. I suggest that when scandal becomes public, there is necessarily involved a more forceful restatement of community values than if the affair remains under cover. This I believe was the village's dilemma. Action had to be taken against individuals who disobeyed moshav laws. Against outsiders they could do this and appear as a unified community but members were reluctant to take action against their own fellows because this both revealed the divisions between members and also might have led to further action against other deviant members. It will be remembered that this same dilemma existed in the early days of the settlement, at a time when conditions were different.

There is one case in the village of a member being transferred from agricultural membership to the status of public worker. This happened several years ago, when a man was caught stealing from the store where he was employed. The transfer was regarded as a penalty, a demotion for the man, confirming the idea of the village that the essential community of Kfar Hefer is its agricultural members. Theft is a very serious breach of moshav life. In a talk David Shauli gave in the village, he expressed the view that the biggest factor in Kfar Hefer's success as a moshav was the confidence of members, one in the other. This is dependent upon a belief in the honesty of dealings between members. The decision in this case was left to the General Meeting, and they decided to transfer the man to the status of public worker. According to moshav law he could have been expelled from all membership in the village, but members were reluctant to do this. I was told that no-one raised this point in the meeting. His demotion signified his failure to behave according to communal and civil law, but to have expelled him from the village would have been to deny the communal values by which members bear responsibility for the welfare of one another.

The controversy surrounding the 'moshav law' which stood before the *Knesset*, centres on this question. This law sets out the rights of members in moshavim and also gives grounds for the expulsion of members. The main reason for expulsion are: (i) unsuitability for the framework of the settlement, (ii) non-cooperation, (iii) non-acceptance of the principle of mutual aid. Opponents of this 'Bill' argue that it is unnecessary in co-operative settlements, where disputes should be settled without recourse to law. Writing in the *Jerusalem Post* of 12 July 1968 a correspondent pointed out that the 'moshav law may menace basic rights'. His concern was that the moshav was a territorial and municipal entity and a co-operative society. Every resident was subject to municipal law but membership of a co-operative was voluntary. The law would give power to a moshav to expel an offender but this was not compulsory, and some feared that this might lead to abuses. The attitude in Kfar Hefer towards this law was mixed: on the whole individuals welcomed the measures but said that they did not apply to the village because they could deal with their own problems.

This statement was one of village ideology, the ideal of the un-differentiated unified co-operative. But I think that the above cases show that there was a good deal of uncertainty and hesitation about the operation of formal sanctions within the village. In an effort to clear some of the doubts a special committee was entrusted with reviewing and bringing up to date the village constitution. Five members sat on the committee—Dora, Ben-Natan, Marks, Cohen and Shimoni. Most of their proposals concerned conditions pertaining to membership in the moshav and the formal structure of committees in the village. Thus, when the proposals for changes were drawn up and presented to the General Meeting they contained provisions for gaining membership in the village; the definition of a quorum for village meetings; and voting rights. The more controversial proposals concerned individual rights in the co-operative; details about the transfer of land to the village; and rights on cessation of membership. Many of these provisions were already contained in the contract signed by the individual member with the Jewish National Fund, on receiving land in the moshav and were simply a restatement in legal form giving force of law to earlier and existing customary law. But nowhere in the document were there details of how these should be enforced, and the initiative was left to the members themselves. This document illustrates, I believe, the thinking in Kfar Hefer about social control in the village. It was stated by many members that all that was needed was a clear statement of rights and wrongs in the village and then all problems would be clarified. But this view ignored the processes which were to follow upon wrongdoing, and here lay the real dilemma in the village. In most cases in the village it was clear when a breach of moshav or community law had been committed: the difficulty was to decide what to do about it. The constitution reflected the idea prevalent in Kfar Hefer that flouting of moshav principles should somehow 'be worked out' in the village, for to define the procedures and penalties would be to tighten and circumscribe the co-operative. But if these procedures were to have any meaning and not be discredited, they would have to be enforced, resulting in the exclusion of members from the co-operative. But it is against the spirit of the co-operative, as understood in moshavim. The moshav as a unity has a legal standing as a co-operative society, but the co-operation of members within this framework is felt to be a chosen working together rather than a compulsive way of life. Ben-Natan summed this up when writing in the village bulletin in March, 1968, he stated: 'There is no doubt that no-one in the village is an anarchist, but there is something of the "anarchist philosophies" in the life of a moshav; people are free to do as they wish.'

This freedom to do as one wishes has another consequence in village life, one which I believe also affects the village's reluctance to lay down strict rules and regulations for members. Within the individual families of Kfar Hefer there have grown up practices which are not strictly in accordance with moshav law and principles. Chief amongst these is the practice of 'outside work'. There are several members who work outside the village and still hold the status of agricultural members. In the main this is the result of personal circumstances—the death of children who were expected to carry on the farm, or ill health which makes it impossible for a member to continue in farming. There are farms where the sons of the family although resident on the farm do not engage in farming. All these have been recognised and tacitly accepted by the village over a number of years. To initiate legislation about the precise conditions of membership would be to start a process difficult to stop. Members accused of failing in one aspect of moshav life could justifiably point to others who failed in other respects. Therefore I consider that the village prefers not to take action against deviant members. So far these activities have not seriously affected the running of the village; indeed I have shown that many members have benefited from the failure of others to be full members of the moshav. However, the legal provisions set out in the constitution, are present as a threat to members who in the opinion of the village go too far in disregard of moshav principles.

A poll organised by the editor of the village bulletin expressed the differences in opinion, between members, and the lack of precision in defining the question, 'Who is a moshavnik?' The first person questioned was a Kfar Hefer son living near but not in the village. He replied that, 'a moshavnik is: "a man who receives subsidies from the government because his father cleared swamps" '. But more charitably and less cynically he added that, 'he is everyone living in Kfar Hefer'. Others expressed similar views. A 'moshavnik is a man who earns all or part of his income from agriculture and lives in a village'. Another added, 'and who brings up his children in the village, sees this as his way of life'. On the question of outside work the most stringent definition came from Ori, the Executive member, who answered: 'Outside work is permitted as long as it does not exploit other persons. I do not think that a shopkeeper could be a moshavnik. Members who work in government or public institutions and continue to work their farms and maintain connections with the village and its institutions are moshavniks.'

These opinions reflect the 'customary conventions' that have grown in Kfar Hefer alongside moshav law. If there was to be a rigid definition of moshav life, then many families in Kfar Hefer would fall outside its conditions. This has an influence on the kind of control that members can use one against the other. And I believe the following example illustrates this.

There was within the village one family which raised poultry for sale but not within the framework of village institutions. This family had a private venture of breeding turkeys for sale, and none of this produce went through the village co-operative. Before the building of the village incubator there were in the village several incubators for hatching chicks. A number of families supplied village needs from their incubators. On the building of the village incubator these were all closed except for the one belonging to Yael, the wife, and her husband Pinhas. They were allowed to continue in production because their farm was heavily in debt, reputedly for over IL.40,000, and it was believed that the incubator would help them pay off this debt. They had made several attempts to reduce the debt, by experimenting with the raising of geese and ducks, but these all failed. Both Pinhas and Yael are 'children of Kfar Hefer'. Yael's parents and her sister live in the village. Pinhas farms his family farm and his mother lives with them. Another reason why the farm was allowed to continue in production were the extenuating family circumstances. Pinhas' father left the village and his mother had to continue alone in the farm, which despite the presence of Pinhas never fully developed. On marriage Yael moved into Pinhas' home and the village acknowledge that the young couple had a very difficult time and lived in poor conditions. The family fortunes began to change when they began the breeding of turkeys: this was a great success and the village bought chicks from them. As the business expanded and they invested in it, the village asked them to close it down. They replied that they were only just beginning to pay off the debt and asked for more time. In spite of subsequent repeated requests they have refused to close down the incubator. The business was a great success and very profitable. In 1966 they formed the venture into a company and entered into a nation-wide organisation supplying chicks, many of them for export. Recently they have built a large house and they have a car, and Yael has full-time domestic help in the house. When villagers spoke of this they admired the energy of Yael; they said that she was the driving force behind the enterprise, but they add that the enterprise was forbidden according to moshav law.

The village incubator was built in 1958 and Pinhas and Yael started with turkey breeding in 1962. When I asked village members why the venture had been allowed to continue and to grow, they pointed out the 'special circumstances' of the farm and said they had no reason to doubt that Pinhas and Yael would not give up the venture when they reduced their debt. Also this was the time of Kfar Hefer's two 'outside secretaries', and villagers said these had paid no attention to the venture, while the villagers themselves were too concerned with their own difficulties with these men to take any action. In 1966 when the company was formed the Executive offered to buy the enterprise and to allow Yael and Pinhas to continue working as employees of the village. They refused.

On the formation of the company, the villagers and the Executive were faced with the problem of how to act. At a General Meeting in 1966 questions were addressed to Dov from the floor enquiring what the Executive was going to do about the development. He replied that the matter was under consideration. At a meeting of the Executive and of the Council, it was said that the village did not recognise the incubator because it was contrary to moshav law. This same meeting decided that the village in furtherance of this policy would not take taxes from the family. Taxes would be raised on their other agricultural production (citrus and dairy) but as they did not recognise the incubator they could not receive taxes from it. This decision was given to the General Meeting and there were many objections. People said that Yael and Pinhas were making a lot of money and they did not see why they should subsidise them. The family only had a small production in other agricultural branches and they still owed a big debt to the village. Their children attended the village school and they attended village activities, so why should they not pay? The Executive answered that they had to differentiate between the village as a municipal area and the village as a co-operative. The family paid taxes to the municipality but not to the co-operative because they had put themselves outside its framework. The meeting eventually agreed to let the decision stand for a year and then review it.

Nevertheless many members were dissatisfied with the decision and throughout the year at General Meetings questions were asked why Yael and Pinhas did not pay taxes. Dov each time answered that the case was constantly under review and would be brought to the General Meeting when final proposals were made. At the beginning of the next year, when the tax committee brought its proposals to the Executive, Oren raised the problem again. Dov said he would refer it to the Council for a decision. Several weeks and several Council Meetings passed but the question was not raised. Finally at the end of one Council Meeting Shlomo said to Dov that he thought some decision should be reached about Yael and Pinhas. He said that he had many times been asked by villagers what the Council was doing about the question. Dov said that they would discuss the question when the tax proposals were brought to the Council.

When taxes for the year 1967/68 were discussed in Council, Oren raised the problem of Yael and Pinhas. He said that the meeting had to decide if they were to be charged taxes this year. Marks spoke in favour of taking taxes from them; he said that he did not want to subsidise their children's education. But Oren and Dora spoke in favour of retaining the tax avoidance. Both said that Yael and Pinhas suffered from this; to which one young member of the Council announced that he wished he could suffer in the same way, he would not mind not paying taxes. But Dora said that she too had held that view but she had changed her mind. She said that she had direct evidence that Yael and Pinhas were very concerned that the village should take taxes from them. After the last Council Meeting which had only briefly touched upon the issue, Pinhas had appeared at her house the next day to say that he had heard they were discussed in the meeting and he wanted to know what had been said. And, she continued, the same afternoon she met Yael in the street and Yael had accosted her and told her that they (she and Pinhas) were no less patriotic about Kfar Hefer than any other member of the village. Dora answered that she was glad to hear it. However, she interpreted this as a sign that Yael and Pinhas felt uncomfortable in the village and would be glad if taxes were taken from them. Dov said that he was always on good terms with Yael, since they had been in school together. Dora added that she too was 'always all right with them' and she added that Yael and Pinhas had attended the annual seder[1] which their street always held.

From conversation with members in the village about the affair, it was clear that everyone protested that they were on good terms with Yael and Pinhas, and their only quarrel was with their private farming. Notwithstanding this, Yael and Pinhas did feel themselves isolated in the village in spite of their kin ties. Members were polite towards them and certainly there was no insulting behaviour directed against them, but equally there was none of the informal visiting which went on between families in Kfar Hefer. At the house warming party to celebrate their new house most of the guests invited were from Gavish and outside Kfar Hefer. A woman in Gavish told me that Yael felt alone in Kfar Hefer and urged me to go to see her new house of which she was very proud. When I did go to see it, I was afterwards asked by other women in the village if it was nice, since not even close neighbours had been inside the house.

Oren urged that they could not now change policy; they could not disown the incubator one year and then recognise it the next year. Others in the meeting agreed but said they felt they should take other action. Dov said that there was no other action, since they could not make the couple leave the village. This seemed to be difficult to believe, and those present said that there must be some other measure open to them. Dov said not and the others did not

[1] Meal on first night of the Passover

know the legal position. In fact according to the proposed law members may be expelled from the moshav, but whether this is the moshav as a co-operative or the moshav as a local authority is not clear. Dov proposed that he, as a friend of Yael, should talk with her, and in the meantime they would agree to continue not to raise taxes on the incubator.

When the topic came up for discussion at the General Meeting, Pinhas attended, the first time I saw him at a village meeting. Dov recounted the history of the affair and said that the question this evening for discussion was: 'Is there a place in Kfar Hefer for a private incubator and a limited company?' He warned that this was an important question for the village which could set a precedent for other private enterprises. This presentation was immediately challenged by Marks who said that the question was 'if the village should raise taxes on the incubator': he said that there was no connection between taxes and recognition, one did not imply the other. Again he reiterated that he did not want to pay for the education of Pinhas' children. Others raised this point and said that taxes should be paid according to income, and Yael and Pinhas were obviously doing well so they should pay their share. Pinhas then claimed the right to reply. He said that he had papers in his possession from the village agreeing to the incubator. Indeed, he added, the village had suggested to them that they should give up geese and change to turkeys. All they had done was to follow the village's advice. He said that in many other moshavim the moshav itself formed a company for various purposes. Then, turning to Oren, the village's tax expert, he said: 'It is a way of avoiding tax, you pay only 45 per cent instead of 60 per cent.' Moreover his wife received a salary from the business and he did not pay income tax because he was an agricultural member of Kfar Hefer. This advice, he added, was given to him by the Moshav Movement. He believed that the incubator was of value to the village; they should, as other villages did, raise more than their quota of turkeys; he could supply chicks to members. In conclusion he said that he thought that the village should take taxes on the incubator, it would be to their mutual advantages. After this speech he left the meeting.

The tone of the speech was not very pleasant hearing for the members present, and after Pinhas' departure there was a storm of protest from those assembled. It was said that the village must take taxes from them and must also bring the incubator within the boundaries of the village co-operative. Dov said that the Executive had taken advice on the matter and there was nothing they could do to compel Pinhas and Yael to give up the incubator. The meeting then said that

Dov should make representations to the Moshav Movement and to the organisations with which Pinhas was associated and enquire if the incubator could be taken over by the village co-operative. Dov said that he would do this and he would speak again with Pinhas.

After his talk with Pinhas, Dov reported to the Executive that they had come to an agreement that the incubator should be brought under the auspices of the co-operative. An announcement to this effect was put in the village bulletin. But two editions later another announcement appeared saying that Dov had received a reply from the organisations saying that they had heard nothing from Pinhas and so they could not answer Dov's question. Commenting upon this Dov wrote that he had spoken to Pinhas and he had said that he had no intention of selling out to the village.

This was the position when I left the village and according to letters to me from the villagers, nothing has yet been settled about Yael and Pinhas' private incubator.

I have dealt at length with this case because I believe it illustrates the central dilemma of Kfar Hefer as a co-operative: co-operation is viewed in voluntary terms, but how does one control a member who refuses to co-operate? The most extreme measure is to expel a person from the co-operative, but even in this case he may remain in the village. In Yael and Pinhas' case the problem was the opposite one: how to bring into the co-operative an enterprise spatially inside but economically outside. Where a member gains his livelihood within the co-operative, individual breaches may be dealt with by social and economic penalties. Here again, there is dispute within the village. The ethics of voluntary co-operation deny the use of penalties against members. Yet in Yael and Pinhas' case their livelihood did not come from the co-operative, nor could members sabotage the venture, as they sabotaged the farming of the young man who attacked the girl. All the financing of the incubator came from outside the village so the Executive could not use economic measures such as those they had used against Ben-David (see Chapter V). Yael and Pinhas had rights as residents in a local authority, so the village could neither cut off the water supply nor refuse their children schooling. The action they did take was to exclude them from the co-operative, action which was effective in making life socially uncomfortable for them but it had no effect upon their economic activities. And village members protested that their relationships with the couple remained good, so that at least superficially, there was no open hostility towards them. Differing attitudes to the affair were taken by Dov and the Executive (with the exception of Marks) and village members. Members were anxious

P

that the couple should pay taxes, because they did not want to subsidise them. Dov saw the problem in a different light, and here the question of 'precedent' arose. Throughout all discussion of the problem Dov was reluctant to have the issue brought up: he tried to delay discussion and even to dissuade members from debating the matter. This, I consider, was because the problem raised many issues which could have far-reaching effects on the village, and which Dov, as the formally appointed head of the moshav and the co-operative, was interested should not be brought into the open. This, I think, was also realised by other members of the village, but they were less concerned with the constitutional aspects of the problem than the immediate economic one.

The village could always have taken the case to the Moshav Movement for a decision. But as I reported in the previous chapter, the village did not hold a high opinion of this body, nor did they feel that ventilating this case in public would enhance Kfar Hefer's reputation as a 'real moshav'. In addition to these considerations, I believe the Executive was hesitant in 'making a case out of this issue' because whichever way the decision went it would have repercussions in the village. Pinhas has documents to say that the village approved of the incubator, and it was true that in the early days they had encouraged it: therefore, it was doubtful if they were in any position to reprimand him. The Executive and the villagers might be accused of what Willner called 'naïveté'[1] in expecting the couple to give up a prosperous business in return for full membership in the co-operative, but previous experience had given them no cause for alarm. Furthermore the Moshav Movement had advised Pinhas on the setting up of the venture so it might be expected that they would approve it, the more so as the practice was not uncommon in other moshavim. As Dov pointed out, if the decision went in favour of Pinhas then this left the way open for other similar ventures in the village, a situation not unlikely in view of the current agricultural market. If the Moshav Movement upheld Kfar Hefer's position this could also cause repercussions in the village because there were other families in the village who did not precisely fulfil all the conditions of moshav life and individuals might be tempted to take action against them. On top of all this there was the reluctance, implied in co-operation, to take legal action against village members. Even if it could be argued that this was in support of the greater good, it would be a break in the village's tradition of co-operation. For all these reasons I believe Dov preferred to ignore the situation and

---

[1] Willner (1960)

possibly to hope that the issue would sort itself out in time, perhaps a forlorn hope in view of Pinhas' intransigence.

This last case points out the ineffectiveness of gossip and scandal, and also of formal measures, in dealing with individuals who are, or have put themselves, on the margin of the community. One of the strengths of gossip and scandal is in reaffirming community values and of exercising social control over those who are interested to remain in the group. This is especially true when, as in Kfar Hefer, members are in both co-operation and competition with one another. Leach writes: '. . . if we repudiate the emphasis on moral rules and jural obligations then the problem becomes much simpler. The constraint imposed on the individual is merely one of patterning and limitation; the individual can do what he likes as long as he stays in the group. The group itself need have no rules.'[1] Other writers have discussed the nature of co-operative bodies. Social relationships in Kfar Hefer are in Weber's words 'either closed or limit the admission of outsiders by rules'.[2] And as Marx has pointed out: 'The various rules of admission . . . serve to define a group's membership in a precise fashion, at least in a formal sense.'[3] But more than this, Kfar Heferites believe themselves to be legally, formally and ideologically equal. Within the wider moshav movement immense changes have gone on in the framework of moshavim so that many are moshavim only in name. For economic and historical reasons the co-operative in Kfar Hefer has remained strong and most members have been interested that it should be so. There was no real alternative within the moshav for them; if dissatisfied, they could only leave it. Thus I believe members could operate, as Leach suggests for the Cingalese village he studied, by patterning and limiting relationships. But I, as against Leach, would suggest that this process operated through moral rules, especially through informal gossip. Yet changes in moshav policies outside Kfar Hefer have affected the perception of moshav life within the village. Kfar Hefer is concerned to maintain her reputation in the movement, but cannot do this by a stricter adherence to formal rules for this would negate the voluntary aspect of co-operation and disrupt the community.

[1] Leach (1961)   [2] Weber (1957)   [3] Marx (1966)

IX
Co-operation

In the last chapter I referred several times to the conception of 'co-operation' in village life. It was a frequently stated belief in Kfar Hefer that co-operation had declined over the years, as witness Ben-Natan's statements about the lack of co-operation to help the 'new farmers' (see Chapter V). Along with the decline in co-operation it is said that 'mutual aid' in the village has diminished, a tendency well illustrated by a current witticism told to me very cynically by a young farmer. The story goes that a moshavnik came to the village and asked if there was mutual aid between members. The answer was: 'Of course, two farmers will always combine to push down a third.' I believe most members of Kfar Hefer would repudiate the implications of this joke, but the 'old' of the village complained that members did not help one another as they had in the past. By this reference was made to the 'young' who were said to be more interested in making money than in helping others. It was said that they had taken on the values of the city to replace those of moshav life. An editorial in a journal published by the Moshav Movement commented: 'Nevertheless, the economic growth and financial security did not strengthen the social stability in the moshavim. In quite a number of them, some of the members are looking over the "fence" of the social framework which the moshav represents, lured by the appeal of city life. This of course has a disintegrating and demoralising effect on the community. It is apt to recall that Berl Katznelson once told members of moshavim that they were, "the guardians of the labour movement posted on its most exposed frontier—closest to the lures of the middle class." ' [1] The editorial concluded that, 'Only a proper balance between economic achievement and spiritual values will maintain the stability of the moshavim; will induce the moshav communities to creative ventures, and will strengthen their ability to develop new and modern farms enabling the moshav to cope with technological progress, social welfare and higher education demands.'

Unlike the kibbuts, which has a greater centralised direction and control and in which individual action is subordinated to that of the community, the moshav gives emphasis both to individual autonomy and to co-operation. And here is the apparent paradox that the kibbuts has been better equipped to incorporate, as it has been to

[1] *The Settler* (1965)

reject, new ways of living than the moshav which is theoretically more open to these. In the moshav, individuals have been affected by new developments but the Executive has tried to ignore these. This ignoring of reality has resulted, I have argued, in village members trying to extend the area of responsibility of the collective and to reduce its area of decision making, while the Executive is involved in exactly the opposite attempt—to act effectively it assumes unity in the village even though this is seldom true. Each member in Kfar Hefer is actively concerned to increase his economic possibilities, and in farming these are channelled through the co-operative. A result of this has been that members as individuals and as groups have gone outside the co-operative to achieve their aims. Through the administrative device of assuming unity within the village the co-operative seeks to consolidate and maintain existing social and economic patterns within the village. Initiative comes from individuals: and the previous chapters have shown how in some cases the co-operative can incorporate these changes into the framework of village life. Thus the 'alfalfa group' and the 'avocado group' went outside the co-operative to introduce changes but their activities take place within the framework of the village. The private incubator is an instance where individual effort cannot be sanctioned by the co-operative but rather than attempt to re-define and re-align relationships the Executive preferred to avoid a confrontation.

These developments have had an effect on co-operation and mutual aid in the village. The traditional explanation of mutual aid is: 'The principle of mutual aid, one of the moshav's main tenets, resulted from the desire of the founders of the first moshav villages to establish a just and humanitarian relationship between one individual and another and between the village and the individual.'[1]

Although emphasis is given to individual effort and initiative it is felt to be just that village members should help one another and show a practical concern for every member's welfare. Responsibility for some of this concern is taken by government and *Histadrut* organisations. All village members subscribe to the *Histadrut* organised health service and they are given medical care and hospital treatment under this scheme. Members also contribute to a national pension fund. The pension is received at the age of 65 years and 60 years respectively for men and women, but 70 years and 65 years if they continue working after pension age. The village also runs a savings fund under which a percentage of annual gross income is deposited in the member's account. The fund was started in 1950

[1] *The Settler* (spring/summer 1963)

when young families began to work in the family farms. It was felt that the older members should have a source of money available to them independent of that of the farm. The fund has grown in size from IL.14,000 in the first year to IL.2,750,000 in 1966. The contributions of older members stop at the age of 65 years, when all the money may be withdrawn. Contributions of the young start at the age of 35 years. Where there are two families in one farm paying into the fund each is credited with 1 per cent of gross income. The saving is tax free and cannot be claimed by the Executive to pay off debts in the village. It provides a useful capital for members when they are no longer earning. Money can be withdrawn from the fund before the age of 65 years; according to the constitution, an amount up to 40 per cent is allowed. In the village there was a lot of uncertainty about this clause: some said that 40 per cent of the given total at any one time could be withdrawn, while others said that the 40 per cent dated from the time of the first withdrawal. All members agreed that the fund was desirable and a fair measure to provide for the old. The disputes arose over the right of the co-operative to claim from this sum to pay off debts after the member's death or on his leaving the moshav. In some farms where there were large debts it was not expected that the sale of the farm would cover these. Therefore the co-operative, in the persons of the Executive, argued that they should have first claim on the savings fund to pay off debts. This was agreed in the village, but the uncertainty about withdrawal rights often resulted in members withdrawing sums from the account which they gave to their children or deposited elsewhere so that the money could not be used to pay off debts.

Most of the members in the village, as in many rural areas, are in debt to the co-operative. This gives the Executive as the chief lender of money in the village a certain control over members' affairs. I have already referred to the minimum sum paid to each family for its livelihood irrespective of the state of its account. This is one of the practical ways in which mutual aid is expressed in the village. Expenditure above this amount has to be requested from Dov, and the state of the farm plus the member's account are considered. Debts of up to IL.10,000 are not considered to be serious on a farm which is producing in all three main branches of agriculture. A good year can pay off this debt. But there are in the village several farms where the family is heavily in debt, IL.15,000 and above, and it is known that this debt will never be reduced. These are usually cases where the family is no longer actively involved in farming and where income is insufficient to cover living expenses and repayment of interest on the debt. In an Executive meeting Ben expressed his dismay at these debts which all had to be covered by the co-operative. One member told him not to worry, since according to economists greater debt signifies greater investment and greater future returns. Ben replied that he would feel much happier if he could believe this.

The support of individual indebtedness by the village is one factor which keeps members in the village, as members of the co-operative, even if they are no longer involved in production. Prices received for the sale of farms vary considerably, according to the state of the house, farm buildings and livestock. Not many farms have been sold in Kfar Hefer, but while I was in the village several members were said to be prepared to sell. Yet, despite the willingness of several young members to buy, not one owner agreed to sell. One widow actually went so far in a possible sale as to have her farm valued. She was offered IL.45,000, a sum which she turned down because she said that she could not afford to accept. She had a debt in the co-operative of IL.20,000 and a large part of her savings fund had gone to settle her children outside the village. As I stated earlier, members are allowed to draw on their savings fund and to receive the monthly amount without enquiry into their financial position. In fact an investigation purely of debt in the village is not very instructive about individual financial situations. Those without debt in the village were not the big producers; in the main they were farmers who had been active until recently in farming and on the sale of their dairy they had paid off the debt. They had no debt but their income was small and their standard of living reduced. The village is unlikely to give them loans for purchases, and where children are living outside the village the parents have often used the money from their savings fund to help the children when these married. An illustration of this is one man who farmed with his son-in-law, with the farm in their joint names. The son-in-law progressively reduced his work on the farm, turnover fell and the debt grew. Eventually the son-in-law decided to leave the farm and to work outside, but he claimed his share of the farm in order to give him capital to buy a house. The farm was sold but the price barely covered the debt; and when the son-in-law moved away the parents moved into a rented house in the village. The man worked part-time in the village since he was old and could not get work elsewhere. His money in the savings fund has gone to set up his other children in lieu of their share in the family farm. As a hired worker the man was not eligible for the minimum sum given to members of the co-operative.

This is an extreme case and the circumstances are deplored by village members who say that nothing of this kind should ever be allowed to happen in the future. But it does bring out some of the reasons why members, predominantly the elderly, who express dissatisfaction about Kfar Hefer, do not leave the village.

In addition to the non-producers who have big debts, there are also some farmers still actively farming who do not reduce their debt. These form the category which gave concern to Ben. Under the ethics of co-operation in the village it is considered the duty of members to help farmers who have difficulty in farming. Usually this task is left to the Executive, who often call in outside instructors to give advice. One young farmer, who had a very big debt of nearly IL.30,000 which was increasing, was called to a meeting of the Executive. Dov, from the outset, said that they were there to help him and not to censure him. According to his account this man lost income on his dairy, his poultry and turkeys, only making a profit on his citrus groves. Dov said that he was very worried about the state of the farm, but felt that the young man, who had to support a wife and two children, should be more concerned. He asked him if he had any suggestions to make. The man answered that, 'Yes, I would be all right if I could double the size of my poultry holding.' Dov reminded him that he was here for his own benefit and warned him that soon there might be a new Executive who would not be so lenient.

Members with debts are the concern of the whole village. Where members were elderly and had little or no income from the village there was no public complaint about the provision of a minimum standard of living. This was felt to be a humanitarian action towards those who had helped to build the village. But there was not much sympathy for the plight of inefficient farmers; many felt this was their own affair and that low income was their just deserts. Some members said that they should give up farming and leave it to those who were successful.

The paying of interest on these farms was difficult, though the village policy was to reduce the interest for those who paid over IL.2,000 interest per year on their debt. In all there was 16 such farms, but the reduction was given only to 'deserving cases'. Inefficiency or ineptitude for farming were not considered extenuating circumstances. Relief was given to those who were farming, yet under difficulty. In the year 1967/68 three farms were given a 25 per cent reduction: (1) a family where the parents and their two sons were engaged in farming, but all were ill and had been for many years; (2) a young farmer who had bought his own farm in the village and had invested heavily, and also helped his father in the family farm because of an accident to his elder brother who was that farm's mainstay; (3) a farm where the main labour force was the youngest daughter. All these cases were felt to be deserving of help, but the young man who wanted more poultry, as described above, was refused aid. Discussing the list the Executive were unanimous in refusing relief to him, since they all said that he was a young man and he should work harder.

Helping others is the essence of mutual aid in the co-operative, but some members complained that they were giving help to so great an extent that they themselves had no incentive to develop their farms.

The main ground for complaint was the village tax system. This was called within the village a 'progressive tax system'. In fact it was progressive in the sense that those with bigger incomes paid more tax, but each pound of income paid the same amount. Earlier I have described the background to the tax, but while I was in the village there were constant complaints about the system. Once again the 'young' of the village were said to be the main proponents for change. The 'young' of the village are, as I have indicated, a social rather than an age grouping. In each situation where the 'young' were said to be involved there was a shift in definition. The young in this case were those who had responsibility for two families on one farm. The young proposed a different system of 'equal taxes' where with a few exceptions everyone in the village would pay the same tax. The exceptions were at the lower end of the scale, so that those with small incomes would pay a reduced amount or be entirely exempted from payment.

Reaction amongst the 'old', who are also really a social grouping of those without the second generation on the farm, was that this confirmed the lack of idealism and ideology in the village's young. These were accused of following private interest without concern for others. In fact as often happened the two categories appealed to moshav principles though they interpreted these in different ways. The 'young' stated that 'equality' meant equality in taxes; the 'old' believed that it was the responsibility of the strong to help the weak.

The appeal by the 'young' to change to a system of equal taxes led others to join in the discussion. Questions were asked at meetings and articles were written in the village bulletin. I was told that in every general meeting in the last ten years there had been proposals to change the tax system, but those advocating change had always been in a minority and were overruled. Several alternative schemes were put forward in addition to that of equal tax. One was a scheme whereby 75 per cent of the tax paid should be equal, the remaining 25 per cent paid according to income. Another more complex suggestion involved members being divided into income groups and according to these tax would be paid. Under this last scheme it was proposed that income up to IL.10,000 should pay the average tax of the village, those with income up to IL.12,500 should pay 125 per cent of the average tax; up to IL.15,000 should pay 150 per cent; and up to IL.18,000 should pay 175 per cent. All these schemes acknowledged that some members should not pay taxes or should pay a reduced amount. This is the practice in the current tax system in the village; members who do not reach the average tax level pay at a rate of two-thirds the amount or even less.

At a General Meeting to discuss the tax situation, a meeting twice postponed because of insufficient attendance, a member of the tax committee opened the evening by saying that the demands for changes in the system had come from outside the committee. No member of the committee at any time had suggested a change in the system. He concluded that some members wanted changes because of the lack of '*haverut*' in the village. Throughout this analysis I have translated the Hebrew word '*haver*' simply as 'member' but the word carries with it more than mere membership in an organisation· The word is also translated as 'friend' or 'comrade'; and to be a '*haver*' of a moshav has connotations of both meanings. Thus this member was complaining that the spirit of friendship, of comradeship, of mutual concern, was missing in the village. The next to speak was Moshe Eden, also a member of the tax committee. He said that he supported the system in the village but a few changes should be made. This was seconded by Shimoni who said that the system needed 'bringing up to date'. The changes proposed by these two men involved a re-appraisal of the two-thirds system, because those who did not reach the average tax paid more per pound than those who did. One of the main complaints of those advocating change was acknowledged: that not all income goes through the co-operative and so some members did not pay village taxes on all their annual income. Further complaints were made that no account was taken of family expenses in paying tax. A farm with six or seven people to support had to meet more expenses than a farm where only a couple lived. This was elaborated by a member from the hall who said that farming families also had to invest in their farms, and he believed that this should be taken into consideration. Shimoni took up this point and said that he was opposed to the 'added value' of a branch being taxed. ('Added value' is an estimate of the increased value of the farm during a year, through the increase in the size of holdings.) The first speaker retorted that 'added value' was income and if this was not taken into consideration then those who bought and sold cattle and made a profit would never have this included in the tax. Emanuel said that professional members in the village should pay more: they paid only IL.40 per month for municipal taxes, a sum which was quite inadequate to cover the services they received. Continuing the argument he added that professional members did not have the expense of farm investment; all the money they received went straight into their pockets. Dov then joined in the discussion. He was in favour of retaining the two-thirds system because the financial situation of those who did not reach the average tax was often as good as those who did. In this argument he referred to members who received pensions and had money in the savings fund. He added that there were enormous differences in taxes paid by members, but there were not such big differences in standard of living. (There were indeed big differences in the amounts of tax paid by members: in the year 1966/67 14 members paid over IL.2,000 in tax, and in 1967/68 one member paid IL.3,000. At the bottom of the tax list were those who paid less than IL.300. All these figures were well known in the village because every year a list of members and the tax each paid was published in the village bulletin.)

On a vote to decide whether to maintain the present tax system or to advocate changes, 15 voted for changes, while the rest abstained. There were about 30 members present, so only half voted for the change. Those who abstained were chiefly the 'old'. The next vote was on the two-thirds system, and it was decided to abolish this. All supporters of the vote recommended that consideration should be taken of the number of people in a farm before deducting tax. It was decided that a special committee to discuss this proposal should be elected to sit with the already existing tax committee, and their proposals should be put to the Executive.

Shimoni's plea to the meeting that the tax system should be 'brought up to date' was the continuing theme of those who wanted changes. They argued that this did not affect systems of co-operation and mutual aid but was simply a reflection of the changes that had occurred in the village's history. This point affected other areas of co-operation in village life. The village recently improved the agricultural supplies store and changes were made to the silo. All agricultural members in the village were required to cover the cost of this investment despite the fact that almost a third of the village did not use these services. Again, a decision was taken in a General Meeting, attended primarily by the young, that the cost of the voluntary kindergarten (ages four to five years) should be covered by the village as a whole and not by the parents of the children attending. After this last decision one elderly member, whose children and grandchildren live outside the village, said: 'Wait, we will have the decision reversed at the Annual General Meeting.'

Co-operation in other areas of village life was also questioned when the scrutinising committee revealed to members that profits from the village store were used to cover losses in other village enterprises, notably the egg-grading station. For tax reasons the village does not want to end a year with a profit on an enterprise and so surpluses are transferred to other accounts. The egg-grading station, which employs many of the village who are no longer farming, consistently ended the year with a loss, chiefly on the salaries paid to these workers. When the scrutinising committee told a General Meeting that profits from the store were used to cover this loss, members decided to demand an explanation from the Executive. Dov, who was not at the meeting, wrote a reply in the village bulletin. This stated that the scrutinising committee were totally misinformed about the workings of the Executive and he denied that this practice took place. Notwithstanding this denial, members continued to write that profits from the store should be distributed amongst those using the store, in proportion to the amount spent. They also argued that if one village enterprise suffered a loss then this should be covered by members using this enterprise.

Aside from the formal aspects of co-operation and mutual aid complaints were made that informal mutual aid was also a custom little honoured. While co-operation in farm economy is a basic tenet in moshav life and mutual aid is included in this sphere, it is impossible to legislate for all contingencies; and co-operation in non-farming spheres does not have the force of 'moshav law'. Older members pointed to the early days of settlement when income had been shared and members helped in one another's farms. In fact a good deal of mutual aid was given in Kfar Hefer; and here common residence as neighbours was important. Between women in the same street there was borrowing and lending of household goods and equipment, baby sitting and joint baking of cakes for birthdays and other celebrations. Men often shared agricultural equipment with their neighbours, though this frequently gave rise to quarrels and the assertion that it was 'more trouble than it was worth'. If a family went away from the village for a day the neighbours took care of poultry; and the borrowing of small amounts of cash between neighbours was common. In times of family difficulties, illness or bereavement neighbours helped one another. The ties of kinship uniting many of the village members also played a part in this. These are all instances of short-term help and members complained about lack of help in long-term need. Members who were called away into army reserve service, often for as long as 40 days, complained that they had to hire workers for the farm. Part of this cost was returned and the member could claim tax relief but nevertheless it was a considerable expense for many farms. Some members urged that neighbours should make pacts of mutual aid in time of military service, as was done in the Six Days' War. But most members were anxious not to be tied to agreements of reciprocal aid, for the nature of present-day farming in Kfar Hefer had resulted in time being the farmer's most valuable factor. And even though farmers may have been glad to receive aid from their fellows they were not anxious to return this by giving of their own time. Therefore in times of need, if the farmer and his family could not cope with the demands of the farm, then the farmer preferred to hire labour rather than become indebted to his fellow farmers.

The Six Days' War of June 1967, reasserted Kfar Hefer's belief that the spirit of co-operation was not dead in the village. Amidst the national rejoicing over victory, Kfar Hefer celebrated the fact that there was 'nothing wrong with our youth and our village; we still know how to work together'. Mobilisation into the army began some time before the outbreak of war and men from the village were called up from 21 May. The first to be called were those who served in maintenance work and as drivers. As more of the village's young men were mobilised their work was organised from within the village. This was done from the village office under the direction of Ben, Marks and Oren. The men remaining in the village took on work in other farms, each receiving a list of duties from Ben. Dov was called to the army in the early days of mobilisation. With the increasing departure of men from the village women took on more of the farm work. Many of them did not know how to drive tractors and they received instruction from a Kfar Hefer girl who was active on her farm. Women could be seen driving tractors, looking after cows, and transporting feed from the fields for the animals. Men helped with the milking in several farms and people remarked on the difference at the village dairy. The dairy was known as the place for the exchange of gossip and news, but no longer did the men stop to talk—they brought the milk in and went back to work. Children were also involved in these efforts. Classes went on as usual in the village school, but children in high school started school later in the day in order to help with milking. Officially children were supposed to receive a letter from one of the Executive if they absented themselves from school. Increasingly this was ignored and many children worked all day in their farms and those of others. The children of Kfar Hefer and all the young people of the area helped in their own and other settlements. Moreover, children from the suburb of Dunia also worked in Kfar Hefer and other moshavim. Often fairly young children could be seen driving tractors and the Executive several times reminded families that even though this was wartime the normal legal requirements were still in force and children under 15 years were forbidden to drive tractors.

As in all the country the men were called up according to their tasks in the army and their army divisions. By the second and third of June most men were called to the army. Those who remained in the village were anxious and wished that they too would be mobilised. When the fighting was announced on 6 June many volunteered and contacted the army to ask why they had not been called. All through the day the radio announced code names of army divisions calling on men to report to their units. In spite of their hard work in the village those who were eligible for army service felt disappointed that they were not involved in military action. A few young men remained in the village—those who were trained for youth leadership in the army, and a couple of young men who were exempted from army service because the family farm could not manage without their labour. Villagers commiserated with them but pointed out that they were serving in the village instead of in the army. These young men did work very hard from the early hours of the day until after midnight, both on farms in the village and in services.

The village was joined with the surrounding area for civil defence and measures in case of attack. In this the Regional Council played a part in co-ordinating settlements. The old, most of whom had not served in any of Israel's three wars, were engaged in tasks of local defence. Men took on guard duty and dug shelters. Sessions for donations of blood and first-aid classes were organised. The women of the village, especially the old, were engaged in a flurry of baking cakes, collecting magazines and books and so forth, to send to those serving in the army. Many of the young women of the village who had left Kfar Hefer on marriage came back to the village to stay with their parents while their husbands served in the army. These women, together with their mothers, maintained a 24-hour telephone service in the village. Those on duty late at night were escorted to and from the office by one of the elderly men of the village. The office, especially at night, was a meeting-place for the women who sat together drinking tea and talking. Those women remaining at home in the evening also gathered together, mainly on a neighbourhood basis because those with young children wanted to be close to home. The meetings were important not only for mutual support but also for the passing on of information. Before the outbreak of war soldiers occasionally telephoned to the village and passed on news of themselves and others from Kfar Hefer. People gathered together to hear news bulletins and those who missed a broadcast eagerly questioned others. The majority of the village listened to the national broadcasts. I listened to the B.B.C. and the five-minute journey, on foot, to the village store often took me as long as half-an-hour as members asked me what was the news from England.

The war was short but the effect on the village was considerable. The death of a pilot born in Kfar Hefer was deeply mourned, as were the deaths of those from the surrounding area. Yet, the main reaction of the village was one of pride, not only in their soldiers but also in the village itself. The co-operation of individuals and the mutual concern were constantly remarked upon with conscious pride. The young children were especially congratulated: they had proved that they were the inheritors of Kfar Hefer's traditions. The young men who had remained in the village were also singled out for praise. A notice in the village bulletin said that it was not usual in Kfar Hefer publicly to praise individuals, but each was mentioned by name, and they were thanked for their contribution to the village.

In this euphoric mood after the war, people said that the differences of the past were over, now they had proved themselves a community and they could begin anew. A national crisis brought people together in co-operation and gave them the feeling that once again they, within the nation, were a real community. The feeling was real and warranted. But it was short-lived. As the village returned to normal conditions the 'normal' differences again re-appeared.

In several ways the war did have a more prolonged effect on the village: it entered into the cultural history of Kfar Hefer. Instances which were believed by some to show a lack of concern for others were now unfavourably compared, not only with actions in the early days of settlement, but also, with recent events. Young people also continued to take an interest in farming that they had not shown previously, in the time before the emergency. This did not always take the expected forms. One man humorously and despairingly complained that his tractor was never there when he wanted it. The young boy, who had worked on the farm during the war, a son of a professional member, felt that he had a share in the vehicle and pre-empted it to take his friends on jaunts around the village and to the beach. The owner asked, 'How can I refuse him; tell him that those days are over?'

'Those days' were over, and the debate in the village continued about the rights and obligations of village members. Emanuel, in a General Meeting, summed up the discussion as: 'The question is to which kind of society we want to belong. Our way is right if we say that all our ways of production are equal. I think that health services, education, culture, and municipal services are thus equal and should be to public workers.' He concluded that, 'There is no absolute justice, but there has to be a minimum.' Cohen put the problem differently: 'The important question is, how are decisions reached and on what are these decisions based?'

It was popularly believed in the village that the 'young' were in the vanguard for changes in the tax system and those opposed to them interpreted their action as their lack of belief in village values. Marks complained that he did not understand the younger genera- tion of the village. His son who was 'one of the good ones' held completely different ideas about the development of the village. The son believed that when a farm became vacant in the village then the village co-operative should buy it and divide the land amongst those continuing in farming. Marks said that this would completely alter the character of the village and destroy all its ideals. When he ex- plained this to his son, the latter always retorted: 'That was all thirty years ago, times have changed.' In fact the 'young' were not attacking the 'old' in their pressure to have tax changes. All who advocated reform acknowledged that some members could not afford to pay more tax. More attention was given to families where there were sources of income from outside farming and which were not account- able for tax. Moshe Eden in an attempt to differentiate between farms in Kfar Hefer said, 'We must recognise two types of farms: one, developed farms which demand large investment in both material and labour; two, farms content with two branches of pro- duction and with a side income from outside work. We cannot com- plain about the old who cannot increase production. But the young, the second generation who work outside, should have their taxes increased.' This statement emphasised the ideas of those who were disgruntled, an idea that was subscribed to by the values of Kfar Hefer, that agricultural production was the essence of village life. This attitude also explains the demands for professional members to pay taxes according to income. For most of the village's develop- ment the returns achieved by farmers were greater than those of professional workers. This has now changed, for although agri- cultural income has risen in the village so, too, have costs of produc- tion. The market situation and the economics of production demand heavy investment for efficient production. Within the village indi- viduals are in competition with one another for quotas of production; the possibilities for expanded output depend both on the farmer himself and on others in the village. I have shown how the land and the quotas of those giving up dairying were used by dairy farmers to increase their output. The situation in poultry in the village also reflected this competition between members. The original nucleus of the 'avocado' group was of members who despite their participation in all farming branches did not have big returns. This latter group, and others associated with them who were in a similar position, formed the bulk of those pressing for changes in the system of mutual aid. These were the farmers who worked hard in agriculture but needed costly investment to reach very profitable levels of production, and in this they were discouraged because as individual production grew, the personal quota of permitted output fell.

The attitudes of this category of farmers in Kfar Hefer were expressed by their counterparts in Nahalal. At a symposium held there, young members gave their views about the moshav as a way of life. A young member of the Executive said: 'The role of the moshav today is to produce agricultural produce cheaply and efficiently, with no hidden unemployment. The policy required of the moshav is to exploit to the maximum the means of production.' Another speaker followed this by saying: 'The aim today in modern states is to reach a situation like that in the U.S.A. where 8 per cent of the population are in agriculture. Today Israel has no further need for more agriculturists and the idea of the moshav does not serve the purpose of the State.' This opinion was shared by many connected with agriculture, and it will be remembered that a *Knesset* member had expressed the opinion that 'ideological reasons' should not stand in the way of improved agriculture.

Those who were seeking to alter the tax system in Kfar Hefer were drawing attention to the difficulties of farmers in a moshav in trying to adjust to these new demands. This view was not shared by those who had retired from full farming. They said that farmers already benefited from extra quotas which were the rights of others; the former were enjoying the rights of others and they should acknowledge this by carrying responsibility for those less fortunate than themselves. Also they pointed to the cars and houses of these members and said that things could not be as bad as they said, or else they could not afford such luxuries. In fact most of these possessions were bought on credit and guaranteed by expectations of future returns. Many in Kfar Hefer deplored this trend, a symptom of what Doron called, 'Israel's national disease—spending more than one can afford'. Kfar Hefer was not immune from this 'disease' and the involvement of members in the wider society of Israel, accentuated by her geographical position in the country, influenced members' thinking about the desirable style of life to be attained.

The third category of members, the main target of those pressing for tax reforms, were the families involved both in agriculture and outside work. They argued that they were doing no more than those fully engaged in agriculture, trying to improve their financial position. And citing the moshav principle of individual initiative, they said that they took a part in farming and contributed to the village, and what they did beyond this was their own affair.

Within the village there existed varying ideas about co-operation and mutual responsibility. These are revealed in the dispute about taxes and in the attitude to village enterprises. Views did not in every case coincide, and each new issue brought together a new clustering of members.

In the widest sense all the villagers were joined in the administratively defined municipality of Kfar Hefer. Within this there existed the 'co-operative' of Kfar Hefer, to which all professional and agricultural members belonged. In the ideological sense of the moshav, all those connected with the running of the moshav share membership in the community, and this includes hired workers, both those resident in the moshav and those living outside. (In part this explains the ideological resistance to the employment of non-Jewish labour in moshavim and kibbutsim, for this detracts from the 'national' quality of settlement.) Aside from the distinction between 'professional' and 'agricultural' members, the co-operative is viewed in moshav law and ideology as an undifferentiated body. Members of the co-operative may have different interests but these are felt to be encapsulated in the all-embracing 'co-operative'. In this study I have drawn attention to the broad lines along which Kfar Heferites divide. (1) There is the division between the 'non-farmers' and the 'farmers'; the first grouping was those who no longer use all their available agricultural rights in the village; the second was composed of those who are fully engaged in all the main agricultural branches of farming. (2) The village is also divided into families which have the continuation of the second generation on the farm, and those who do not. The generations are said to be divided in Kfar Hefer, and popularly the distinction between the 'first' and the 'second' generation was clearly drawn. Factors linking the Kfar Heferites include: (i) common membership and residence in Kfar Hefer; (ii) kin and neighbourhood ties; (iii) economic interest, including production quotas, mutual aid, political affiliation and the negative factor of the unprofitability of selling a farm; (iv) a commitment in the broadest sense, to the ideal of moshav life; even those who criticised Kfar Hefer did not denigrate the moshav as a way of life.

Those are the broad interests and links which tended to unite all Kfar Heferites and also to divide them into various groupings. In some instances these interests coincided, and indeed, there is, by and large, a direct causal link between the groupings of 'non-farmers' and 'those without the second generation in the farm'. The attitudes and interests of village members were affected by their particular social characteristics and economic interests which placed them into the above categories. Thus all 'farmers' were opposed to the move by the 'non-farmers' to regain their lands from the village. But seldom, if ever, did the village divide on such clear-cut lines. Not all the 'non-farmers' were opposed to the village using their lands; some had found employment elsewhere and were not interested in farming; the movement to reclaim lands came from those who did not have alternative employment. Similarly there was no clear opposition of the generations in Kfar Hefer: in most two-family farms the relationship between the generations was amicable.

The social attributes which made an individual belong to one category did not guarantee that he would act primarily in terms of these characteristics. Each individual held a variety of interests, and these were not necessarily of equal weight. Even if the assumption is made that economic interests are of primary importance to the individual, this does not mean that his interests are the same as those of the grouping with which he is broadly identified. In some situations an individual's interest unites him to those with whom, in other circumstances, he has little contact, or to whom he is even opposed. The differing attitudes expressed about mutual aid and reciprocal aid reflect this process. The shifting alignments and allegiances on this issue show how members acted in terms of their varying interests. Thus, firstly, on the tax issue big producers supported the proposal that investment on the farm should be taken into account when computing taxes. But they split on the issue that account should also be taken of family size, and that tax relief should be given to those with many dependents. Those with big families supported the proposition, but big producers with small families joined the single-generation farms in their opposition to the proposal. Secondly, on the question of reciprocal aid, the alignments also showed difference of opinions between 'the young' and the 'farmers', categories which are usually regarded as congruent in Kfar Hefer. Farmers who had recently bought a farm, or those who were trying to build up a family farm, advocated the promotion of schemes of reciprocal aid. Established farmers preferred to hire help rather than to incur a commitment to give time to another farm.

The relative strength of these various ties and the resulting clusters of individuals which they produce is seen in the operation of several new ventures in the village. Economic demands and interests are the most powerful of these ties but in themselves they do not automatically override all other ties. Where there is a coincidence with other groupings then this strengthens the economic principle. This can be seen in the emergence in Kfar Hefer of spheres of co-operation within the moshav framework. The 'alfalfa' and 'avocado' groups illustrate this tendency. It appears that within the village there is a growing coincidence between certain economic and social groupings. And in the last few years distinct clusters of individuals have acted as pressure groups within the village for the promotion of their interests. Concomitant with this, co-operation and mutual aid have become increasingly formalised. I have referred to the assumption by the government and the *Histadrut* of some of these duties. The growing use by the village of insurance schemes to guarantee members' production aims to transfer this responsibility away from the village on to formal agencies.

The acknowledgement that there existed different interests within the village caused concern to many members, who argued that this signified the decline of the community. 'Community' and 'harmonious social relationships' are almost synonymous in Kfar Hefer, where it is believed that identity and unity of purpose are the hallmarks of true village life. Dov, writing in the village bulletin, said: 'For those members who have no continuation there is no interest in contributing to the development of certain large enterprises in the village. We have to say this openly, that there are members who have no interest in the economic development of the village. Many settlements have broken up because some members have lost all interest in the development of the community economically. Only if those members who have no continuation in their farms continue to regard the village as their home will they see the general interest as their interest.' And continuing he added: 'Then there are those members who say openly (although not in writing) that they are waiting for the reduction of the number of farming units in the village.' In conclusion he warned the village: 'It is apparent that there are two sections in the village and this is a very dangerous development for the future of the village.'

This was known in the village but never precisely stated in these terms, for disputes were normally fought out in differing interpretations of moshav ideology and law. Each of the various interest groups was convinced that if only it explained its case sufficiently well, and those in opposition paid careful attention, then all misunderstandings would be cleared away, and the village could harmoniously proceed with its affairs. After a long and noisy meeting in which opinions on many topics were exchanged, my neighbour in the village hall, a young farmer, turned to me and said: 'Oh, these old men; and they are not fools you know.' The appeal was that I as a young person would see the infallible logic of the arguments of the 'young' and realise that the 'old', while well-meaning, were being obstinately obtuse. The differing interpretations were not simply the pursuit of self-interest. The differences over co-operation in the village show that all acknowledged that it was the duty of members to help those who could not help themselves. The absence of private marketing in Kfar Hefer, a phenomenon prevalent in other moshavim, indicates the recognition by Kfar Heferites of the value of the co-operative. Their attitude to their neighbouring moshav shitufi, Gavish, forcibly expressed their appreciation of their way of life in Kfar Hefer. One young farmer, 30 years of age, told me: 'My generation is all right on ideology, but I am worried about the next.'

Gavish held an attitude of mixed admiration and amusement towards Kfar Hefer; their achievements in building the state and the moshav were admired but Gavish felt the members' staunch insistence on individual effort resulted in an inefficient system. They tell the story how in the early days of their settlement when they tried to drive through Kfar Hefer, its members would slowly drive their tractors in the middle of the road so that they could not pass. This story is indignantly denied by Kfar Heferites who say that they would not be guilty of such ill-mannered behaviour, but add, 'If that is the way they feel, then they must believe that they are inferior.'

The differences in attitudes in Kfar Hefer towards co-operation sprang from a differential involvement in agriculture. Those whose full income came from agricultural production, the traditional mainstay of Kfar Hefer, tried to have this recognised in the village. In the sphere of village investment they usually succeeded because the village's financial strength came from her position as a big and efficient producer. Individuals could not become big farmers in the sense of holding more land, and limits were set upon their production by internal village rules, but with the increasing pressures on agriculture from the national level they attempted to transfer some of their responsibilities and costs to the wider community. Those without continuation on the family farm, commonly designated 'the old', also felt the pressure of national agricultural policy; but its effects were attributed to the failings of the 'young' of Kfar Hefer. They argued that if the young were the true inheritors of Kfar Hefer, then they would share their quotas with those who had not enough for livelihood. Thus the two categories worked with different terms of reference: the young with a set of economic relationships drawn from the national arena; the old with the more circumscribed relationships of the moshav as a social and economic entity. The clash of these two separate frameworks took place in village meetings and I believe that this situation supplies the reason why each category claimed to fail to understand the other. Hence the young man's remark about the 'old', and the 'old's' frequently asserted belief that, 'We do not know where these young people got their ideas; certainly not from Kfar Hefer.'

Dov, in his role as internal secretary, can be seen as the figure connecting these two sets of relationships, and hence we may understand why he was constantly criticised by both 'young' and 'old' alike.

This struggle went on within the setting of moshav values and principles which both categories interpreted as vindicating their demands. In spite of the competition between 'young' and 'old' and differences within these categories, all needed the co-operative for their livelihood and each category attempted to influence village policy. In this the 'young' were in a stronger position for all were interested in increased production and increased efficiency. They succeeded in building the village silo at a cost debited to all agricultural members; they 'persuaded' Ron as the head of the land committee to use the land of others on their behalf. The 'old' were divided amongst themselves, for many were not interested in farming, and some had found work elsewhere. Numerically they were in a minority and their numbers were depleted by those who failed to take any part in village life. I have shown how not all the elderly of Kfar Hefer were called 'old', but the failure of those whose sons were farming to take an active part in discussions enabled the different interests to be termed a struggle between 'young' and 'old'. The old expressed the idea that they were the trustees of Kfar Hefer, the keepers of the moshav spirit, and attempts to change this were attributed to the dilution of this spirit in the less idealistic youth. Through this the myth of the trouble-free days of the past was maintained and of a spirit which, if it could be recaptured, would put an end to village strife. Differences were said to spring from lack of commitment to moshav ideology: this was seen as the cause and not the symptom of conflicting interests. Thence the belief that if they could once and for all lay down rules of conduct and begin afresh then they would be all right. This ignored the fact that social, economic, friendly and kin ties were not separate entities, but that the intermingling of all these serve at the same time to define the community and to make precise delimitation of its framework impossible. Because of the manner in which all these ties intermingled to form the community, it was felt that Pinhas and Yael had gone over the 'reasonably drawn line' of community relationships; but because of the impossibility of precise delimitation of what was and what was not included in moshav law the village found it hard to take effective action.

Conclusion

'Today the moshav is not the same as the moshav of Eliezer Jaffe. And to our regret we cannot turn back the wheels of history, and it seems that the moshav of the future will not be the same as the first moshavim.' This was the view of the editor of the village bulletin, printed and distributed to members in an editorial. This prognostication was dismissed by one member because 'he works in Tel Aviv; he has ceased to milk cows; and he does not attend village meetings'.

In this analysis I have been concerned to record, interpret and analyse life within Kfar Hefer during a short period of time. I have attempted to show how Kfar Hefer as a moshav, as a community, and as a collection of groups and individuals, pursued policies and reacted to events both in the village, and outside in the wider Israeli scene. These responses have been interpreted in the light of village history; moshav ideology; co-operative and customary law; demography; and the economic facts of life.

The above quotation highlights one of the central problems with which this study has been concerned: how Kfar Hefer, who believed herself to be a community and a 'real moshav', responded to the changed conditions surrounding the moshav, economically and socially, in Israel.

Writing in 1952 Talmon-Garber emphasised: 'It should be stressed that the co-operative village together with the communal settlements form an integral part of an active and conscious elite.' [1] Today, in 1968, Kfar Hefer still believes herself to be a leader though this opinion is not always shared by those outside the village. Israel is a small country, and the line of direction from government to local level is short, although seldom direct. Various associations and organisations with which Kfar Hefer is joined influence and implement government policy. It is open to these organisations and the individual settlement to attempt to divert and mitigate the full effects of government directives; but the power residing in government, especially in economic affairs, makes this the chief deciding factor on local life. In the past, in the *Yishuv* and in the early years of the State, the interests of national government and established

[1] Talmon-Garber (1952)

settlements more or less ran concurrently. As the population grew so too did demands for agricultural production and communities like Kfar Hefer benefited, particularly as they formed a part of national leadership. Over-production at home and competition in overseas markets have made the position of agricultural producers more difficult, as has the growth of a national leadership not drawn primarily from settlements. These settlements still exercise an influence on policy and values of Israeli life, and membership of an old-established settlement still holds high status in national values. But the development of cities and the growth of industry and professions no longer guarantee first place in national social and economic rankings to communal and co-operative settlements.

Within the village this has affected community relationships. During the time I was in Kfar Hefer members were consciously involved in debating the cultural, social and economic structures of their community, usually summed up as, 'our way of life in the moshav'. Existing processes of administration and legislation were called into question and attempts were made to re-define moshav principles. In this, two main categories were identified, 'the young' who urged changes, and 'the old' who tried to reaffirm tradition and accused 'the young' of being less idealistic and more materialistic than was suitable for the heirs of Kfar Hefer. I have shown that 'the young' and 'the old' were really social and economic groupings. Farmers who were still involved in all three main branches of agriculture clustered together to form 'the young'; 'the old' were those families in only one or two of the agricultural branches. Full farmers were anxious to increase production and raise efficiency, but because of national policies which set a limit on production and because of internal village allocations of production this could only be achieved at the expense of others in the village. As one farmer gave up production in one area of agriculture so his quota was transferred to the remainder to be divided. Those giving up production were the families where there was no second generation continuation in the farm. The farms where full production continued were two generation family farms and farms bought by a second generation member. In all cases it was the labour force of young people in the farm that was decisive, and so the division was popularly called one between 'young' and 'old'.

The co-operative, especially the Executive, and particularly Dov, were intimately involved in this differential involvement in agriculture. Both categories were concerned to ensure for themselves an adequate standard of living. But the strength of the co-operative lay in its role as the co-ordinator of agricultural producers; and to act

effectively in internal affairs and external relationships it was concerned that the village should be a strong producer. In effect this
gave primacy to those still engaged in all branches of farming. The
provision of improved agricultural services, the building of the silo,
and the improvements to the supplies store, at a cost borne by all
agricultural members, reflect this trend. This gave rise to disgruntled
complaints from those not involved in these activities.

For the moshav is not simply an agricultural co-operative: it is
also a social unit and there are certain tenets which are basic to it,
such as mutual aid, concern for the welfare of others, equality
between members. Those who had given up dairy farming stated that
the primacy given to the needs of full farmers went beyond these
provisions to such an extent that they themselves were exploited. This
argument was not placed in the setting of national economic affairs
but in terms of moshav values; 'the young' were accused of being
unaware of moshav principles. Those without full farming also felt
the pressure upon agriculture: they too were affected by external and
internal policies, but citing the moshav principle of equality they
argued that they should be compensated for the rights they had
renounced in the dairy by corresponding increases in poultry holdings. Both categories felt the Executive, in its attempts to satisfy all
demands, was acting without heeding their interests. This feeling led
to a demand for the check on the powers of the Executive and a
demand for the formulating of moshav principles.

This discussion all took place in terms of moshav ideology. I
have shown how this culture was not the mere rules and regulations
of moshav life but also the outcome of the multiple ties existing
between individuals and the body of 'customary law' which had
developed with the village. The Executive and Dov resisted the
attempts for clearer definitions of moshav culture because of the
repercussions that this would have had in the village, and on the
moshav's standing in the wider society. This latitude of interpretation in moshav life, helped by such technical devices as imprecision
in the writing of minutes and the failure to record decisions, served
to preserve a unity within the village.[1] Yet it also weakened the
power of members to take action against recalcitrant individuals,
such as Pinhas and Yael; thus the presentations of relationships to
the internal and external systems were at odds. Outside, the village
was concerned to present a united front, for ideological and sound
economic reasons. Inside this was to some extent a facade which
could not always be maintained. Until recently this has not been a
contradiction, for the strength of the co-operative in outside dealings

[1] This is reported for another community in Frankenberg (1957)

had brought prosperity to village members. This, I suggest, is why Kfar Hefer did not become involved in the new agricultural developments in Israel. Village members had a direct interest in maintaining village production at a high level and each benefited from Kfar Hefer's historical position as a big producer. This may explain Ben's statement to me that, 'Kfar Hefer has never been a pioneer'.

Village interests have been well served by the unity of village life in the co-operative and this has consolidated and increased the members' livelihood. I believe that this pattern is now changing, partially because of national economic policies and partially because of demographic patterns within the village. In this the significance of numbers is important. The 'alfalfa group' and the 'avocado group' were successful ventures because the above conditions combined to unite sufficient members, who despite their differences felt enough common interest to combine together. It is significant, I think, that initially both these groups appealed not to the Executive for help but to outside professional bodies. The Executive as the consolidator of achievements cannot act as innovator, it can only recognise and endorse innovations. Thus there seems to be a process within Kfar Hefer whereby pockets of co-operation are growing up within the formally defined overall co-operative. I believe that this process will continue, especially as the third generation come into farming. On some farms there will be an excess of labour, more than is needed to work the existing branches of agriculture. And I consider that these farms will venture into new forms of production; I suggest moreover that these will not be individual efforts, but will be achieved in co-operation with other farmers. The justification for this belief is based on the evidence submitted: demographic patterns within the village will bring together a number of farms and the past experience of working together through the co-operative will reinforce this. Kfar Hefer is a strong moshav amongst moshavim and the influence that this brings serves members' interests.

But these are future possibilities and at the moment the village is in the process of incorporating these trends into village life. This took the form of an endless debate about moshav principles and ideology. All in Kfar Hefer subscribe to the idea that there should be a community. The first generation hope to see the second generation, their successors, as the transmitters of village culture and community life. But no longer are they the pioneers closely involved with agricultural production and their lack of intimate involvement in this sphere of village life makes their appreciation of village problems different from that of the young. Nevertheless they are still members of the village and the co-operative, and as the founders of Kfar

Hefer they believe that they should advise on the village's way of life. Pressures for change are viewed as attacks on the principles by which they have lived. In fact, as I have recounted the emphasis on individual action in the moshav has enabled many practices to develop which are not in strict accordance with moshav law, but which have been sanctioned by village custom. National policies have sharpened existing differences between individuals with which village systems of government have been unable to cope. This has led to demand for the re-definition of moshav law; the cleavage along lines of economic differences is believed to call for a new definition of moshav life. In the past 'co-operative' stood for unity of like family farms and now it has to contain and even represent differences. The dilemma facing Kfar Hefer's members is that the moshav cannot be understood in simple economic terms: relationships from all other areas of life spill over into the economic sphere. A re-definition of economic relationships invariably carries with it a re-definition of other ways of life. This is the paradox of Kfar Hefer: as members of a real 'moshav' the 'comrades' (*haverim*) cannot afford to define too closely the relationships which bind them together, but the absence of this definition curtails community action in dealing with violations which fall beyond the 'reasonably drawn line' of the moshav law and culture.

Postscript: two years after

In late 1969, a year and a half after I finished my field work in Kfar Hefer, I returned to live in the village. Although I was engaged in new field research, not specifically on Kfar Hefer, my residence in the village did give me a further opportunity to observe events in the community and to notice the changes which had taken place during my absence from the field.

Outwardly the village had not changed very much; some houses had been extended and improved; more people owned cars; about half the houses had television sets; and more houses had a telephone. The impact of television on the village was considerable, for in place of the twice-weekly film shows of the past there was only one film show per week at which the attendance was very poor. It was also alleged that television had affected the attendance at village meetings; as reported above, this was always low, but it became even lower and many meetings were cancelled because too few members were present.

Dov, the internal Secretary when I was in the field, resigned on completion of his term of office. This did not surprise village members because during his last year in office he had often said that his responsibilities to his family and to the family farm made it difficult for him to continue in the job. Apparently there were difficulties in finding a replacement: it was said that the younger generation did not want a member of the parent generation to fill the position, while not one of themselves wanted to take on the job because each preferred to devote his working time to farming. Eventually a candidate was found, Assaf, who had been a member of the village Council. Assaf was a young member of the village and he, like his contemporaries, was not willing to give up farming to take up the job on a full-time basis, but he agreed to take on the duties of internal secretary in addition to his work on his farm. After the appointment of Assaf as internal secretary there was a change in the pattern of village government: unlike Dov, Assaf did not work a full day in the village office and the village Council which had met frequently during Dov's period of office was seldom summoned to meet. One result of this state of affairs was that more and more of the day-to-day running of the village was directed by Ben, the external secretary, and the permanent staff of village office-workers. In the text of the study I reported the trend that I observed from my earlier field work, namely the diminishing influence of village members over the formulation of policies affecting village life. During Assaf's period of office, this problem, for so it was seen by villagers, took on another aspect. The failure by Assaf and the Executive to implement the article of the village constitution which stated that the village Council should be called at least once per month resulted in less formal participation by the elected representatives of the villagers in the direction of village affairs. Assaf did not stand for re-election after the completion of his term of office and Yoav took over the position of internal secretary. Yoav, a young man, was married to a Kfar Hefer girl and lived on her family farm. He had worked in the Moshav Movement for several years and in the past had refused nomination for the job of internal secretary because of his job in the Movement. However during Assaf's term of office Yoav left his job and returned to work on the farm with his wife and parents-in-law. His father-in-law was still active in farming and this may have been a reason why Yoav felt able to accept the duties of full-time internal secretary in the village, but he was widely regarded, both within and outside the village as an able and well-qualified person for the job. There was the belief that not only his personal qualities but also his connections outside Kfar Hefer established during his work in the Movement would be assets in the performance of his new job and thus poten- tially useful to the village as a whole. The main hope was that he would introduce changes in the village that would lead to a greater economic development of the moshav: changes that would bring economic benefits to the individual farmer and greater economic strength and power to the co-operative.

The two Executive committees which were elected after I left the field were both composed solely of young members. Similarly the two village Councils elected during the same period were both domi- nated by the young of the village: in the first new Council, out of fifteen members, only two members were drawn from the older generation, and in the second new Council there remained only one member of the older generation. The older generation have also been removed from paid employment in the village administration. It will be remembered from the above text that several elderly farmers who no longer worked their farms were given jobs in the village offices, but shortly after I left the field in 1968 it was decided to mechanise various processes in the administration of village affairs. It was argued that the new system which included the preparation, by an outside agency, of all village accounts on a computer would lead to greater efficiency, would give better information to the individual member and would reduce the need for clerical workers in the village. The redundant workers, all elderly farmers, were given a small amount of severance

R

pay on completion of their duties. In fact the new scheme did not lead to a reduction of office workers because several trained female workers from outside the village were engaged to operate the new accounting machines. But clearly, both in the formal framework of democratic representation and in village administration control has passed into the hands of the young.

I have argued above that there has been a strengthening of the trend for actual control of village affairs to pass from elected representatives to the permanent salaried staff of the village, and from the village to outside agencies. An illustration of the latter was the decision, taken after I left the field, to join a scheme run by the Ministry of Agriculture and various government departments. This scheme, the Consolidated Credit Scheme, operated to give loans for agricultural development. However, there were certain conditions laid down for participation in this scheme: it was not open to individual farmers to join this scheme, only the whole co-operative of a village: all the financial affairs of the co-operative had to be handled by one of three banks nominated by the Credit Scheme; the village as a whole had to present a yearly plan of future agricultural developments in the village and to report on the state of the village economy in the past year; and, in addition, each family had to present its own planned agricultural production for the coming year. On the basis of these production plans the Credit Scheme gave loans and allowed an agreed amount of agricultural expansion subject to the scrutiny of their own economists and agricultural advisers.

When the Credit Scheme was conceived it was not intended for the use of well-established settlements like Kfar Hefer. The purpose of the scheme was to help newer developing settlements to obtain credit on more favourable terms than was available from existing agencies, and also, significantly, in view of the analysis above, to give the government a firmer control over agricultural production. The prevailing opinion during my earlier field work was that Kfar Hefer did not need the assistance of the Credit Scheme for the village was believed to have sufficient economic strength and resources to readily receive credit from other sources and thus avoid the governmental control of production implicitly involved in the Credit Scheme. However, in the years 1968–71 not only Kfar Hefer, but also other economically strong *moshavim* and *kibbutsim* decided to join the Credit Scheme and thus placed themselves under government direction. I think that the reasons for this change of mind and policy can be found in my preceding study of Kfar Hefer. Throughout my analysis there are references to the vagaries of the market situation at home and abroad, and hence to the resulting changing policy of government to the various kinds of agricultural production. The lack of advance certainly about quotas and support of production affected agricultural development throughout the country.

I have argued above that Kfar Hefer's farmers were able to withstand the effects of the restrictive aspects of government policy because of the advantages that accrued to them from their large share of national markets, from their political and economic influence, and from their relative economic independence of government aid. Notwithstanding this, it will also be remembered that many individual farmers in the village did suffer a drop in income as a result of changes in government subsidies, pricing policies and quotas, and that for many the margin between profit and loss on production was very slight. Furthermore, farmers who had shown an interest in moving into new branches of agriculture had found it difficult to get credit from the village co-operative because it was reluctant to finance ventures which it considered to be risky. This situation had not changed during my two years' absence from the field and, if anything, it had become even more pronounced: interest rates had gone up and banks and other financial institutions showed greater reluctance to lend money for agricultural development. Thus, government policy in the wider economic field brought about changes in the agricultural arena which policies specifically designed for agriculture had not achieved: Kfar Hefer and other settlements have relinquished more of their economic and planning independence in return for government guarantees and favourable loans.

The consequences of this decision affected villagers in several ways and caused some discontent in Kfar Hefer. In the past Kfar Heferites were accustomed to request and usually receive loans from the Executive for a variety of purposes not necessarily connected with farming. The ruling of the Credit Scheme was that members who were indebted to the co-operative were allowed only the minimum allowance guaranteed by the *moshav* to all its members. In addition, under the Scheme, members were allocated their production for the year as a whole and were not later granted supplements as they were in the past. In answer to my asking villagers why they had joined the Scheme if there was so much opposition, I was told that Ben wanted to introduce the Scheme into the village and the Executive of the time was weak. Indeed, the Scheme was introduced into Kfar Hefer during Assaf's tenure of the internal secretaryship, when Ben, the external secretary, was *de facto* running the village. I believe that Ben may have used this particular period of time to press for agreement to join the Credit Scheme, knowing that consultation and participation in decision making were weakly organised in the village. However, I find it difficult to conclude, as many villagers did, that this was the mere personal whim of Ben decided upon for his convenience, irrespective of village wishes or needs.

Earlier I have referred to the differential perception of events and processes by individuals: differentiated according to the varying statuses and peculiar circumstances of an individual which cluster together to indicate his 'social position' in regard to particular events. Thus, Ben; the Executive; the village Council; and Kfar Heferites were all united in agreement that improvements in the economic standing of the village were needed, but they differed in their respective interpretation of how these improvements could best be achieved. On the whole Ben favoured the co-operative taking advantage of the financial inducements offered by government to develop production in new agricultural ventures: villagers, on the whole were wary of committing themselves to follow government directives which in the past they had found change with a high degree of frequency making investment an uncertain activity. Kfar Heferites therefore tended to support the idea that they should retain the traditional pattern of farming using their considerable economic and political resources to obtain the best possible terms for their production.

In my study I have suggested this policy when put into practice within the village produced, due to a specific set of circumstances set out in the text above, a series of conflicts over the principles of organisation of co-operative life. I have shown above how various categories and groups within the village interpreted 'co-operation' in different ways and how each attempted to have its understanding of 'co-operation' accepted by the village as a whole. I have further argued that the competition for resources within the village was affected by changing demographic patterns within the village and by the pervasive influence of government whose decisions, although emanating from 'outside' the village played an integral part in shaping events in Kfar Hefer. On the basis of my previous fieldwork in Kfar Hefer and my observations when I returned to live in the village I would suggest that; (1) the increase in number of 'elderly farmers' who gave up cultivating their land with the consequent transfer of this land to those who were still farming; (2) a situation where strict quotas were still imposed by government and rising costs of production encouraged greater output in order to benefit from economies of scale; (3) the determination of the 'big farmers' in Kfar Hefer not to forgo their output in favour of fellow villagers; and (4) the increasing effectiveness of government policy on financial institutions in Israel, all combined to produce the necessary conditions for Kfar Hefer to join the Credit Scheme.

I was not present at Kfar Hefer when the decision to join the Scheme was made and I cannot say if my suggested analysis of the reasons for the village joining the scheme is sufficient, nor can I say if any one factor was of greater significance than any other. However, it may be significant that other well established settlements with different demographic patterns from that of Kfar Hefer also decided to join the scheme at this time, and this may point to a general tightening of the availability of credit other than from government departments and agencies. It would seem that the act of joining the Scheme was the formal recognition by Kfar Heferites that the focus of economic growth and devlopment was in government and not in the village itself or in any of the institutions with which the village has been associated in the past. In fact, during my earlier field work the villagers did realise that ultimately power resided in central government but they believed that through their multiplicity of links with associations, such as the Moshav Movement and the various Growers' Associations they could influence government policy in their favour. Why, in this instance it appears that these links were not sufficiently influential I can only attempt to answer by pointing to the fact that although the member settlements of these associations combined to make representations to government they were also divided on many issues and often in competition one with the other, and, furthermore, that many of the country's settlements were already involved in the Credit Scheme and thus directly under government direction.

Despite the close government control over the village and the need for the co-operative to keep within the quota of production for each year, the Credit Scheme has in some ways eased the Executive's problems in dealing with individual members. In the past refusals by the Executive to give loans or to grant extra allocations of poultry to individuals were often countered by accusations of favouritism on the part of the Executive: since joining the Scheme the Executive's refusals were couched in terms of its having to obey government orders on pain of having loans withdrawn. Thus the Executive have used the Scheme to overcome some of its internal difficulties with village members.

But one problem which was not yet overcome was that of the operation of the private incubator in the village. This enterprise was still working independently of the village's co-operative institutions and the village continued its policy of 'non-recognition'. During my absence from the field the operations of the incubator grew in scale, and Pinchas and Yael hired a full-time manager for the enterprise.

All attempts by the Executive to reach an agreement with the couple failed: the protracted negotiations which were taking place when I left the village in 1968 foundered because Kfar Hefer insisted on the incubator being incorporated into the economic system of the co-operative, a proposal to which the couple steadfastly refused to agree. The village co-operative continued to refuse taxes from the couple despite their eagerness to pay the taxes. The operation of the incubator seemed no longer to be an important issue in Kfar Hefer and most village members appeared to be content for the situation to continue as it was—an attitude of mind summed up in the pragmatic statement, 'There is nothing that can be done about it'. The passage of time and the failure to take action because of a genuine dilemma about what action could possibly have been taken, seem to suggest that nothing will be done about the incubator.

The two new economic ventures which were started during my earlier field work still continued. The 'old men's' venture growing alfalfa was in its second year; and in 1970–71, in contradiction to the gloomy forebodings of the original members, the growers enjoyed a small profit. This profit was in the main due to the favourable weather which allowed additional harvests of the crop.

It will be recalled that when the alfalfa venture was launched the chaotic state of land registration in the village was revealed; and in this situation one of the stated aims of the alfalfa group was to investigate their own land-holdings. In fact two of the original alfalfa group who wished to start planting were not able to do so because they were told by the Executive that they had no land. This matter of land holding and registration of land continued to be an issue in the village, though it was only the two members concerned in the alfalfa scheme who pressed their claims. None of the 'landless' members wanted to sell his farm, and so the issue did not become a real crisis for most village members, who were content to let the problem ride until it became pressing.

The avocado group had less immediate success than the alfalfa group. The parcel of land that they set aside for growing avocadoes was not approved by the Ministry of Agriculture and only after they made several improvements to the land were they allowed to go ahead with their plans. The first plantings took place in 1969 and it will be several years before it will be known whether the venture will be economically successful.

In my main analysis I predicted that other clusters of co-operation would develop in Kfar Hefer, but at the time of writing this had not happened. The change in the system of financing agricultural production had an effect upon this possibility. Members felt that if the

Consolidated Credit Scheme gave loans for production, this production was to some extent guaranteed by the Scheme and so the incentive to move into other areas of production was weakened. Notwithstanding this, there was evidence that a process of internal specialisation was taking place within the village and the results of this process were similar to the co-operative ventures of alfalfa and avocado growing. The raising of turkeys for meat and for breeding became increasingly profitable, partly because of a government decision to cut down on the imports of frozen beef in an effort to save foreign currency. Correspondingly the government attempted to persuade the consumer to buy turkey meat instead of this beef which was mainly imported. Six farms in Kfar Hefer began to concentrate almost exclusively on breeding turkeys, an operation which demanded a high capital investment in equipment and buildings. It seemed likely that the number of farmers engaged in this project would grow because of a suggestion that the village should go into partnership with a nearby *kibbuts* to set up a joint plant for slaughtering and processing the turkeys by the two settlements. This last-named development was interesting because it marked the first direct venture by the co-operative into industry. Kfar Hefer was associated with a regional industrial scheme, mentioned above, which involved all settlements in the area but the involvement was on a purely financial basis and the regional plant did not take any of Kfar Hefer's produce.

The venture was also interesting for another reason—the link up between a *kibbuts* and a *moshav* in a joint economic venture. In my discussion of Kfar Hefer's relations with the Moshav Movement I drew attention to the fact that many members of the Movement shared a greater similarity of interests with *kibbutsim* rather than with other *moshavim*. This is not to suggest that Kfar Hefer's interest in the Moshav Movement was lessened, rather to point out that due to the changes that had taken place within *moshavim* the Movement no longer served as the single centre for the clustering of interests common to all *moshavim*. Thus, Kfar Hefer[1] used other existing linkages and attempted to establish new ones to further the village's interests: there was a selective mobilisation of resources according to each particular instance. The new venture would seem to provide at least a partial solution to the demands of those within Kfar Hefer who pressed for an economic diversification within the village economy, and also to the wishes of those who felt that the village's interests could best be served by expanding existing forms of production. Absolute specialisation was not achieved in the village because even those farmers who bred turkeys still maintained their

[1] See introduction to Mitchell (1969) on mobilisation of network links.

dairies and worked their fields: it seemed that those who were best equipped to take advantage of the new opportunities were those who were already economically strong. Undoubtedly the aim of the new venture was to provide benefits for all *moshav* members. How far this could be achieved depended on a complex series of factors, not least being the willingness of farmers to overcome their hesitations about complete specialisation in one branch of farming to the exclusion of others, and this in turn depended on another set of factors amongst which the demographic variable was important: some farmers in Kfar Hefer already had a labour force made up of three generations and it seemed possible that specialisation within the village would develop not only between farmers but also within a single farm on the basis of generational differences. Equality of access to the means of production existed in Kfar Hefer but, as I have shown above, considerable differences in the ability of farmers to exploit these resources also existed in the village. It was these differences operating within the system of national and local policies that gave rise to the conflicts about the principles of *moshav* organisation which I have recorded in my study of the village.

Bibliography

(*Works cited in the text*)

Arensberg, C. M.—(1936, reprinted 1959) *The Irish Countryman: An Anthropological Study*, Smith, Gloucester, Mass.

Colson, E.—(1953) 'Social Control and Vengeance in Plateau Tonga Society', *Africa*, vol. xxiii.

—(1963) *The Makah Indians: A study of an Indian Tribe in Modern American Society*, Manchester University Press, Manchester.

Coser, L. A.—(1963) *The Functions of Social Conflict*, London.

Deshen, S.—(1970) *Immigrant Voters in Israel*, Manchester University Press, Manchester.

Eisenstadt, S. N.—(1960) 'Patterns of Leadership and Social Homogeneity in Israel' in *International Social Science*, U.N.E.S.C.O., Paris.

Frankenberg, R. J.—(1957) *Village on the Border*, Cohen and West, London.

Gluckman, H. M.—(1955) 'Frailty in Authority' in *Custom and Conflict in Africa*, Blackwell, Oxford.

—(1963a) 'Gossip and Scandal' in *Current Anthropology* vol. 4.

—(1963b) *Order and Rebellion in Tribal Africa*, Cohen & West, London.

—(1964) (Editor) *Closed Systems and Open Minds*, Oliver and Boyd, Edinburgh.

Institute of Farm Income Research in co-operation with Central Bureau for Statistics—(1967) *The profitability of various farm branches in Israel in the years 1964/65*, Tel Aviv.

Israel National Committee of the International Dairy Farmers—(1967) *Israel's Milky Way*, published for the 52nd Annual Meeting of the I.D.F. in Israel, September 1967.

Jerusalem Post—Morning newspaper, Jerusalem.

Kfar Hefer Bulletin.

Labes, E.—(1962) *Handbook of the Moshav*, Haikar Haoved and the Youth and Hechalutz Department of the World Zionist Organisation, Jerusalem.

—(1967) 'Moshav Sons knocking on the door', *Jerusalem Post*, 7 April 1967.

Leach, E. R.—(1961) *Pul Eliya: a Village in Ceylon*, Cambridge University Press, Cambridge.

Marx, E.—(1966) *Bedouin of the Negev*, Manchester University Press, Manchester.

Mitchell, J. C. (Editor)—(1969) *Social Networks in Urban Situations: Analyses of Personal Relationships in Central African towns,* Manchester University Press for Institute of African Studies, University of Zambia.

Orni, E.—(1963) *Forms of Settlement,* Youth and Hachalutz Department of World Zionist Organisation, Jerusalem.

Paine, R.—(1967) 'What is gossip about? An alternative hypothesis', *Man* N.S. 2.

Rees, A. D.—(1951) *Life in a Welsh Countryside,* University of Wales, Cardiff.

The Settler—A quarterly published by Haikar Haoved.

Shatil, J.—(1966) 'The Economic Efficiency of the Kibbutz', in *New Outlook Middle East Monthly* vol. 9, No. 7.

Shokeid, M.—(1971) *The Dual Heritage: Immigrants from the Atlas mountains in an Israeli Village,* Manchester University Press, Manchester.

Shoresh, S.—(1965) 'Change in the moshav', in *The Settler.*

Talmon-Gaber, Y.—(1952) 'Social Differentiation in Co-operative Communities', *British Journal of Sociology* vol. 3.

—(1961) 'Aging in Israel: a planned society', *American Journal of Sociology* vol. 67.

Tlamim—The Moshav Movement journal, published by *Tnuat Ha'moshavim.*

Weber, M.—(1947) *Theory of Social and Economic Organisation,* Collier-Macmillan, London.

Weingrod, A.—(1966) *Reluctant Pioneers: Village Development in Israel,* Cornell University Press, New York.

Weintraub, D.—(1971) *Social Change and Rural Development: Immigrant Villages in Israel,* Manchester University Press, Manchester.

Williams, W. M.—(1956) *Gosforth: the Sociology of an English Village,* Routledge and Kegan Paul, London.

Willner, D.—(1960) Ph.D. Thesis, University of Chicago, published as (1970) *Nation-building and Community in Israel,* Princeton University Press, Princeton, N.J.

Yedict Ha'Ezor—published by Regional Council: Kfar Hefer.

Index